BREATHE DEEPLY, MY SON

The Library of Holocaust Testimonies

Editors: Antony Polonsky, Martin Gilbert CBE, Aubrey
Newman, Raphael F. Scharf, Ben Helfgott

Under the auspices of the Yad Vashem Committee of the
Board of Deputies of British Jews and the Centre for
Holocaust Studies, University of Leicester

BREATHE DEEPLY, MY SON

The Library of Holocaust Testimonies

Editors: Antony Polonsky, Martin Gilbert CBE, Aubrey
Newman, Raphael F. Scharf, Ben Helfgott

Under the auspices of the Yad Vashem Committee of the
Board of Deputies of British Jews and the Centre for
Holocaust Studies, University of Leicester

My Lost World by Sara Rosen
From Dachau to Dunkirk by Fred Pelican
Breathe Deeply, My Son by Henry Wermuth
My Private War by Jacob Gerstenfeld-Maltiel

Breathe Deeply My Son

Henry Wermuth

VALLENTINE MITCHELL

First published in 1993 in Great Britain by
VALLENTINE MITCHELL & CO. LTD.
Gainsborough House, Gainsborough Road,
London E11 1RS, England

and in the United States of America by
VALLENTINE MITCHELL
c/o International Specialized Book Services, Inc.
5602 N.E. Hassalo Street, Portland, Oregon 97213

Copyright © 1993 Henry Wermuth

British Library Cataloguing in Publication Data

Wermuth, Henry
  Breathe Deeply, My Son
  I. Title
  940.53

  ISBN 0-85303-246-7

Library of Congress Cataloging-in-Publication Data

Wermuth, Henry.
  Breathe deeply, my son / Henry Wermuth.
    p.   cm.
    1. Holocaust, Jewish (1939–1945)—Personal narratives.
  2. Wermuth, Henry.   I. Title.
  D804.3.W44   1993
  940.53'18—dc20   91-41748
                                                        CIP

All rights reserved. No part of this publication may be reproduced in any
form or by any means, electronic, mechanical, photocopying, recording
or otherwise, without the prior permission of Vallentine Mitchell and
Company Limited.

Typeset by Regent Typesetting, London

Printed and bound in the United Kingdom by
Watkiss Studios Limited, Holme Court, Biggleswade, Beds.

To Ida and Bernhard Wermuth – my dear parents

To the six million unarmed Jewish men, women and children who were murdered in the cruellest manner during the greatest crime in human history

and especially

to Hanna – my beloved little sister who so wanted to live

"You took the initiative,
And, like your brother,
You were determined to survive.
Alas,
At the tender age of 13,
At the very first hurdle
Luck deserted you
And cruel fate tore you from my side
forever."

Contents

The Library of Holocaust Testimonies

It is greatly to the credit of Frank Cass that this series of survivors' testimonies is being published in Britain. The need for such a series has long been apparent here, where many survivors made their homes.

Since the end of the war in 1945 the terrible events of the Nazi destruction of European Jewry have cast a pall over our time. Six million Jews were murdered within a short period; the few survivors have had to carry in their memories whatever remains of the knowledge of Jewish life in more than a dozen countries, in several thousand towns, in tens of thousands of villages, and in innumerable families. The precious gift of recollection has been the sole memorial for millions of people whose lives were suddenly and brutally cut off.

For many years, individual survivors have published their testimonies. But many more have been reluctant to do so, often because they could not believe that they would find a publisher for their efforts.

In my own work over the past two decades, I have been approached by many survivors who had set down their memories in writing, but who did not know how to have them published. I realized what a considerable emotional strain the writing down of such hellish memories had been. I also realized, as I read many dozens of such accounts, how important each account was, in its own way, in recounting aspects of the story that had not been told before, and adding to our understanding of the wide range of human suffering, struggle and aspiration.

With so many people and so many places involved, including many hundreds of camps, it was inevitable that the historians and students of the Holocaust should find it difficult at times to grasp the scale and range of the events. The publication of memoirs is therefore an indispensable part of the extension of knowledge, and of public awareness of the crimes that had been committed against a whole people.

Martin Gilbert
Merton College
Oxford

Introduction

A shot rang out and the bullet, missing my body by inches, mowed down one of my two companions. Two more ominous thuds followed and I realised that my destiny was sealed.

It was in the late summer of 1943, a few days after the above brush with death in the infamous *Zwangsarbeitslager* (forced labour camp) of Kraków-Plaszów (a camp that will be familiar to readers of Thomas Keneally's *Schindler's Ark*), that I first resolved to write my autobiography. I felt I already had enough material to fill a sizeable volume. Pen and paper were not then available, at any rate to me. Later, pondering over my past, I found I had already forgotten so many names, dates, even events, that I could offer only an incomplete picture.

This excuse was only one of many reasons that held me back from telling my story for the next 40 years. No writer, no poet, no matter how distinguished or eloquent, could ever successfully convey the extremity of anguish, the enormity of what really happened in situations unimaginable to anyone except the participants. How could I even attempt to describe all that wretched misery, the death-cries of millions of innocent people, the open and secret tortures, the agony of parents seeing their babies dragged away and thrown like discarded rubbish on to lorries, sometimes alive, sometimes killed, their limbs torn apart or their heads smashed in? How could I, or anyone, put into words the last moments of even one family inside a gas chamber, stripped, degraded, humiliated, embracing and looking into each other's terrified eyes, the strongest of them forced to see their loved ones dying slowly and in agony?

At last I was persuaded by my cousin Kalman Benyamini that it was my duty to overcome my doubts and reluctance and write my story. As I committed my first thoughts to paper, a torrent of images and impressions came flooding back in a tidal wave of memories.

1

A friend of recent date, Michael Spencer, consented to be my sounding board in the initial stages of my first venture in writing a book in English. Having, by the grace of God, not lost any members of his immediate family in the Holocaust,* he was ideally suited to help and, being born after the war, he came up with the right questions. In common with so many others he confessed that he could not accept unquestioningly the slaughter of so many millions with apparently so little resistance. The Warsaw ghetto uprising in itself is also an answer to this vexing puzzle. With hardly any weapons, without proper organisation, it was not a fight to win; it was what I dreamed of when death seemed inevitable, to die fighting, with a weapon in my hand and taking with me as many of those evil murderers as possible.

The questions I have been asked were manifold: 'Did the Nazis start the killing right after the invasion of Poland?' 'How did you make a living before you were thrown into a concentration camp?' 'Were you ever really close to death yourself?' 'What did it feel like?' ... and many more in this vein. Within the natural limits I have just mentioned, I shall answer them all. I shall also endeavour to analyse my feelings and reactions during situations that a normal person, living in normal times, would neither encounter nor experience.

To ask 'Who wants to read about these atrocities?' begs the question of who we want to read these accounts of Nazi outrages. I, for one, would like to think that on the whole readers are genuine students seeking to solve the puzzle of how a leading country of the civilised world could have let itself be dragged to such a low that its shame can never be eradicated. Then, I wish this book to be read not only by my children and theirs, as well as the children of my and future generations, but also – or even more so – by the children of the perpetrators.

All that I relate in these pages, therefore, are my own experiences and impressions. It is my firm conviction that a comprehensive account of the full horror of the *Churban* will never be told, owing to the sheer multitude of tragedies, each in its own way a story that

*I prefer to describe the indescribable as '*Shoah*' or '*Churban*' (pronounced 'choorban' with the 'ch' as in 'loch'). To be precise I should call it the second Churban; the first, which initiated two millennia of misery and persecution unequalled in history, was the *Churban Beth-Hamigdosh*, the destruction of the Holy Temple in Jerusalem (what's left of it now is called the Western or Wailing Wall), and the dispersal of the Jewish people from their homeland into the Diaspora.

ought to be documented. But, of course, they never will be because the closest witnesses to violent and forcible death are dead.

I have my own ideas of what I would like this book – and others like it – to achieve. Alas, it is wishful thinking. The reverberations of the agony and death-cries of millions, the helpless silence, the tears of the bereaved, can find only a faint echo now. It is only the few remaining survivors, the eye-witnesses, with whom this echo remains, as it will remain until the last of us has gone. Then, history and time will step up the speed of a process which has already begun – the ever-lessening impact, the constantly diminishing significance of these momentous events.

How different the effect must be on the various types of readers. Those who had no personal involvement; those who lost close relatives, the children or grandchildren of those murdered or of those who survived; those who, like myself, were in the midst of it all and are not only reminded of it but also made aware that others have experienced (hard to believe) even greater mental or physical torture.

One category of readers whom I really dislike are those who read a book about Nazi atrocities as others watch a horror film, for their entertainment. On the other hand, maybe I am too harsh in my judgement; perhaps, after watching this horror film, they appreciate that such things happen outside their safe, comfortable lives.

My main aim is to counter those people who, incredible as it sounds, are hard at work in diminishing the dimension of the unspeakable crimes, to whittle down the figures of those killed – or to deny the *Shoah*, or *Churban*, altogether. Six million is, of course, a rounded-off figure. Personally, I think that the real figure might well exceed this, as Jews who were not affiliated to any community are usually not counted. What questions should we ask these doubters? Would they be happy with say, five million? ... four? ... a trivial three or two? Would this lessen the crime?

Yet another reason for writing is that, in common with most survivors, I found it impossible to tell my children. It never seemed to be the right time to speak of this subject; in any case, I found it impossible to hold on to a story without veering off again and again until I lost my thread altogether.

Finally, this book is written as a memorial to my dear parents and darling little sister Hanna. There can never be an adequate memorial for the 1½ million children who died a forced death not even knowing why. Dare I hope that it will also contribute to warning future generations of the excesses a wanton dictatorship can produce?

Note: If my memory has a deficiency, it is in remembering names. Those who appear in this book are mentioned in the hope that they, their descendants or relatives, might read about them and – if they know of their fate or whereabouts – contact me.

Henry Wermuth
London, 1992

The photographs shown in this book, with the exception of the last, were obtained by the author from relatives who managed to emigrate before the war. His family's own were left behind and lost, together with most of their cherished possessions, when they were deported to Poland.

1

A Young German Patriot

'*Deutschland, Deutschland über alles – über alles in der Welt ...*

In 1932, in a Jewish school, a class of nine-year-old boys sang the German national hymn. Among them, with a fervour and enthusiasm, not to be surpassed by any German patriot of the Aryan race, I sang, with pride swelling my chest, the song that imbued me with the spirit that 'my country' was 'über alles in der Welt' (above everything in the world). I had no presentiment then that within this beautiful country, to whose culture the tiny (less than one per cent) proportion of Jews had contributed enormously, lurked a murderous virus that would soon embed itself in the murkiest recesses of the minds, not only of the deranged, the ruthless opportunists and the sadistic, but even of ordinary people.

Even today I feel quite sentimental when I hear or remember Germany's soul-moving songs and poetry. How strong were my feelings of patriotism when I sang the old Andreas Hofer song, of the Tyrolese hero who was tried, court-martialled and shot in Mantua. How deeply and acutely I felt – and still feel – with the soldier who lamented the death of a comrade in the song '*Ich hat' einen Kameraden ...*'! How captivated I was by the song of Siegfried, the young hero of the *Nibelungenlied* who left his father's castle to learn the skills of swordsmanship, and whose adventures I used to dream of emulating.

Among the philosophers, poets and composers whose work brought eighteenth- and nineteenth-century Germany to the fore-front of culture and civilisation, Schiller was my favourite poet and I still know his 'Die Bürgschaft' by heart. The recitation of this poem lasts over ten minutes and it always moves my listeners, when the tyrant, the villain of the piece, mellows as he discovers the strength of loyalty between two friends who would suffer death by his hand

5

rather than allow him to think that a betrayal had taken place between them – when he finally utters the plea to accept him as the 'third' in their alliance with the immortal words known to every German, young or old:

Ich sei, gewährt mir die Bitte
in eurem Bunde der Dritte.

No such sentiments could be expected from the tyrant who out-witted the ageing President Paul von Hindenburg and persuaded him to entrust him with the chancellorship of the German Reich. Adolf Hitler (we called him Schickelgruber after his father who was illegitimate by birth), cunningly duped the ailing old man.

It is almost inconceivable that, within such a country as the civilised Germany of this century, a brutish clique of men – and women – who were brought up with and sang the same songs as those I loved so much, and who were schooled in the same culture, would then grow up to become the perpetrators of the most gigantic crime in human history; they would also become *my murderers*. The 'me' who survived in May 1945 was not the same 'me' who entered the camps. The innocent, fun-loving, well-brought up young man who believed in the goodness of mankind and trusted in God was no more.

And yet I could still have loved, and forgiven, my country Deutschland, if only it had become *Nazirein* (purged of Nazis) and brought those guilty to trial.

* * *

In July 1929, during my first school holidays, my parents sent me to Konigstein im Taunus, a spa much favoured by Jewish people, especially from Frankfurt am Main and the surrounding area. When I returned I was presented with a brand-new baby sister, Hanna, whom we called Hannelore, or even, with the added term of endear-ment, Hannelorchen. Not very far away and about a month before little Hanna's birth, another little girl had been born. Thirteen years later, when this other child, Anne Frank, went into a well-concealed flat in Amsterdam, where she and her family survived for two years, little Hanna, at about the same time, also entered a hiding-place – but Hanna's was ill-prepared and she was to stay there for only one night. But of what significance are the stories of two little girls among

6

1 Left to right: The author's Aunt Minna, father and mother on an outing before he was born

2 The author aged five, with his parents

a million, give or take a few thousand, murdered children and a thousand such parallels?

Up to 1930 we lived in the Rotlindstrasse in Frankfurt am Main. Although I attended a Jewish school, all my playmates in the street were Christians, but I experienced no antisemitism. In any case I was too young to know what antisemitism was. One day, one of the boys, Seppel, who was shunned by most of the others because of his dirty appearance and his coarse manner of speaking, came out with a taunt, a rhyme which made fun of the word Jew. It made no sense, but the dirty words contained in that ditty caused me a couple of sleepless nights, until I found a suitable riposte. So armed, I awaited Seppel's next encounter. When it came I parried it with the same type of language, unaware that, in fact, I was insulting the rest of my Christian friends as well. It shut him up – and, more significantly, the others didn't seem bothered.

I was too young to concern myself with business. All I knew about my father's trade was that it had something to do with textiles. Late in 1930, we moved into a larger flat in the Bäcker Weg and into a somewhat better area nearer to my school.

The unease I felt early in 1933 when the Nazis came to power must have been a reflection of the atmosphere among the adults surrounding me – my parents and relatives. I had no real idea what Fascism stood for. But I learned fast. The songs I could now hear, when the infamous Brownshirts were marching through the town, were unambiguous – and spine-chilling.

'*Wenn das Judenblut vom Messer spritzt, dann schmeckts nochmal so gut*' – when Jewish blood splashes off the knife, then the taste is twice as good. Or *Köpfe rollen, Juden heulen* ... (Heads are rolling, Jews are crying ...).

Did the Jews still regard this as rabble-rousing when the rabble-rousers were now the government? Why did the Jews not flee, to a man, when the Nazis' intention became clear? Perhaps they became used to hearing these songs and, as yet, no Jew had actually been murdered.

It is a well-known fact that German Jews were proudly patriotic. Many a family recalled their active participation during the First World War. Many produced their medals, quite a few Iron Crosses – First Class – among them. They felt sure in their belief that even a Nazi government would heed such distinction. How wrong they

7

were. I remember the sadness and the pride I felt when I learned about the 12,000 Jews who died fighting for their German fatherland.

Some Jews did leave in 1933, but the vast majority stayed on, waiting – for what? Everybody had their reasons. However trivial, in comparison and by hindsight, they loomed large and weighty at the time. Also, it must be said, that many countries, if not closed altogether to immigrants, had been erecting barriers – such as quotas.

My family's reasons for delaying emigration were manifold. We did not have the financial resources to settle somewhere else; we did not speak another language; we were waiting for an American entry visa (our quota).

In 1935 we sold all our furniture and many other belongings – ready to leave for the 'promised land'. A letter arrived. Aunt Golda Brauner (mother of Professor Kalman Benyamini) wrote that the Arabs are a 'bit restless' and we should wait 'a little' until they settled down. Having sold everything, we moved into one-roomed accommodation in the Uhlandstrasse – ready to leave at short notice. I do not know why, in the end, we never went. After a few months the time for my 13th birthday and my barmitzvah drew near. The Nazis were boycotting Jewish shops and removing Jews from all important positions, relentlessly tightening the screw but – so far – I had learned of no killings.

My parents took a large flat in the Roederbergweg – only a few houses from my school – which we then shared with another Jewish family by the name of Kraus. They had a son slightly older than myself and a daughter slightly older than my sister. The father was an apothecary by profession – very respectable people.

Because I was born in the middle of the Passover festival, when no barmitzvahs take place, it was postponed for one week. But it also resulted in four boys celebrating together, with each one reading a portion of the week's Sidra – a chapter in the Torah. Three thousand people were gathered to hear us in the Börne Platz Synagogue, one of the two very large synagogues which, together with large schools of religious learning, gave Frankfurt the aura, and the reputation, of more religious observance than other big German towns.

When my turn came to do the reciting and show what I had learned, nature's urges made themselves felt – irresistibly. Three

8

thousand people waited and wondered whether I had absconded. It was a relief for all when I reappeared and, to the pride of my father and mother, acquitted myself with honours.

I was not to obtain such great honours at school, though. To be acclaimed as a good footballer by one's classmates made more sense than being praised by the teachers – except, of course, at those dreaded times when I had to take home my less than glorious reports. My last tutor, by the name of Katz – we called him *'Kater'* (Tomcat) – displayed a distinct dislike of me. No wonder: my indifference to everything he tried to teach us – especially the holy scriptures – must have made him angry. I still remember the expression on his face during our last week at school in the spring of 1937 when he found that I was the only one, in a class of over thirty boys, who had a proper job waiting. I did not disclose the fact that my apprenticeship as *portofeuiller* (making handbags etc.) was in my uncle's factory.

My daily journey of 20 kilometres to the village of Heusenstamm (near the town of Offenbach, world-famous for its leather goods), took half of my wages of 5 marks 28 pfennigs. I was allowed to keep the 28 pfennigs and had to borrow another two if I wanted to go to the cinema. Soon, without telling my parents, I began cycling to work. After five weeks I had saved enough money to buy what I had always wanted – a 'Diana' air rifle.

I was the only Jew among 15 workers. Of course, I felt uneasy but in fact there was no hint of antisemitism in their behaviour towards me, not even after my uncle, Sigi Müller, sold out to a German in the spring or summer of 1938.

At about this time, in preparation for our future either in America or Palestine, my parents spent some hard-earned money for me to learn English by private tuition.

Father had ceased his textile business and was now selling oil products. He used to travel the country on his motorbike, away from his family for weeks on end. Inevitably, he would come across Nazis. 'We don't mean you, we're after "the others",' they would assure him, without, however, telling him whom they meant.

Besides the Jew-baiting speeches of Hitler and his propaganda minister, Goebbels, the most devastating effect on the gullible German mind came from some so-called newspapers whose contents consisted of nothing but the vilification of Jews. The most notorious was *Der Stürmer* whose editor, Julius Streicher, was

9

hanged after the Nuremberg trials. There was no need to purchase this paper, it was displayed like placards in many public places.

One of these displays was outside the *Sturmabteilung* (SA) offices (or headquarters) in the Friedberger Anlage, a park-like promenade which wound – and still winds – like a giant horseshoe around the town centre, beginning and ending at the river Main. I passed it regularly on the way to my English lessons. One day when I arrived early, I had time to gaze at the ghastly and distorted pictures. Stepping off my bike I soon became engrossed in reading about people whose deeds created in me an instant feeling of dislike. Their artfully uglified features added to my disdain – until I suddenly realised that these hateful people were Jews just like myself, my friends and my parents. It was then that I understood how hatred could be manufactured by hostile reporting.

The following week, as if possessed by a strange fascination, I was again reading this trashy literature when two boys, aged about eighteen, came strolling along. A look into their eyes told me what they were thinking. Is that a Jew-boy reading our paper; if so, how dare he?

Should I brave it? I let them come nearer, then, with a short run and a jump, I was off on my bike. Having won so many races against friends, I felt very confident about my ability to get away – fast. My pride, however, was hurt and, like a mischievous little boy, I rode around the block and finished the interrupted article. The boys, of course, were nowhere to be seen.

Dreamily I pedalled on. At the next corner I saw them racing towards me. They came from the front and there was no escape. When one of them gripped my handle-bar I jumped off. They ran after me and, looking back, I noticed a toy pistol aimed in my direction by the one nearest to me. Since I had once possessed one of these myself, I knew that it was only dangerous when fired near one's eyes. Seeing that I outpaced him, he fired. The action and the noise were realistic – and ominous.

The bike I found completely demolished in a nearby street. Two women who had witnessed the incident tried to console me. '*Viele Hunde sind des Hasen Tod*' – Many dogs are the death of the hare. That proverb brought me no comfort at all.

10

2

Deportation

The date was 28 October 1938; the time six o'clock in the morning. Shrill and persistent ringing woke me up with a start. Still drowsy, I heard my father opening the door. Three men in civilian clothes (Gestapo, I thought) entered our flat. *'Anziehen – mitkommen'* was the short command, yelled by one of the intruders. We were to get dressed and go with them. Our bewildered queries as to what it was all about, or where they were taking us, met only the sharp reply – *'schnell, schnell'* – quick, on the double. Soon this order, bellowed and often accompanied by the crack of a whip or enforced with rifle butts, was to become the dreaded audible scourge all over occupied Europe.

Before very long these words would be used to hound people to their death. 'Get dressed, *schnell, schnell'*, 'Get packed and out of your home, *schnell, schnell'*, 'Get into the train, get out of the train, dig your grave, get undressed, lay out your belongings neatly in front of you, die, *schnell, schnell!'*

These would be the last words heard by hundreds of thousands before the machine-guns began their mowing action, and, for millions of others, before the heavy doors of the gas-chambers shut with an ominous thud.

I dressed myself almost mechanically. My mind, numb and without coherent thoughts, was jerked back into reality by the shrill sound of my alarm clock at exactly ten minutes past six. I recollect looking at the policeman and saying sheepishly to him, 'I have to go to work now.' Was I, in my childish mind, trying to impress or even sway him?

Next door, in my parents' bedroom, I heard my mother pleading and saying something about bad health. Perhaps it worked; I remember leaving our home with my father only – my mother and sister were allowed more time but soon had to join us.

11

A few hours later, we were all on a train with hundreds of other unfortunates who, like us, had been torn from their homes at a moment's notice. But whereas mother and Hanna had been able to collect and bring some of our belongings, many of our co-travellers had to leave everything behind.

Listening to conversations, I gathered that the reason for this deportation was the German reaction to a declaration by the Polish government invalidating all Polish passposts whose owners had not been to Poland for a certain number of years. Though both my parents held Polish passports, my father was only nine months old when his parents emigrated to Germany, and my mother had come to Vienna with her family when she was 14. My sister and I, both born in Frankfurt, had no identity papers of our own and were entered on our mother's travel document.

Unlike the indescribably cruel journeys inside the infamous cattle-trains, of which, mercifully, I had as yet no inkling, we travelled in comparative comfort. Thinking back, I felt almost elated with a sensation of freedom and adventure. I was, of course, too young to appreciate that, at a stroke, we had lost all the intimate links with our past. Now it is the loss of all family photographs that still hurts me most.

*   *   *

We arrived at the border town of what the Germans called Beuthen and the Poles Zbaszyn. There we joined an enormous queue of people – most with suitcases and the maximum amount they could carry. Some, however, had no luggage at all. Probably they had been forced to leave their homes in the clothes they stood up in, just as my father and I were compelled to do.

The next nine hours were among the worst of my life. An underground passage, which led to the Polish side of the station, was crammed, sardine-like, with deportees. Once we had entered that passage we were wedged in, unable to budge. Every 15 minutes or so we moved a mere few inches.

For a while the prospect of leaving Germany kept my spirits up. However, after two hours of hardly any progress at all, surrounded by masses of despondent and sweating fellow-sufferers, and with no end in sight, a sort of claustrophobia began to grip me. As we had shifted only a few yards after all this time it appeared that our ordeal

12

could last for days. Hunger and thirst were not my biggest worry but when nature's urges manifested themselves, I began sweating too.

Although the next seven hours, however distressing, were almost insignificant in comparison with later events, I did learn a valuable and significant lesson: my body had a discipline of its own and could take far more than I expected.

*   *   *

When we finally reached a kind of barrier, which appeared to be the crossing-point for the train into Poland, there were still hundreds, maybe thousands, in the tunnel behind us – among them, as I learned later, many relations and friends.

Suddenly there was a sound like a disturbed beehive. News spread like wildfire and, while I was sitting on a suitcase, listless and unconcerned, everybody else was busy discussing what was obviously of momentous importance. At length, my parents, unable to agree what to do for the best, turned to me: 'The Poles are closing the border but we can still go through. The question is: should we proceed to an unknown destination or should we return to Frankfurt – back to our home but also back to Nazi Germany?'

My answer was unhesitating: 'Let's go on – let's go to Poland!'

My parents, in their deliberations, were thinking of all that they were leaving behind, as well as the anxiety of looking after the family in an unknown place. Without knowledge of the native language and with very limited funds we should be relying on relatives and their ability or inclination to come to our assistance. Whether my parents had ever met any of these relations I do not know – I certainly hadn't. No wonder they were so indecisive.

I had no such scruples. My motive was adventure. All the things I had left behind – a bicycle, a 'Diana' air-rifle, a football – I gladly forfeited for the prospect of living in a new country.

'Let's go on – let's go to Poland!' This answer of mine still haunts me today – and will never cease to do so. However unwittingly, with this decision I sentenced them to misery and death. I derive little consolation from the fact that the same fate would probably have befallen them had we decided to return. There were a few, however, of the many who did go back, either willingly or because the Poles

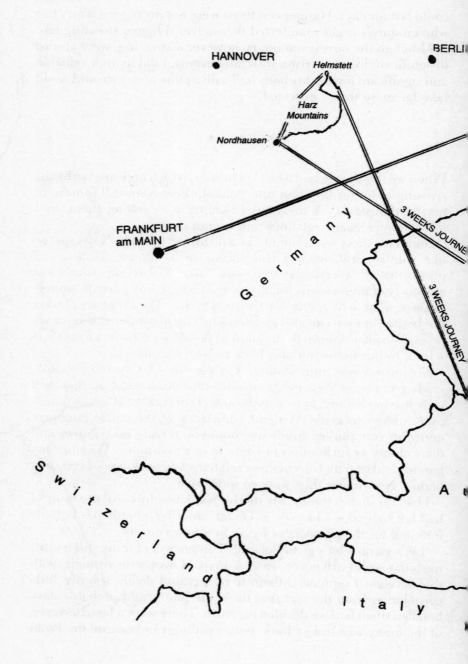

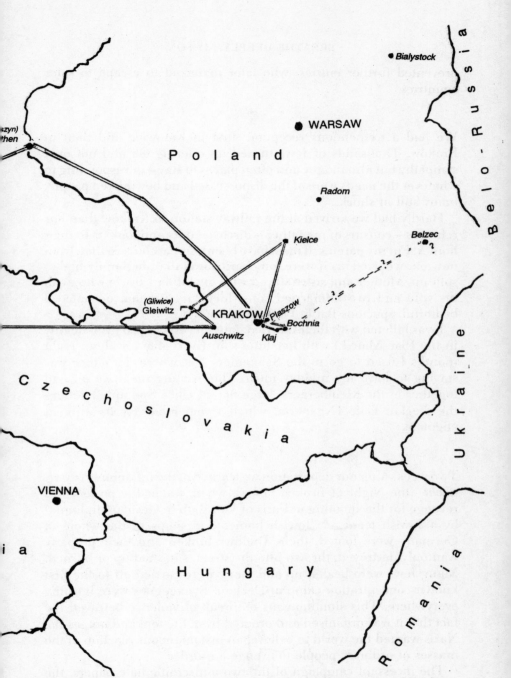

Map showing the extent of the journeys across Europe endured by the author during the course of the war

prevented further entries, who later managed to escape to safer countries.

* * *

We had a tremendous reception, first in Katowice and then in Kraków. Thousands of Jews turned up offering tea and not only sympathy but also money and often places to stay – or responding to whatever the needs were of the dispossessed and bewildered people, many still in shock.

Hardly had we arrived at the railway station in Kraków than our relatives – cousins of my father – discovered us and took us to their homes. For my parents, it must have been of great concern that, from now on, we lived, as it were, on charity, and that the family had to split up. Mother and sister stayed with my father's uncle who, with his wife and two unmarried sons, Idek and Roman, occupied a beautiful, spacious flat at Ulica Spitalna 36.

I was billeted with their married daughter Elza, who lived nearby in the Plac Matejki with her little son. Every day for about eight months I used to go to the Schneiders' flat where my father was staying to have my midday meal. The evening meal we all had together in the Kleinbergers' large flat, at Ulica Spitalna 36 above the elegant Café Cyganeria, which I remember for its affluent clientèle.

* * *

Two weeks after our deportation we learned of the infamous 'Kristalnacht' (the Night of Broken Glass), when, under the pretence of revenge for the shooting in Paris of Von Rath (a German diplomat) by a Jewish teenager, Jewish homes and shops in the whole of Germany were looted, their windows broken and their property wantonly destroyed, thrown into the street, smashed up or burned. Many Jews were beaten up and many were carried off to the first known concentration camp at Dachau. Synagogues were burning everywhere. This simultaneous outbreak of violence betrayed the fact that it was organised and ordered from the top, and not, as the Nazis wanted the world to believe, an instantaneous reaction of the masses of ordinary people to avenge a murder.

The incessant campaign of the two antisemitic hate papers, the *Voelkischer Beobachter* and *Der Stürmer*, must have had a devastat-

14

ing effect, not only on the impressionable young but also on many adults. The Germans themselves had coined a phrase to describe their average compatriot – *'der Deutsche Michel'*. A person so described would be utterly gullible and would sway with the political wind, and I would say that this was characteristic of the majority of the German population. Hypnotised by Goebbels' propaganda speeches, influenced by the daily outpourings of hate literature, teenagers with ordinary teenage activities had to join youth organisations where they were further indoctrinated. They were told that they belonged to the master race, Aryans, whose racial purity was 'wilfully' sullied by those inferior Jews.

It did not take long for this virus to fester; by the time war came, these brainwashed boys were put into uniform – ready to do their bit for the 'master race', to conquer the world and to destroy the 'inferior' races. Jews were the first and suffered the most, but there were others on the agenda. It must be said that not all Germans fell for these perverted teachings. After the pogrom, when the true creed of Nazidom had revealed itself to the most credulous German, many were heard to say 'This cannot be right'. Such people were reviled in the SS paper *Das schwartze Korps* as 'worse than the Jews'.

3

Kraków

Left to my own devices, I had only to appear punctually at meals. For me, it was my one teenage year, a year of maturing, a period of awakening and adolescence. I spent a lot of time in a nearby club frequented mostly by other teenage refugees. None of us had any money, and going out with a girl meant an afternoon stroll, no more.

So, with absolutely no conception of the future, no career, no ambition but also no worries, I drifted along – idly, but comparatively happily. Perhaps our plans to emigrate to America prevented us from making greater efforts to integrate and settle in Poland. Poland or America – what did it matter? I was looking for anything life had to offer – preferably adventure.

This being essentially an autobiographical account with the events of the Second World War as its main theme, I should move on to September 1939. But first I want to dwell just a little longer upon the short (much too short) period of normal teenage activities, unburdened by Nazi oppression.

Whiling away my time at the youth club, I discovered that I could entertain parties with jokes and conjuring tricks. I began by wrapping a match in a handkerchief, then offering it to a keen-eyed friend to break. Then, instead of the conventional abracadabra, I would select my favourite girl to blow into my hand. 'If it doesn't work it will be your fault,' I proclaimed. But, of course, it did work; the unwrapped square of white linen showed a perfectly sound, unbroken match. I praised the young lady for her skill which, I said, was absolutely instrumental in performing this miracle. On one such occasion I took the opportunity of playing a prank on Alfred, my first rival, very good-looking and, except for one slip, very bright and a good sport too. He wooed the same pretty girl as I did.

16

After I had performed more magical feats, including restoring a piece of rope, cut by Alfred with his pocket-knife and 'repaired' for all to see by Martha's 'skilled' blowing (how lovely she looked with her pursed lips), the onlookers were ready to believe anything. As a *coup de grâce*, to top everything they had ever seen, I announced that I was going to cut off all the buttons from Alfred's trousers and, by just whistling three times, restore them all to position. (In those days, braces were held up with buttons, and most trousers had buttons instead of zips.) To ward off any hesitation, I claimed that I would stake my reputation as a magician on the success of this performance.

Alfred dared not refuse when Martha proceeded to remove the buttons holding his braces but insisted on cutting the other buttons himself.

To make this trick more effective, I announced that I would leave the room and they would hear my whistle from outside the door. Turning around before leaving, I saw Alfred standing in the middle, holding up his trousers with both hands and looking very apprehensive. On the other faces I could read expectation and amusement.

'Please count aloud,' I said and gave the first whistle. 'One' they shouted before I closed the door. Ten seconds later I whistled again and the chorus roared 'two'. Then I decided that I didn't want a career as a magician anyway – and left for home.

I revelled in the short-lived popularity that followed these exploits, except, of course, with Alfred. He did not appear in our circles for the next two weeks and Martha, so I thought, had been left with only one suitor – myself. When he finally came back, he ignored Martha and me completely.

One afternoon the discussion was about the customs in our new surroundings. While the practice of kissing a lady's hand was on the wane in other countries, it was almost a 'must' for the Polish gentleman. Alfred and I had made up and became friends again, especially as the cause of our rivalry, Martha, had chosen to associate herself with Paul. 'A smooth talker and braggart' Alfred used to call him (I wondered what he had called me only a short while ago). We all agreed about the extremely difficult and slow process of learning the Polish language.

'It sounds like hissing and spitting,' Paul exclaimed angrily.

'Tonight our relatives are giving a special party for my family and I cannot exchange more than simple greetings with them,' he continued miserably.

My waggish nature took over again. 'You can be helped,' I butted in eagerly, also grasping the opportunity to show off my greater knowledge of the vocabulary we were all struggling with. Not waiting for his reply, I continued: 'First make your grand entrance and call "*dobre wieczór*" – good evening ...' 'We all know that much,' Paul intervened, '*dzien dobre, dobre wieczór, do widzenia* – good day, good evening, goodbye – were the first words we learned, that doesn't get me very far.'

'I cannot teach you whole conversations,' I continued, 'but I can teach you how to impress your relations that you are a "man of the world" – a gallant gentleman – if you want me to.' He accepted my offer and I proceeded to explain how to approach the lady of the house: 'Take her hand to your lips, then, while looking warmly into her eyes, say with sincerity "*pocaluy mnie w dupie*"', which, so I told him, was the equivalent of the French '*Enchanté*'. After repeating it a dozen times or so, he became really fluent. He was still repeating it when he left.

Those with some knowledge of the Polish language have had their chuckle. To others I should explain that what I taught him was the equivalent of the English 'kiss my backside' – only ruder.

I cannot report how the party went, but I was told I had better keep out of his way as he promised to kill me, and also to beat me up into the bargain. Well, I did keep out of his way for a couple of weeks, then I heard that our meeting-place had been transferred to another part of the town. Except for Alfred, I lost contact with all the others. Alfred did not survive the war, I wonder if any of the others did.

*   *   *

In common with other teenagers, I often mistook infatuation for real love. One late afternoon, as I entered the house where my mother and little sister stayed and where I spent most evenings, I saw a group of actresses or dancing girls arrive, undoubtedly for a cabaret act in the Café Cyganeria.

Scanning the variety of these glamorous females, my eyes were solidly fixed onto one bronzed beauty, whose classical features were enlivened by a pair of deep black eyes. A description of their fiery glances, had I not seen them myself, would fall into the category of poetic licence.

She spotted the spellbound incredulity in my young face and rewarded me with just a hint of a smile, but enough for me to launch a thousand ships. Seconds only, then I lost sight of her as the group entered the restaurant. How I wished to be old enough, rich enough, to follow her inside.

'Not even Rembrandt could have painted such eyes,' I murmured as I climbed the two flights of stairs leading to my relative's flat. On top of the first flight was a landing where I previously noted a metal door which had always puzzled me. It was definitely not an entrance to any of these elegant flats but seemed too high to belong to the café below. Passing it, I noticed light shining through the crevices. 'I never saw any light there before,' I thought before my mind wandered off to the angelic vision I had seen minutes earlier.

As I was not touching my food, I was asked questions as to my well-being. I hardly heard them. I was well and truly smitten with her beauty and before long withdrew to find a place to be alone with my thoughts. Through the well insulated floor I could hear gypsy tunes with all their inherent romanticism. I left later than usual to walk the five minutes to Elza's abode in Plac Matejki. Descending the stairs slowly and deep in thought, I heard laughter and giggles coming through that mystery door. As if pulled by an irresistible force, I was drawn towards the source of these merry noises. Furtively, I looked back to ascertain that no-one could see me from the flat I just left, then I bent down to look through the keyhole.

What I saw would probably, by today's standard of female exposure, not cause a young man to take a second glance but, in those more guarded days, a group of girls changing their dancing costumes for their normal attire kept my eyes glued in rigid fascination.

Because of the low position of my spyhole I could see only the heads of the girls bending down towards me (needless to say, if they bent the other way I did not see their heads). Since the exquisite creature who only three hours ago had invaded my mind as if to occupy it forever did not seem to be among them, I concentrated on the sea of thighs in motion only a few feet away from me, all excitingly well-shaped and not a face in sight. Then, the girl nearest

19

to me, barely an arm's length away, bent down to adjust – to adjust ...
who cares what she did, it was her – it was her ...

Was it an Elysian dream? Certainly not. The pinnacle of frustration – that's what it was.

Only an arm's length from ... oh that damn door. But for this
obstacle, I could have shaken her hand or something and told her of
my admiration and undying love. Perhaps I could even ... There was
a noise, I heard voices coming from below. Two people had entered
the house and were coming up towards me. I straightened up and
walked nonchalantly past an elderly couple, bidding them *'dobre
wieczór'*.

True to my age, the 'unhappiest man alive' feeling soon subsided.
Why be so sad? 'After all,' I thought, 'beautiful though she is, age is
creeping up on her; she must be all of 24, maybe even 25 years old!'
Still, she must have made quite an impression to be so vividly
remembered 45 years later.

Her image was eventually replaced by an even more ludicrous
event. One evening, on my way home, I had to cross an open space
with trees around its edges. A tall and comely lady in her late
twenties approached me and asked me something in Polish. As a
well-mannered young man, I instantly took off my cap (I can still see
the picture) and clasped it in front of my chest ... *'Ja nie umie mówić
dobrze popolsku,'* I answered apologetically, telling her that my
Polish wasn't very good.

She then spoke in German. In just three words she asked me, in
the coarsest way possible, but with a friendly and slightly amused
smile, if I wanted sex.

To be confronted with such a direct question, which I could never
have imagined coming from the lips of a lady, created a whirl in my
head and a shock to my system. Notwithstanding this reaction, I
replied, fully composed and in the manner of a worldly and experienced gentleman, *'Ile kosztuie* (how much)?', knowing full well
that I didn't have a *grosze* to my name, let alone a *złoty* in my pocket.
'Finnef złoty.' This multilingual businesswoman was now replying
in Yiddish, accompanied by a quizzical look and, probably, by now
realizing that five *złotys* might be beyond the means of her prospective client. 'Very reasonable,' I mumbled, while searching my jacket
for a non-existent wallet. With a grand gesture and a few suitable

words, I motioned her to wait. I would be back in *finnef* minutes as I had left my money at home.

* * *

A few days after this episode, I encountered Idek (who, for some reason was usually called Pucek), leaving the flat just as I was entering. 'A young man ought to have some pocket money,' he said simply, handing me five *złoty*. What timing, I mused as I wondered what made him give me just this amount, the only money I had had since arriving in Poland.

Since I was not spending anything on food or transport, as I walked everywhere, the purchasing power of five *złoty* in those days represented riches to me. The only other example I am able to give – other than the one just quoted – was the price of hiring a billiard table: one *złoty* for one hour. I quickly developed a flair for this game and, since only the loser had to pay, I managed to stretch my capital for many hours of this lovely pastime. It is often said of people good at this essentially recreational sport that this is the result of a misspent youth. If only I had had more of it.

* * *

By the middle of 1939, after seven months staying with relatives, my parents rented a flat in the main square of Kraków named Rynek Główny – the main market (perhaps the equivalent of 'square' or 'circus' in English). For a while we all continued eating where we ate before. Father and I had our main meal at precisely one o'clock with the Schneiders, a well-to-do family whose maternal head was my grandfather's sister. With their two grown-up sons, Olek and Idek, they escaped the German invaders and made their home in Israel. The Kleinbergers also fled but were somehow split up. The parents stayed in Warsaw and, so the story goes, despite frantic efforts by their sons who sent the petrol needed for the vehicle to take them out of Poland, which was then lost, stolen, or sold on the black market, were left stranded there and subsequently perished with all the others in the infamous ghetto. The Kleinbergers' two sons with their married sister Elza found their way to Brazil where they still live.

Although the younger generation is not young any more and the older ones have passed on, I feel it appropriate to express here my sincerest thanks to all of them for helping my family on arrival in

Poland and for the first few months of the war. By then the Schneiders had already left.

I cannot help wondering who enriched themselves with all the lovely things that were left behind. I remember how my fastidious great-aunt in the Ulica Spitalna opened the door to make sure that visitors used the mat to clean their shoes; how she had the expensive carpets covered with white linen sheets to keep them clean and preserve them ... for German officers.

*　　*　　*

Memory takes me into someone's flat where I find myself sitting at a sewing machine, diligently making two lines on leather belts – one on each side and one millimetre from its edge. How I got this job I cannot recall. I had never done any sewing at all – at least on a machine. The lines were an embellishment: one moment of less than 100 per cent concentration and the belt would be ruined. Why I was trusted with this work I didn't know, but I learned fast and damaged only a very small amount.

A week later, my employer – a kind Jewish man – hired another refugee and my heart somersaulted. She was a girl of exceptional beauty. Her name was Hanna Tänzer. He made the mistake of placing her next to me, doing the same work on another machine. Not surprisingly, my work suffered; 100 per cent concentration was no longer possible.

I slowly conquered my shyness and invited her to come for a walk. She seemed to like me all right but fate intervened.

My parents had placed me on the list of an organisation that gave children of Jewish refugees the opportunity of a holiday. I was one of about 40 or 50 chosen. The destination was Zakopane – the world-famous ski resort. When I announced this to my boss, and learned that Hanna was going too, I could not have been happier.

We set off on a train journey to Zakopane. Our group was spread over two coaches. Far from seeking out Hanna, I avoided her as much as I could, greeting her briefly and walking away from her – backwards – into the adjoining wagon. I sat down, probably the saddest person aboard. The explanation for this behaviour? Vanity! The morning before departure my beloved, practical and ever so skilled father had given me a haircut. The front was not too bad, but I hated the back. In no circumstances could I bear my dream girl to see me with such a hairstyle. Oh, how I suffered. Without knowing the reason for my sudden withdrawal, Hanna may have been bewildered and saddened too. I shall never know.

On arrival we were placed in a hotel where we spent the night. The next day, after breakfast, most of us were placed with families who volunteered to receive us.

Mine was a family of four. Though I recall nothing of the parents and son, I do remember the daughter of 17, from whom I learned the valuable lesson that beauty is only skin-deep. Of very ordinary appearance, she had the gift of pleasant and easy-going conversation. When she spoke, the store which I, as a young man, put on beauty seemed to shrink into irrelevance. So much so that when I left after three weeks, her looks were not unappealing any more.

Hanna I met on two more occasions; the first, when we were leaving the hotel. She was in the company of a lady and her son, about 17 or 18 years old, very strong and handsome. Seeing Hanna next to this blond Adonis brought on a pang of jealousy. 'They really look good together,' I admitted to myself. I waved to her but could not attract her attention.

At the second meeting, the last time I ever saw her, something happened which ensured that I should never forget it. There was a gathering with most of our group of refugee children present. Hanna introduced me to her new friend. His family name was Schildkraut. His father, so I was told, was a lawyer and he had an uncle in America who was an actor. After the war I heard and saw this actor on the screen on several occasions.

This handsome young Schildkraut then invited me to a game of arm-wrestling. 'Never heard of it,' I told him. 'What is it about?' He asked me to lie down on the grass – belly down – and lift my arm in an L-shaped position; he showed me how. He then gripped my hand and, before I knew that this was meant to be a contest of strength, he unceremoniously pressed it to the ground. I had lost – and Hanna had seen it all!

Most of our group left after three weeks. My parents somehow managed for me to stay on for another three, explaining that the clean mountain air of Zakopane was good for my lungs.

I remember two more people whom I met in Zakopane: a girl of 17 and a young man of 21. The former could have changed the course of my life dramatically – the latter did.

23

The girl's story is short and sweet. We met a few times. Once she took me home to meet her parents, bankers from Katowice on holiday with their daughter. They were going to emigrate to America shortly and invited me to go with them. I don't know if this would have been possible, nor do I know whether they made it in time, as it was only about three weeks before the invasion of Poland, and Katowice was quite near the German border. Anyway, I declined the invitation.

The young Pole's story was initially even shorter. He impressed me with his 1200cc motorbike with a side-car, in which he gave me a hair-raising ride up and down narrow mountain paths. On one occasion I would swear that, while swerving round a sharpish bend, the side-car, with me in it, was hanging in thin air over a 200-foot precipice! Four months later, Janek and I were to meet again – back in Kraków.

*   *   *

Before leaving Zakopane I want to mention that it was also the watershed of a certain 'thinking process' – as I was still only 16, I feel I was too young to call it a philosophy. On the last day before my departure for home, I decided to go for an extended evening stroll towards a descending sun already stooping low in its course. Wandering aimlessly into the fast-approaching darkness, I observed the gradual illumination of the stars as if to compensate me for the now distant and diminishing lights of Zakopane.

I stretched out in the long fragrant grass. Gazing up at the infinite span above, with its uncountable celestial bodies, winking, inviting, mocking, I felt a strange yearning to penetrate the secrets with which mankind had wrestled since time immemorial.

It was a similar experience to one I had had seven years earlier. Then, in my childish mind, I was determined to unravel all the enigmatic questions which nobody (not even my erudite father who, for me, epitomised the sum total of knowledge) could answer satisfactorily. I was looking for answers to the beginning and end of time, of space, and of God Himself. Why did God create the world? How old was He when He had this idea? And, why did He select this planet and no other – or did He? If there were people or thinking beings on other planets (I always believed there were), did He reveal

24

Himself to them too? Did He also give them the Torah, the Law, to live by?

I wanted to turn belief into knowledge – doubt into conviction. At the age of nine, I decided that, if no one else, it would be I who, by deep thought, determination and willpower, would solve the unsolvable. Seven years later in a Polish spa, my aspirations had widened to take on the equally profound but unexplained puzzle of heaven and hell, life after death.

Again I sent up a prayer for enlightenment, this time more devoutly and with deeper emotion. The intensity of my entreaties grew in fervour. My head felt on the point of bursting with an ever-increasing whirl of desires, hopes, supplications and requests; prayers engendered by the awe-inspiring expanse above and the awareness of my own nothingness; an overwhelming desire to be lifted heavenwards. I was reaching out – soon I would acquire the knowledge, learn and understand the reason for it all: the reason for life, the reason for death. It seemed all so tantalisingly near – yet utterly out of reach, and my plea for response went unheard – unanswered. Not a sign, not an echo, came back to reassure me that my prayers had reached anything but a void.

The sound of a noctural bird rudely interrupted my contemplation. I rose, shaking in anger and in sadness – I had received my 'enlightenment'. Never, never, never, would mankind have the answers to any of these questions. Never again, I decided, should my mental activity include any metaphysical speculations which are – and forever will be – unanswerable.

*　　*　　*

The first day of September 1939 passed for me as unremarkably as most days. Everybody, including myself, seems to remember the exact place where they were when the news of President Kennedy's assassination broke. The German invasion of Poland, news of equal, if not greater, magnitude, left no such lasting impression. First Austria, then Czechoslovakia; people had become accustomed to these annexations.

Somebody mentioned the strength and preparedness of the Polish Army; somebody else heard that the invaders had received a bloody nose and been rebuffed. But what did I understand about propaganda, battle lies, rumours? The overriding event of the day filled my

25

mind: I was determined to beat my old friend and adversary Julius 'Lulu' Rubinstein at billiards.

The first thing I do remember of the Second World War – and I don't even recall whether it was the first, second or third day – was when an air-raid siren sent the panic-stricken tenants of our block scurrying into the cellars. Nearby explosions shattered the silence of our underground shelters, somebody shouted 'Gas!' and out came the handkerchiefs, an obviously futile gesture. My eyes anxiously scanned the door and crevices at the top of the walls, expecting deadly clouds to seep through and engulf us. Soon it became clear that the panic-provoking word had been shouted by someone whose nerves had cracked at the first sign of danger; before panicking he had proudly proclaimed that he was a *'Volksdeutscher'* (an ethnic German) and so, whatever the outcome, he would be safe.

For a few tense moments, I thought this was the end of my young life. On close examination of my feelings during this imagined brush with death, I have come to realise that never during what followed did I fail to retain at least a tiny spark of hope. My brain always came up with all sorts of imagined and real reasons for sustaining hope when, by all normal calculations, there was none.

Afterwards I heard that the bomb dropped during the above-mentioned raid, less than a kilometre away from where I lived, was the first of the Second World War. It was the one and only time that I recall going into the cellar. The German progress was swift and, in just about a week, Kraków was overrun.

Whatever we had anticipated that the Germans would do to the Jews, nothing much happened immediately; in fact, harassment started slowly. During the initial stages of the German occupation of Poland, they were busy consolidating their position. However, with the Allies entering the war, the Nazi screw of oppression was turned slowly (but unremittingly) at first, then accelerated during 1941 and culminated in relentless and sustained slaughter in 1942.

There were occasions when I spoke to German soldiers – one at a time, of course, because when there was more than one they were unapproachable supermen, harshly spoken. On their own, the very same men opened up and spoke of their grievances, saying how much they disliked being in the war and wanted to go home as soon as possible. In other words, they had the same feelings and sentiments as any soldier in the world.

During the winter of 1939/40, Jews were stopped in the street and ordered to clear certain areas of snow and ice, but, as there were usually more people rounded up than there were tools available to work with, our ordeal did not normally last very long. Nobody liked it but nobody resisted. If one had to be on the street in pursuit of one's daily business, then trying to dodge these unscheduled unpleasantnesses and delays was what one had to contend with. It was then that I heard, for the first time, the fatalistically philosophical words: 'If only it doesn't get worse, one can bear it.' This phrase was repeated after people had become accustomed to each and every new twist of the oppressors' screw.

When the edict was issued that all Jews had to live in ghettoes, some said with characteristic stoicism: 'Our fathers lived in ghettoes', and so the phrase changed slightly from 'one can bear it' into 'one can survive it'. This typically Jewish attitude was best expressed by an equally typical old Yiddish saying: '*Az men gevaynt sech mit de tsoores leybt men mit zay in fryden.*' Loosely translated this means: 'When one gets used to sorrows, one can live with them happily.'

With the arrival of the special *Einsatzgruppen*, who roamed from ghetto to ghetto and each time left between 50 and 300 dead bodies, the mood changed from dread to mortal terror. The sayings which were meant to prop up sagging morale were not heard any more, but even then people had no idea what lay before them.

Meanwhile, in 1939 and 1940, although with nagging fear of the future, we managed to make a living. When the Germans invaded Poland, the Kleinbergers and Schneiders disappeared and I heard no more of them until long after the war. Another uncle of my father's, Ignatz Kleinberger, had arrived from Frankfurt am Main. We found him in charge of a huge stock of pickled cucumbers in 5-kilogram metal containers and an enormous amount of jam in tins of an equal weight; these had been left behind by his brother-in-law, Jakob Schneider, when he fled the country. He engaged my father to help him sell off this stock. Helping in this enterprise gave me my first experience of commercial vending. It was very easy since everybody wanted to buy foodstuffs and the price was not dictated by the usual criteria of having to restock. Thus the first few months went by in comparative ease.

In December 1939, around the time of the last sale, I met up again with my Polish friend Janek, from Zakopane. This enterprising young fellow had been buying gold and jewellery cheaply in his home town and had come to Kraków to dispose of it. Inspired by my success in selling cucumbers and jam, I asked my father to offer him the hospitality of our home and, of course, to try to sell Janek's merchandise.

To conduct business on the black market is, of course, a punishable offence. But this is one illegal activity where buyers and sellers are mainly people who, in normal circumstances, would not dream of breaking the law. It often starts with parents' inability to provide sufficient food for their children. Inevitably, however, trading in this manner, born of need, degenerates into profiteering – by some, at least.

Currencies (English pounds, US dollars, German marks) were sought-after trading commodities. In this way the rich and the super-rich safeguarded their surplus, steadily devaluing native currency, and a host of lesser fortunates were enabled to feed themselves – by selling their valuables at inflated prices or by being middlemen in these transactions. Those who were dealing in valuables carried their business in their pockets. They stood around in little groups in certain streets in the Kazimierz quarters of Kraków. More and more joined these groups until – it had to happen – in a major raid by the Polish police, a number of men were arrested, searched and, if found in possession of 'illegal' goods, held for punishment. Needless to say, they also lost all that had been found on them. Once the police and their German masters had found that such raids not only 'served the law' but also provided them with a lucrative new income, a whole new sinister game developed. Some of the arrested, in order to regain their freedom, made a deal with their captors – they became 'moossers' – informants.

When, back in 1939, I handed to my father the gold that Janek had brought from Zakopane, I also, so to speak, introduced him to the black market. There were no jobs, there was no welfare, and we were glad when our Polish friend, pleased with his first success in 'business', promised to continue his valuable deliveries. Once introduced, and not knowing if and when Janek would return, my father made use of his new connections – he became a middleman.

During this time I also managed to make some pocket money. It actually started shortly after my return from Zakopane. My interest in billiards and chess took me frequently to the Hotel Royale which was about ten minutes' walk from where I lived. There was a sizeable hall with two full-size billiard tables but card games were preferred. Before the war, chess was the favourite recreation but now people's interest in games of concentration seemed to have dropped. I once witnessed a display by a billiards champion who scored 2,300 cannons (points) in one turn.

Perhaps because of the hotel's inability to replace their stock of playing cards, or for whatever reason, I was offered the job of cleaning them when they became grubby. I also had to replace damaged ones from an incomplete pack. For this I received a small amount of money. The perks that came with this occupation were that I could make use of the billiard tables whenever they were unoccupied – and that was most of the time. Mostly I played with 'Lulu' (Julius) Rubinstein but my greatest joy was when I played against my father. Because of the many hours of practice I soon became a better player than he was. He didn't mind, as he also didn't mind (he even liked it), when I eventually began to beat him at chess.

Nothing enjoyable lasted for long in those days. Soon German *Wehrmacht* officers moved into the hotel. For a short while, they did not bother us, whether because they were unaware of the large Jewish clientèle in the afternoons, or because they were moving on too quickly, I do not know.

At the reception desk of the hotel, another acquaintance of our family, a Mr Stieglitz, also from Frankfurt, had worked there from before the war. His tall, thin figure and sharp facial features would not necessarily denote his Jewishness. The fact that he conversed in faultless German, spoken, almost exclusively, by Jewish immigrants or those deported from Germany, would, if anybody had given it a thought, have been a significant pointer. It must have crossed the mind of many a German officer. Maybe, as weary travellers, they were glad to be served, politely, efficiently and in their own language. Maybe they did not care. I often stood at the entrance, observing the comings and goings of the guests, by now all in uniform. I wondered how long it would be before a dissatisfied customer – and there is always at least one in a big hotel – or a rabid antisemite would make use of his position as a member of the conquering 'master race', with the inevitable consequences.

A major arrived. 'You are a Jew!' he bellowed and – since there was no denial – 'What is a Jew doing in a "German" hotel?' he exclaimed indignantly. Stieglitz, his wife and daughter, who had lived there in staff quarters, had to leave. I never saw them again. From then on German rule established itself firmly and no more Jews were allowed inside the Hotel Royale.

*   *   *

New laws: Jews had to wear the *Judenstern* – the Star of David – on an armband. A nasty bit of legislation, not easy to get used to, and intended to mark and degrade. A further turn of the screw. There was no designated colour scheme, at least not at first and not in Kraków. Ironically, their manufacture provided a new source of income for some enterprising Jews. With typical ingenuity, the finished product was, with the right clothing, not too noticeable as it consisted of a dark blue star on a piece of material made of dark grey celluloid and held in place by a length of black elastic. The virtue of this design was that it could be swiftly pushed round to the inside of the wearer's arm, thus rendering it practically invisible, which could be an advantage if, for instance, there was a need to visit the Polish section of the city.

If there were still any optimists among us they were, by now, surely filled with the foreboding of impending calamity. We were trapped, there was no more emigration, no escape. 'But, what will they do with us? Take away our livelihood? Force us to work for them for little or no wages?' These and other, in retrospect, very naive speculations were the type of conversations then circulating among the Jewish population.

In response to the question I have often been asked – 'Why didn't you leave the armbands off? Who would know that you were Jewish?', first, quite a few, including myself, delayed the moment when they donned the star for the first time. Without it, in Jewish quarters, you were almost the odd one out; in other places, the Poles, having as yet nothing to gain by it, left you alone whether you wore the armband or not. Nothing extraordinary happened; you weighed up your chances of being caught without it and decided that it was safer to wear the star than to risk punishment. Although it was meant to mark and degrade, it did not, after a while, feel like that at all; there were so many.

Second, in Poland at this time, the slightest accent or semitic feature could be fatal — sooner or later. Not even an Aryan appearance would help you in the long run if you did not also have the correct documents. Pitiably few survived the war on forged papers. (Among them, though I did not even know of her existence, was a relation of mine, a namesake — a lady whom my wife met by chance on Yom Kippur, 1984, sitting next to her in synagogue.)

Many Germans who did not have the desired Aryan look wore larger than average swastikas in their lapels. As a matter of fact, quite in keeping with my adventurous nature, I sometimes considered wearing this hated sign myself to test the possibility of mingling undetected with the enemy if the need should arise. Father, mother and sister, though not particularly Nordic-looking, had no specific features to stand out in a crowd of average Germans. I had very dark eyes and (so I was told) Garbo-like eyelashes: together they would be a give-away.

Thus conditioned, it weighed heavily on my mind when, in the near future, I was planning to escape from forced labour or concentration camps.

* * *

The winter of 1939 was quite severe. As Jews, we were often rounded up and ordered to shovel snow, mountains of it. I remember one occasion, father and I, together with a dozen others, were to clear a major thoroughfare. It was bitterly cold. The guards, German soldiers armed with rifles, were changed every 15 or 20 minutes. One of them informed us that the temperature was $-30°C$. We worked hard just to keep ourselves from freezing to death. When a fellow worker touched the metal part of his shovel his hand stuck to it. I was glad to have followed my father's practical advice always to carry spare socks in my pocket for just such an emergency. With two pairs of socks over my well-worn gloves, all I suffered from this ordeal was a sore throat. Those who were caught a few times quickly learned the art of dodging, and again one would hear people say, 'If only it doesn't get worse ...'

Spring arrived and so did Janek — with another quantity of gold. As before, my father successfully disposed of it for him and, as before, he slept at our place. He was given my bed and I slept in the kitchen. As a Pole, he had freedom of movement. Being young and with plenty of money in his pocket, he was never without a bottle of vodka, and progressed slowly towards a state of permanent intoxication. It became embarrassing to have such a friend but this was no time to dissociate oneself from the 'goose that laid the golden eggs'.

While I easily resisted his offers of a drink, I once accepted his invitation to go out and look for girls. It was a pleasant evening after a very warm day; I was wearing a white suit – one of seven that Idek Schneider left behind, and the only white suit I have ever possessed. Needless to say I was not wearing my armband but carried it in my pocket.

We strolled along the banks of the river Vistula. The light of the moon, mirrored by the flowing waters, was the only illumination by which we could discern shadowy figures of people, seemingly moving in patternless directions. My eyes, growing accustomed to the darkening surroundings, could now make out figures beginning to pair up. Before long, we had to walk carefully lest we stumble over couples lying indiscriminately on grassy patches. 'Let's go home,' I suggested to Janek, only to find out that he was not with me any more.

I turned around and walked back. There he was, making advances to a blonde with dishevelled hair. I also noticed with alarm a group of figures moving menacingly in our direction. I shouted a warning. Janek jumped to his feet and we both sped away as fast as our legs would take us. The mob followed, screaming abuse and throwing stones at us. The adventure had turned into a 'flee-for-your-life' situation.

We soon outraced them, however, and, resuming our normal pace, we tried to guess what had gone wrong. Maybe the blonde was someone's girlfriend or sister, maybe it was my white suit that attracted the attention of hooligans or maybe just high-spirited youngsters – out for kicks. Janek was ready for further adventures, but I had had enough excitement for one evening and turned homewards.

It was getting late and, it only now occurred to me, my parents must be worried. As I hastened my pace, I noticed that there were not many people out and about and again regretted the white suit, fearing it might attract more unwanted attention.

Three minutes to go and I would reach the safety of my home. Slightly out of breath, I approached a rather noisy group of two men and one girl, the latter screaming 'Let go of me' and the two suitors pulling her by her arms – in different directions. Suddenly a pail of water, probably thrown by someone disturbed in his sleep, cascaded down and drenched the three revellers. As I passed by, the girl managed to free herself and disappeared inside an open doorway, with the two men in hot pursuit.

'What a night,' I thought. 'This, at least, I can tell my parents.' I turned the last corner and almost bumped into three German soldiers. '*Verdammt*' ('damn') – the German word slipped out thoughtlessly. Rallying fast, and before I was asked questions for which I had no satisfactory answers, I turned and beckoned them to follow me. 'Quick, quick, come and help me, two Poles are molesting my sister!' After only a few steps, we could hear the shouting going on unabated. Hearing the sound of a damsel in distress made two of the musketeers overtake me. I ran after them (a ridiculous situation), leaving the third, slightly staggering and probably the worse for drink, behind. I prayed for the door of the quarrelling threesome still to be open – it was. 'Second floor on the right,' I said brazenly, waving them towards the stairs and the sound of the commotion, which came from somewhere above.

What next? I could, of course, follow them upstairs and bluff it out, relying on the two parties not to understand each other. No I couldn't. I had committed myself by saying 'Second floor on the right', which was simply a shot in the dark. Luckily a fearful scream urged my two companions into action. Taking two steps at a time, they rushed upstairs. It was now or never; I peeped outside prepared to confront number three. He stood outside, five paces away – relieving himself. '*Ich rufe die Polizei*' – I'm calling the police – I told him as I rushed away, hoping he would not interrupt the flow of his activity. In seconds I was across the road and out of sight.

Another story to excuse myself to my worrying parents. I was still reprimanded about my inconsiderate behaviour; frightening mother and father out of their wits by being out late at night in such dangerous times – and without even wearing my armband.

'Janek has gone on to see some of his friends,' I mentioned casually. 'He sends his regards, he will be back later.'

No wonder sleep evaded me for hours; my head was filled with the events of the evening. Where would I be now, had I been caught?

The next day Janek left again for Zakopane, promising to return with another parcel of golden trinkets in about a month's time. We never saw him again. He had helped us immensely until well into 1940. I wish that I could meet him again to tell him of my gratitude.

* * *

The black market was now our only source of income – it was also a trade fraught with the danger of being arrested. That must have been why my father refused to take me with him whenever he went out to meet the people with whom he traded.

'I wish we could find another way of making a living, Bernhard,' my mother used to tell him anxiously. 'It is sheer torture always to wait and wonder whether or not you will come back today.'

'What else can we do?' he would reply. 'We are like frightened animals forced to leave their hiding-places for food.'

All went well – for a while. Almost daily, we heard of people we knew being arrested, while my father seemed to lead a charmed life for a very long time. (A long time in those days could be just a month – a week.)

Then it happened; my father did not return. Mother, distressed but determined, went straight to the police. My father had been found in possession of 800 Reichsmarks – an incarcerable offence unless he denounced those from whom he had obtained this money. As he told us later, my father pretended to agree. By so doing, he avoided further beatings and the menacing behaviour of his captors became, for the time being, almost jovial. The next day he went, accompanied by two plain-clothes policemen, probably Gestapo, to the street where black-market dealings took place. People stood around in small groups, apparently just chatting. Rarely now did anybody carry any incriminating items on him. Arrests were usually made as a result of being informed on.

Eventually my father spotted the person from whom he had obtained the forbidden currency. The man wanted to speak to him but understood at once when my father gave him a warning stare and, ignoring him, walked straight past, followed by the two strangers. Realising that my father was under arrest, he disappeared immediately, and the police did not get their prey.

My father was sentenced to six months' imprisonment. By pretending to play their game he had achieved three things: they stopped beating him, his business friend was saved – and was probably able to warn others – and, most importantly, there was no one to contradict him when he told the judge that this was his only deal and that he had acquired the Reichsmarks because he had lost confidence in the fast devaluing *złoty* – not knowing that it was against the law.

At this time it was still all so 'civilised', seen against the cataclysmic events that were to follow, that we were even allowed to bring him home-cooked food every day, without, however, seeing him – not even once.

* * *

Once again, I was working at a sewing machine to produce something for the war effort. The name and personality of the man who ran the factory are deeply engraved on my memory. Whenever we saw this elegant, good-looking fellow dealing with the Germans as they walked through the factory in their uniforms, inspecting the set-up and the product, we, the workers, had a temporary illusion of security.

Sallo Greiwer treated his *Wehrmacht* guests like a latter-day businessman selling his produce to his most valued customer. Perhaps we do have a future after all, we thought. We do important work here. I later heard of many such industrial undertakings and the more important they became, the better the relationship that developed between the management, Jewish or otherwise, and the *Wehrmacht* – and it also became even more likely that the Gestapo or the SS would step in and give it short shrift.

There was no such thing as a safe place for Jews, even if their work was essential for the war effort; the destruction of the Jewish race took precedence. When Sallo Greiwer headed these inspections, every inch the tycoon, with a high-ranking entourage in his wake, it was as if all the laws pertaining to Jews did not apply to him.

Collaborator? Traitor? These words cross my mind but I may be doing him an injustice. Perhaps he was just trying to save us and, of course, himself. The fact that he enjoyed entertaining his German clients lavishly could well have been the means to an end – until the Gestapo became aware of it – and he was arrested.

* * *

With my father in prison, our situation quickly became desperate. We would now have to start selling our belongings just to eat and to

35

pay our rent. Fear of penury, hunger, homelessness was gnawing at every parent's heart.

There are many degrees of desperation. At our stage, without any income, we were running out of hard cash fast; however, we still had many items in our wardrobe and even some jewellery. The hiding-place my father had made for the family valuables was most in-genious. In those days, we were heating and cooking not only by coal, and coal products, but also with chopped wood. My father selected one or two larger pieces, split them in half and hollowed these out on the split side. He then put the trinkets and baubles, few in number and of no great value, inside the space and then glued or nailed the two matching halves together, making it impossible to detect their contents. Placing the now valuable chunks of wood among the others in the stack posed the tricky question of how to know which was which. Although I memorised the special logs, for safety reasons we made two heaps, one of them not to be used. Every time I put one of the pieces in the stove, I was worried that somebody might unwittingly have mixed them up.

With the worsening of their situation, Jews had increasing dif-ficulties in obtaining accommodation. I soon found a young couple to whom we let the room next to the kitchen, thus displacing my sister into my mother's room. The fact that we had to pass through each others' rooms, there being no corridor, was perhaps the first taste of worse, much worse, to come. The law forcing Jews into certain parts of the town, and then later, after squeezing a bit more, into the ghettos, was not far off. Meanwhile, life went on with my mother and myself taking turns to bring provisions to my father.

Although the payments made by Mr and Mrs Eis, our lodgers, almost covered our rent for the flat, there was certainly not sufficient to feed us as well. Fate intervened again, this time in the shape of a man called Berel, the younger brother of Mr Eis. When he lost his accommodation, he moved in, first into the room of his brother and sister-in-law, then into my room. I now had to make do with the divan in the kitchen. Far from being annoyed, I liked him very much even though he did not pay any rent. He looked 'a real tough guy', the type who fires the mind of an impressionable youngster and makes him think that this is the stuff that heroes are made of. He performed no heroics, but he put himself out to help support us.

It is, perhaps, difficult to imagine that, at a time of such oppression, people were still looking for leisure activity. There were no official places of entertainment open to Jews, and so it was not difficult for 'Bear', as we called him, to organise little groups who would then come to our place to play cards. These were not just friendly family games but gambling, often for very high stakes. The game they played was called Okker (this may not be the correct spelling but that is how they pronounced it). It was played with four cards and had certain similarities to Poker, as the betting starts with two cards and continues after the remaining two have been dealt.

Every time a big kitty developed and the winner was not yet certain, 'Bear' would take one high denomination bank-note from the top of the pile and put it aside for the hostess, my mother, who in turn would provide the gamblers with light refreshments. Our family thus gained more money than we had ever had at any time since arriving in Kraków. My father, who of course benefited as the quality and quantity of his food improved, must have wondered how we did it.

One day a second cousin of my mother, Paula Bodner (now Schechter), and her one-year-old baby son arrived from Tarnow, where, according to her, the situation was even worse than in Kraków. She had plans to meet her husband, and to flee the country. Although our flat was already pretty crowded, a second bed was provided for them in the kitchen, where I slept. They stayed for three days and then Paula and little Ariel (whose name was emblazoned in red letters on his bib) left us. They managed to cross borders and eventually reached Belgium. If only my father was here, maybe we could have all gone together, I thought wistfully.*

Jews were now being cleared out of many places and the Rynek Główny was one of them; especially as it was being renamed Adolf Hitler Platz. We lost our flat, we lost our friends – we lost our livelihood.

Our new quarters were one room in a flat belonging to a family of four – two parents with their two children of school age. We now

*As the story was later related to me, fate caught up with them. The Gestapo, looking for somebody else, found Paula and her husband, and they ended, I believe, in Bergen-Belsen. Ariel, by his parents' wise foresight, had been entrusted to the care of a Catholic, Belgian couple, who became so fond of him that after the war, the Bodner family, who had survived in England, experienced difficulties in regaining custody of the child. Later I met Ariel in London; the baby who had slept in our kitchen in those distant, almost unreal days, is now happily married and proudly introduced me to his charming wife and two lovely daughters.

lived in a district of Kraków almost exclusively Jewish. No more walking about without armbands – that would be too conspicuous. Whether the family were compelled to take us into their flat or whether it was a voluntary act, I do not know. Such things were arranged by adults and so were over my head.

By now hunger had arrived at our door: not the hunger of peacetime when, for one reason or another, one had to miss a meal or two. This was different; it was accompanied by fear that, from now on, the pain in one's stomach would be permanent – with the inevitable consequences of illness and death. The time had come for personal items to be traded for food.

Although we still had several suitcases full of wearable clothes, every item was irreplaceable, and it is a dismal feeling to see one's possessions dwindle, and foresee the time when nothing would be left to trade or exchange. There were, of course, the two hollowed pieces of wood with their golden contents (my parents' wedding rings, one other ring, a bracelet and a pocket watch), which, however, did nothing to lessen the ugly feeling of impending doom. There was also one ordinary pocket watch which I will mention later.

Mother made the decisions as to what we could do without. The first thing to go was my father's old overcoat. How much food did it provide? I could not say; what is more, after some involuntary fasting, my mind ceased to worry about tomorrow and concentrated on the meal in hand. Tomorrow became a far-off time; today and today's meal was the focus to which, to the exclusion of everything else, our attention directed itself. People's natures changed. To obtain a meal, sometimes just a piece of bread, they would go to lengths they would never have believed possible. Yet, by today's standards, morals were still high and there was almost a complete absence of crime to the person; mugging or street robbing were simply not heard of.

Kindness, if anything, was even more prevalent, or so I thought when 'Mutti' (as I called my mother till the day we parted forever) came home with the joyous news that she now had a part-time job carrying bread to a number of households in the morning. One would have thought that, at times like this, people would be queueing for such a commodity, not having it delivered to their homes. But it is possible that it had been baked secretly and obtained by a regular round of people with sufficient money to pay high black-market prices, or that my mother was given the job to disguise the fact that she was the recipient of charity. At that time, I learned the Polish saying: *'Nim tłuste schudni, chudy zdechni'* – by the time the fat become lean, the lean are dying. Yet, death by starvation was still rare in the latter part of 1940. One can only marvel at the endurance of the human body, fed only occasionally with scraps.

We had bread. For weeks we had bread for breakfast, for lunch, for supper; no butter, no margarine, no cheese, no jam – nothing to go with it – well, not quite. The family in whose flat we stayed apparently had a shop. I never saw it, nor did they let on what they were selling, but I guessed that dairy products were at least part of their business, for, whenever mother sold an item of our clothing and we had enough money, she purchased milk or even some butter from them. The daily excursions to the prison had almost stopped but when, after disposal of another item, we had a change of menu, my father received his share. By the diminishing frequency of our visits and the deteriorating quality of the food we sent him, he could make his own deduction as to how the family fared.

Adjoining the kitchen, which we had the use of, was a walk-in larder. Inside were four shelves, empty but for two plates. One with a chunk of butter – about a quarter of a pound – the other with a piece of white cheese of similar size and weight, belonging, of course, to the host family. When I was alone in the flat, I used to visit this storeroom clandestinely and feast my eyes on the precious commodities but I did not touch. Upbringing prevailed for several weeks.

Every time the dwindling portions came to an end, they were replaced immediately by other quarter-pounds. Then I noticed that the top of the butter, as well as the cheese, showed markings which I guessed were designed to betray whether anyone had interfered with the pattern.

The challenge to outwit the designer was too much: I could resist no longer. I lifted the butter, carefully sliced about two millimetres from underneath and put it back precisely where it had been. It would have taken a tape-measure to detect the missing one-twentieth. There I was, with the loot in my hand, and, at that moment, no bread to go with it. Should I hold on to it, tell my mother? I dared not. Who remembers the taste of a slice of butter after 40 years? I do.

Conscience about my misdeed was suppressed by the fear of detection. Nothing happened. This, as every criminologist knows, could well be the first step on a slippery slope – and so it was. Every few days, especially when a new supply appeared, I raided the larder, using the same method each time but alternating between butter and cheese. My conscience was soothed when I observed that replenishments kept coming in undiminished amounts, indicating that the family suffered no deprivations themselves. No time-honoured invitation to us to partake in a Sabbath meal was ever forthcoming. On the other hand, deep in my heart, I could understand that the instinct for survival was paramount.

Less than two years later, when the *Churban* started in earnest, when people were often rounded up from the ghettos, and when life depended on being young, strong and unburdened by helpless little hands, stark self-preservation took over and, in some isolated but extremely poignant cases, the instinct for survival eliminated even that other most powerful instinct – mother-love. Children, thus abandoned, disavowed, bewildered and crying, were put, sometimes thrown, on to lorries like so much rubbish, sometimes killed on the spot. The destination of these loaded vehicles can be imagined.

Who dares cast the first, or any, stone at such parents, wretched and mourning for ever (if indeed they survived) unless he has been in such a situation? Staying alive – alive for the moment – was the all-powerful motivation for the basest instincts, unimaginable and unreal at any other time, to emerge from the hidden depths of human nature.

* * *

'*Now* she becomes a good eater.' All our lives, until we left Germany, my sister and I were constantly told how naughty we were for not finishing up our food. Hanna was the worst offender. I emphasised '*now*' in that wistful remark, believing that, had she continued to eat as little as she used to, I would not need to rise from our meagre repasts still as ravenous and unsatisfied as when I sat down.

No sentence I have ever uttered during my lifetime has been regretted as much as this one. You would think that after more than 40 years I would be ready to recall the past without the choking lump in the throat that ended all earlier attempts. But I still miss Hannelorchen, and she will never be forgotten. I gave my younger daughter the Hebrew name Chana in Hanna's memory.

I remember how, in the autumn of 1940, waiting for my father to be released, we used to play cards every day for hours on end. What surprising capacity quiet eleven-year-old Hanna displayed, winning far more often than could be ascribed to mere luck. I can still visualise the dexterity of her little hands when shuffling the deck.

I remember one particular hand I had, like a poker player who will never forget his royal flush or the highest stake he played for. I can still see the three of us, mother on my right and Hanna sitting opposite me. We were playing the previously mentioned game of Okker, and I had what every gambler dreams of, a hand on which you (so every gambler believes) could safely stake your last shirt. So, apparently had Hanna, though I never found out. Mother threw in her hand. 'You continue,' she said, 'I have something to prepare.' We carried on, challenging each other and raising our stakes in the true old fashion of the Mississippi gamblers.

Mother busied herself at the cooker, while on the table the kitty of matches grew and grew, and so did the excitement. Suddenly, we both threw our cards away, not caring where they fell; an aroma had pervaded the kitchen and the ecstasy it aroused could not be equalled even by a royal flush. Eggs!

(My younger daughter, Tricia, picked up the manuscript. Reading the last few paragraphs she exclaimed, 'What a let-down – all this excitement just for an egg.' How can one explain to the children of this age of plenty that the mere anticipation of a scrambled egg could cause such a stir?)

*   *   *

How is it that I am unable to remember the moment of reunion with my father? All I know is that by now he had been released from prison, the word 'ghetto' was in the air, and my parents decided that we should move to Bochnia.

The period running up to our departure is highlighted in my memory by one incident I would prefer to forget. Stealing butter and cheese might have been forgiven in the conditions then prevailing; stealing money would not. The smallness of the amount would have soothed my conscience were it not for the fact that punishment came in a most unusual form less than two years later when my dear grandfather, not even living in Poland at the time, was, by the oddest coincidence, accused of the misappropriation.

The owners of the flat were, as usual during the daytime, absent.

The toilet looked like a million others except that there was a flowerpot next to the pan. It was filled with earth and a withered stem. Even today I am unable to say what made me probe the soil with my fingers, but the envelope I found hidden there contained 3.500 *złoty*; a small fortune for people with no money at all. I put it back – all of it, nice and neat.

Mother's bread round had come to an end with the inevitable consequences – no more extra bread rations. I overheard my parents talking. The grimness of the situation, which I was well aware of, seemed even more desolate when I heard them discussing the list of items to be disposed of; how long we could live on these; and whether there was any other way of keeping away starvation. Naturally, in the true fashion of loving parents, none of the items to be sold or bartered was mine – or my sister's.

Shortly before we left for Bochnia, I took 200 *złoty* out of the envelope. The official value of the dollar was then about 35 *złoty*, on the black market the price was 150 *złoty* for the dollar – and rising. To me, however, it seemed much more. I thought that I could be a rescuer in dire need – and it constantly appeared that this would soon happen. I had not, however, reckoned with the resilience of my dear father. Somehow, for the next few months, we ate; not opulently, hardly ever a piece of meat, but we did not starve.

4

Bochnia

It must have helped our food situation that we were now living in a small town. We stayed with a Jewish family by the name of Vogelhut I think they were farmers though all I saw at the time was a not very large yard at the rear with some chickens, a dog on a chain and a cow. Also inside that smallholding were some insignificant box like buildings of various sizes; the larger ones had probably held horses or cattle in better times. There were probably fields too but I never saw any. The lady of the house had all the signs of a faded, gypsy-like beauty. Her husband was of very amiable disposition. They had two sons, both slightly older than me.

It was spring 1941. Although the laws against the Jews were country-wide, they seemed less direct, and therefore less oppressive, in Bochnia – for the moment, that is. However, knowing what was going on elsewhere, the anxiety for the future was the same. There was again talk of a ghetto and speculation as to where it would be, but there were very few German uniforms in sight. I was much happier here than during my last few months in Kraków.

We were on the border of the town and it occurred to me that running away, should the need arise, would not be difficult at all. The four of us had one large room (approximately 5 by 3¾metres or 16½ × 12 feet) to live, sleep, wash and cook in. There was a small stove for warmth, just big enough to place one cooking pot on top; it was fuelled with coal and wood. The privy was a little wooden shack at the furthest end of the yard.

For me, there was a respite from the loneliness of the last few months. I met boys and girls of my age, including, by one of life's coincidences, my former partner in billiards and cards, Julius Rubinstein, who with his parents and younger brother moved into a place almost across from us in the same street.

News of atrocities against the Jews became more frequent yet, strangely, Bochnia, for reasons we could only speculate on, was overlooked. Something like a social life developed among us youngsters. There were lots of gatherings, the main ingredients of which were discussions, singing, party games and flirting. Music was very rare, dancing almost non-existent. However unreal these happy gatherings seem to me now, in those days they were our expression of defiance – to get on with life without taking account of tomorrow.

With the increasing awareness that the Nazis were not just interested in isolated killings (at that time 'isolated' meant between 50 and 300 corpses at each of their raiding excursions), there were reports of a gradual loosening of personal morals, but in our group there were no signs of licentiousness. However, 'To hell with tomorrow which we can do nothing about' was the watchword among the younger generation who felt betrayed.

Discussions everywhere centred on the grim future. Right from the beginning the Nazis had disseminated the most vicious hate propaganda against the Jews to a growing and receptive generation, instilling into them the concept of master-race against subhumans, and they had now raised sufficient, only too willing helpers in their avowed aim to solve the *Judenfrage*, the problem of the Jews.

Discussions in our young circle went from the philosophical to the revolutionary but always ended by recognising that, without weapons and proper organisation, we were doomed to destruction. 'What will they really do with us?' was the constant question. The way they were meting out death now – 300 to 600 a week was our estimate, a horrific 15,000–30,000 a year – one in ten of us would be eliminated if the war were to go on for ten years.

'They will shoot every male of combative age but not the harmless old, the women and the children' was a common assumption. There were still quite a few voices that could not conceive of the wanton mass destruction of people; 'ghettos' were their solution. They would put us into ghettos, as in the Middle Ages, and have their sadistic satisfaction in our humiliation. Ghetto laws had already been implemented in other places. It was easier in bigger towns, with large sections of the Jewish community living in certain areas, to force the remainder to join them in designated quarters. Jewish councils were created to help the Germans in this task.

Were they traitors or just so-called '*machers*' – doers? The kind of people one could always find to do an important job, and who would feel elevated among others by a position of responsibility; well-meaning people, perhaps, who imagined that, by co-operating with the Germans, they would be able to improve the lot of their fellow Jews and, of course, of their own family – and often they did. That was their starting position. They were mostly, I would venture to say, normal, even decent people. Little did they know that their initial task of allocating living accommodation and regulating food rations would soon change into being instruments of their masters, helping them in their gruesome task of selecting people to be transported to the 'East', to destinations initially unknown.

That is where I learned the now internationally used word '*protekcja*' (pronounced protectsia) – patronage. The saying 'it is more important who you know than what you know' was never more true. Be it food, living or working conditions, there could be a vast difference between having or not having vital connections – *protekcja*. Later, it was not living conditions but life itself that might depend on such patronage. And that is when 'normal, even decent people' became 'collaborators'.

Neither my father nor I was ever in an elevated position (though later, in the camps, I made it my first task to seek out such patronage), yet I have often asked myself: 'Had I been in a position to save my kin, even only for the moment, how far would I have gone?' Thank heaven that this is only a hypothetical question, impossible to answer in complete honesty – could you? It must have been appalling to be confronted with 'either you deliver or we take yours. ...'

That night, when others were languishing in cattle wagons, they were once more at home with their family, safe. They could not bear to think what would happen ultimately when there was no one else to send. Then it would be their turn.

* * *

We were 'lucky'. We did not have to move when, finally, the Bochnia ghetto was outlined. Now we could also expect a visit from the special *Einsatzgruppen*, the roving assassins, whose brief stay meant the already mentioned death-toll of between 50 and 300 victims.

In the midst of it all we had a new arrival – my grandfather joined us. He had come from Frankfurt am Main – how and why I shall never know. He, of course, took up some of our inadequate accommodation. The initial joy of having one more member of the family with us soon gave way to tension and when, for what seemed to me the most implausible reason, he married an elderly lady and brought her into the one room we all occupied, tension changed to hostility. Although we lived in an era when compassion and understanding for your contemporaries, and especially for family, grew out of the wretchedness we all suffered, self-preservation was an over-riding factor. So when we caught our newly acquired grandmother smuggling a home-baked roll and some pieces of bread out of the house, the understanding we would normally have, that she had to help support a married brother with two children, did little to mitigate our wrath.

In normal times we surely would have welcomed her with open arms. She would have made a perfect companion for our grandfather. Sixty-seven years of age and a widower for more than a decade, he would, at other times, be congratulated on his good luck and good taste. In our heart of hearts we understood, but any charitable feeling we might have had floundered when we began to suffer in our stomachs from the shortage of food that she had secretly stolen. She was an outsider, an intruder and, notwithstanding the fact that we would have done the same if we had been in her position, we resented this extra burden fate had bestowed on us. Her 'other' family probably had less than ours and what she took might well have been bought with grandfather's money. Nevertheless times were such that we were not open to reason.

The old man stood by his chosen wife and, to our great surprise and relief, found alternative accommodation. They moved just outside the loosely defined lines of the ghetto-to-be. This was also a sign that the Bochnia administration, with regard to Jews, was less severe than in most other places. 'And there they lived happily ever after' would have been a good ending to this somewhat bizarre story. But social visits were not on people's agenda and I have never seen my step-grandmother nor my grandfather again.

When my grandfather used to live with us and we expressed our fear of starvation, he repeatedly said, '*Der esserdicker malach shlooft nisht*' – 'the angel of sustenance sleepeth not'. And, amazingly, whenever we were hungry, food appeared from unexpected sources. There were no shops as such where one could buy edibles and, again, connections were more valuable than professorships. Poor indeed were the ones who had neither *protekcja* nor money.

Money or goods to trade were the key to life and both became increasingly scarce in our household. The 'angel of sustenance' stepped in, his name was 'Urbach'. By an arrangement made, probably by my grandfather before he came to Poland, Mr Urbach would give us money, in return for which, if he survived the war, he would be paid by Aunt Fanny Muller (father's sister) in New York. A splendid arrangement, except that Mr Urbach lived in Kraków. He was a *Treuhander*, a sort of manager, in his own shop of electrical goods. This arrangement was a way out of the dilemma of losing one's business: a *Volksdeutscher* (ethnic German) was the new boss who claimed that the previous Jewish owner (Mr Urbach) was indispensable to the running of the firm and, for a considerable time, this ruse worked well for everyone concerned.

Mr Urbach, apparently, had more money than he needed and it would suit him well to be paid in dollars for Polish currency. The problem was how to transfer cash from him to us. One could not trust any stranger and Jews were not allowed to travel. Hanna, who would be most suitable to lose herself in a Polish crowd, was, at 12 years old, a bit too young for this task. It was decided that I would join her in this adventure.

We dressed up as best we could as Polish peasant children, and, with great anxiety, our parents sent us on this dangerous but vital mission. Hannelorchen bought the tickets. We boarded the train with some trepidation, found two vacant seats and tried to appear unconcerned and inconspicuous. I felt sure everyone was looking at us.

'I think we should go back,' I whispered with sinking heart.

'What's the matter, don't you like a bit of adventure?' came her seemingly insouciant reply, accompanied by a smile which would make any observer think that she didn't have a care in the world. ... Hanna had certainly mastered her role and it was up to me not to let her down.

When the ticket inspector came, I was 'fast asleep', my cap pulled well down. So far so good. We reached the familiar streets of Kraków, apparently without anyone taking any notice of us. Our confidence soared. Familiar streets, however, did not produce familiar faces. Not a Jew in sight – not even marked with the Star of

David. We found Mr Urbach's shop – or rather his former shop – easily. He was not surprised to see us, almost as if he had expected somebody – but not youngsters.

I tried to act in a businesslike way and in less than half an hour we left with 20,000 *złoty* – a fortune. (Here I should mention again that, on the black market, the dollar would fetch between 150 to 175 *złoty*.) I later learned that my grandfather, on arrival in Kraków and before coming to Bochnia, had received the identical sum. This time it was going to be shared.

Hanna concealed the money and we returned home to our delighted parents. It had been a very worrying day for them.

*   *   *

Hunger in Warsaw at that time was so acute that even potato peelings were fetching enormous prices. Although we did not have much else to sustain us, we managed to obtain plenty of potatoes, and always threw away the peel. It is ironic to think that nowadays potatoes in their skins are valued for their vitamin content.

Polish peasants defied the authorities and came into our quarters. A Christian blacksmith who lived just across the road, received permission to stay there and carry on his work as before. He was visited by Poles who took the opportunity to do business with Jews. In exchange for an item of clothing and some money, they would sell us a 'mug of butter'.

There were no precise weights or measurements and it was then that I learned the psychology of bartering. Our suppliers were usually old women clad in black. Prices for eggs and butter were exorbitant. They knew we had little alternative. But we did not let on. We pretended that we could get it cheaper somewhere else and so made them drop their prices. Often, a sort of poker game developed, a game of nerves really. We did not show our eagerness and they pretended to walk towards the door. Whoever stopped first lost – pricewise. The old *baba* would turn at the door and quote her very lowest price before leaving. It was, of course, still much too high, but if we offered her just slightly below what she was asking she usually accepted. (If she had not, we would have run after her.) The old women were no fools but they liked the items we offered, rather than the money.

We parted with each item of clothing with a heavy heart. We knew it would not be replaced and supply was not unlimited. But it was a minor feast when we had something else with our usually plain potatoes.

* * *

Bochnia ghetto had now become fully fledged and more and more people were being squeezed into increasingly rigid confines. For us, who already lived in the 'designated quarters', the change came without disturbing us too much. However, it was different for the owners of our bungalow as they had to give up their bedroom to a couple with a 20-year-old daughter.

* * *

Historians differ about when the real *Churban* started; for me, but only in retrospect, it began with the news of special commandos, *Einsatzgruppen*, roaming from town to town, from ghetto to ghetto, killing people at random. The result, a 'mere' 50 corpses, soon had to be bettered and, with each new visit, the numbers grew. What heroes they must have felt, shooting down unarmed, bewildered and hungry civilians. What pride must have swelled their medal-seeking chests in reporting their increasing 'successes' to Berlin.

I do not know whether these killer commandos were the first consequence of the infamous conference at Wannsee – where the Final Solution, the satanic scheme to eliminate millions speedily and economically, was hatched – or whether these *Einsatzgruppen* were too slow and messy for the meticulous Teutonic mind and therefore this high-level gathering took place to expedite matters.

I do know that even the first 50 murders struck terror into our hearts. After further reports of more of these raids, only days apart (why did they take days off – did they need time to recover from their strenuous task?), we lived in perpetual expectation of a visitation. If anybody still believed that only a tiny fraction had been killed and therefore their odds of survival were favourable, they had to correct their calculations with every piece of news from now on.

* * *

'The ghettos are overcrowded and a "resettlement" programme will have to be set in motion', the Germans said when they started their mass transportation of people to the East. Nobody knew where they went, the exact destination was not disclosed. Families tried to stick together, while those who could not, hoped for news of how their relatives were settling down. One of the more naïve assumptions was that a large number of workers was needed for the harvest in the Ukraine. Now that we knew what the Nazis were capable of, doubt crept in right from the beginning but, in the absence of any news, people willed themselves to believe these rumours. Also, they could not help observing that the old and infirm were often among the first to go while many of the younger generation, those who already did slave labour, remained. For the moment, these events happened somewhere else; Bochnia, maybe because it was among the smaller ghettos, had, to our amazement, neither suffered from roaming killer squads nor had any deportation taken place. The time was June/July 1942.

Some months previously, the Bochnia *Judenrat* – the council of Jews who headed the ghetto – had been obliged to provide a number of able-bodied men to build roads for a new ammunition depot in, or near, Klaj (pronounced Cluy), a small town about 10 kilometres from where we lived.

I had been assigned to this group and after a few days' hard work, without any reward other than a slightly larger bread ration, I formed an ingenious scheme to get out of this back-breaking job. I went to a Polish doctor and gave him all the details I had learnt about the symptoms of tuberculosis. Without access to an X-ray machine, he issued me with a certificate which exempted me from work. (Ironically, this ruse returned to haunt me when, after the war, I was refused a visa to the USA – but by then I had had the real thing.) At the time TB was a killer disease, and so it was no wonder that I could read sympathetic concern in the good doctor's face as he made out the work-exemption document.

When, however, it became known that persons employed in work on the new depot were not to be sent to the East, I managed to rejoin the group of labourers. We commuted daily, by train, to Klaj where, in a nearby wood, a number of the above-mentioned depots were being built for the storage of ammunition. The buildings, all of them connected by a series of rails, were sited in an irregular pattern to make it more difficult for them to be detected from the air – and hence to be bombed – and, furthermore, if one of the stone-built barracks were to explode, the others were sufficiently distant not to be affected.

While cattle-trains packed full of people, destined for mass destruction, were already rolling eastwards, for me a period of boyish adventures had begun. Let me hasten to say that, although we were full of dark forebodings about the future of these transports and this 'Resettlement Programme', the full and tragic truth was not known to most until after the war. The mind developed its own logic: 'The Germans like slave labour, they need slave labour – everybody can see that. What about the women and children? Well, they also need cooks and cleaners – and someone will have to look after the children too.' As for myself, even in my darkest thoughts there was the spark of hope that although many would die, many would also survive. That a system had been put in motion to annihilate everybody in death camps simply could not be accepted by the mind – certainly not by mine.

Meanwhile, other trains, those that stopped at Bochnia Station each morning, were also full to capacity. More often than not, many of us could not get inside and had to travel on the steps outside the wagons, grimly clinging to the vertical bars on each side of the doors. This gave a real fillip for my natural inclination to court danger. Places, even on these small footholds, were scarce – and often fought over. I can recall several incidents that I certainly would not want my children to try to imitate.

The train, as usual, arrived full; there was nowhere for my two feet to stand on. But I had to be at work; excuses were not accepted. The train started to roll. Frantically my eyes searched for a toehold. I grabbed at and grasped the handrail and flung myself on to a few inches of space at the very end of the running board. My neighbour would not, or could not, move. With the train already at full speed, I swayed rather precariously, with one leg in the air. There was no way that I would be able to hold on like this for the whole journey.

In desperation, I started a performance which would not have disgraced a trained acrobat; I swung to and fro like a pendulum until finally, and successfully, I reached over to the next wagon and held on for dear life to the other handrail. Next, I managed to pull my other foot over and placed it on the edge of the other running board. With an elation that only betrayed my immaturity, I looked around proudly to ascertain that my achievement was duly observed. Thus, riding on two carriages simultaneously, I felt slightly more secure and, for the moment, rather pleased with myself. When the train negotiated a curve to the left, my legs actually came closer together; but then came a right turn and I felt my arms and legs spreading more and more. My hands were sliding to the very bottom of the rail as otherwise they would not reach. The gradual parting and stretching of my arms and legs created a peculiar, as well as frightening, sensation. I knew that there must be a limit to the curve's acuteness but there was also a limit to how far my arms and legs would stretch. I am sure that it didn't last more than 20 or 30 seconds but in this spreadeagled, almost crouched position, it seemed an eternity.

On another occasion – and again with no chance of getting aboard, not even with one foot – an idea struck me: 'What about the other side?' No sooner thought than done. I quickly slipped between two carriages, under the buffers and out to the other side of the stationary train. To my surprise, I seemed to be the only one with this idea. The pride of achievement barely compensated me for yet another uncomfortable ride in an upright position, as well as being drenched by a downpour and whipped by an unseasonal wind which, by the time of my arrival, had drained me of all the strength which I had to employ in just holding on.

My crossing over had been observed and was soon imitated – with a tragic result. It happened when, for the third time, I stepped from the low platform and, going under the buffers, crossed the rails. Two men followed me. To our horror the train began to move when we were still between the two carriages. I flung myself easily out of harm's way, immediately turning round and reaching out to pull the next one clear. The third was decapitated. The horror of the situation held us rigid – but only for seconds. Reality and our subconscious took over swiftly. The man was dead – we had to be at work. Shaking off the shock and still half-dazed, we managed to jump on to the last wagon. The man I had helped was a work mate of mine but the one who was killed we did not know. We decided that, should this situation arise again, it would be better to lie down flat between the rails and let the train pass over us.

Curiously, on the way back, travelling inside the coaches was somewhat easier to achieve, and it would have been only natural to compensate ourselves with a riskfree journey home. Not so.

We were working in the woods and were allowed to take back as much firewood as we could carry. 'Allowed', maybe, was not the word – rather, nobody objected. In modern terms this would be called the perks of the job. We needed wood for cooking and, of course, for warmth in the coming winter.

We were naturally limited as to what we could carry. Also, we could hardly take a sizeable bundle of wood into the carriage of a train. That, however, did not stop us. We – a few of the foolhardy ones – placed our oversized bundles across the buffers, sat ourselves on the small ledge which could be found at each end of these wagons (not linked by walk-through doors to the next) and, by pressing our feet against the branches of wood, we held ourselves and our precious cargo in position.

Everything seemed just fine and my mood joyous when, in my mind, I anticipated the praise of my family for my forward thinking and enterprise. Then why did I suddenly start to sweat with horror? One of the larger pieces of my badly tied bundle had worked itself loose and bounced happily and independently on the two buffers. Every few seconds, when the wheels passed over the point where each rail met the next, it gave a little jump. My hands were useless as I needed both of them to steady myself on my precarious seat.

Would it derail the train, kill us and a number of other people into the bargain, or would it just snap? It wasn't falling just yet. Having bounced a few inches to the right, it began dancing to the left, then right again. My eyes, and those of my companion who sat opposite me, with his feet steadying a much smaller load, followed the antics of this wretched object with hypnotic fascination. Six to seven feet long and about three inches in diameter, this gnarled and knotty piece of future firewood seemed to enjoy its independence and, mockingly, scared us out of our wits. Suddenly, of its own volition, it positioned itself right in the middle again. This opportunity must not be lost! I pushed it with my foot against the other smaller and thinner pieces – some of which promptly escaped harmlessly between the rails.

*   *   *

Our work in Klaj presently consisted of building a road. We were not actually constructing it but changing one made for the horse-and-cart age into one that could serve modern and heavier traffic.

The roadbed was made of thousands of tree-trunks, all about 6–10 inches in diameter. These beams, lying close to each other, were loosely covered with sand and gravel. Our task was to remove this old foundation. The foreman, a German civilian, showed us how. He took a pickaxe and embedded it at one end of the trunk, then two or three men would grab the pick handle and pull the timber out on to the roadside. It was hard work, but we were rewarded with a quarter of a loaf of bread and a soup which was compensation enough to carry on working without the weakening – and eventual demise – of the body, which would shortly become the established policy.

It has been said that the subconscious has a speedier reaction than the conscious mind. I can vouch for that. I swung the pick and, with a mighty blow, buried it deeply, or so I thought, into the tree trunk. Two men stood by. With the usual heave-ho! heave-ho! we combined our strength to dislodge the stubborn log. The first move is usually the difficult one – then it slides more easily. But after the first heave-ho and simultaneous mighty pull, the pickaxe dislodged itself. Two of us fell backwards into the ditch, the heavy tool following me in semi-circular flight, with the sharpened, wider end in the direction of my face. It was then that automatic reaction saved me from death or disfigurement which, in those days, equalled death.

My arm shot up and grabbed the deadly missile near its metal head but, unfortunately, I could not entirely counter the velocity that we had created by our forceful pull. The fearsome thing hit me in the face, cutting off my left nostril. It was literally hanging by a thread of skin.

My first reaction was not pain, fear or anxiety about the spurting blood – it was the vision of myself going through life with only one nostril – people, especially girls, averting their eyes from such an ugly and pitiful sight. Resolutely I pressed the loose piece of my nose back into place and held the stuck-on piece in position with my hand. When, eventually, the blood had dried, it stayed in position. A rolled-up handkerchief (blue with a white border, I remember) around my face and head protected my 'DIY' surgery on the way home. I can still see the amused glances of the other passengers on the train. I did not take along any firewood that night; but I did go to work the next day. The nostril soon healed back into position – probably helped by the thread it was hanging on. The scar is still visible, though very faint.

* * *

That was some time in July 1942. By this time messages, news and rumours were coming in thick and fast. Bochnia had so far been spared by the roaming *Einsatzgruppen*, who spearheaded the drive into the death-trains to annihilation. In fact, although daily expected with trepidation, they never came. Nobody knew the destination of these transports, but the rapid depletion of the population in the larger ghettos could not be kept secret.

Everybody racked their brains – where did all the people go? 'Resettlement' – the official version – was doubted, but there was as yet no proof for those who believed otherwise. The arguments went on. If the Nazis intended to kill everyone, then why take them away to do so? Why waste train space, so crucial for supplying their armies at the Eastern Front, when they were already so extremely adept at massacring large masses of people on the spot? Surely nothing could be as important as winning the war, the 'Total War' as Schickelgruber had declared? Maybe they did make use of slave labour in their newly won territories – we had to hold on to such illusions, as we could not contemplate the alternative.

On many occasions, during deep discussions within our family, we encouraged each other and tried to cheer ourselves up. Sometimes the news of setbacks in the advance of the German forces gave us a glimpse of hope: 'The war cannot last forever.' Far-fetched reasons were brought up in an attempt to ease our utter despair. It was not even a fool's paradise that we lived in, but unadulterated misery and desolation. We all fell silent now, with no more artificial encouragement of hope. Everybody lived with their dark and depressing thoughts and fears. My father, my mother, my sister, myself … what was to become of us and what were our chances of survival? These thoughts kept me, and I am sure many others, awake. Escape? But where could we go, especially since mother was not at all well lately? Maybe the expected Special Commando of killers would never come to Bochnia after all. A drowning person holds on to a piece of straw.

We discussed the possibility of leaving the ghetto, which would not be difficult as we lived on the outskirts of the town and there were no fences. But where should we go and, even if we were just to stay in the fields, for how long should we stay there? How should we sustain ourselves? There was too the real fear of being discovered by Germans, with their tracker dogs, and shot – even if we were found by Poles, the vast majority would almost certainly betray us to the authorities. These reasons, and many more like them, would not have counted if the Nazis, with their habitual cunning, had not planted a false seed of hope in people's minds with their 'Resettlement – somewhere in the Ukraine'. Had we but known for sure that these transports were leading directly to death, then we, and thousands of others, would have taken measures, any action at all, to have avoided them. As it was, when the order went out that people had to be at the station on a certain day – they went. Whole families arrived together, in their thousands.

More Nazi cunning: by being allowed to bring their belongings, people were lulled into believing that, like their forebears over the centuries, they would be able to start a new life somewhere else. Little did they know that their quite justified fear of being shot if they did not comply with orders to assemble that day at the station would have been a kinder fate by far than that which awaited them. The Germans could then reward themselves for having annihilated many hundreds of thousands – who would, of course, be carrying their most valuable possessions on them, enriching their murderers beyond counting.

Someone said: 'Goebbels has announced that two million Jews have already been liquidated. What is going to happen to us?' I did not believe that the German Propaganda Minister could make such an announcement officially. However, now came one of the two most memorable remarks from my parents during the war – the first from my mother and the second, two years later, almost to the day, from my father, near the gas chambers of Auschwitz.

My mother's comment was: 'What is going to happen to all Jews is going to happen to us.' This resigned attitude stirred something within me and my unspoken response, which made her pronouncement so indelible, was: 'If there is only one left alive, it will be me.' In an inner upsurge of determination, I almost felt that I had not only the will to do so, but also the power. Now that I have survived, I know that this depended a great deal not only on luck but also on the spirit, without the indomitable will to stay alive – even in the most hopeless situation or when suffering the obscene extremities of pain – mental or physical – the chances of survival were nil. Luck had to be supported by the combination of all the senses given to us and by developing these natural abilities to extreme limits only possible in the extreme conditions in which we found ourselves – let no survivor say otherwise.

Aloud, in response to my mother's dire prediction, I suggested: 'We have to find a hiding-place, or perhaps build one.' Whereas I was immediately gripped by this idea, almost ready to get up and start implementing it on the spot, I sensed reluctance and resignation in my mother's reaction. If only I had asked her about her reluctance and so quelled my nagging feelings that, by doing so, and perhaps arguing about it, things might have been different.

We were by now aware that it was only a matter of time before Bochnia was on the list of whoever directed these transports. The idea of a hiding-place grew, and became more urgent every day. We knew from other ghettos that once one or more transport trains had been filled to capacity and gone, a number of people were left behind and, by now used to living on a day-to-day basis, carried on with their lives as best they could. Arrangements were made for my father to join me in Klaj. It was for my mother and sister that I tortured my brain to find a way out – any way to avoid their being transported into the unknown, maybe forever. None of my plans was accepted because they all had, in one way or another, some shortcoming or flaw. There was no safe hiding-place and we had no material with which to construct anything underground.

The hiding place that I had in my mind to build, though far from perfect, was quite suitable for escaping detection by a casual searcher. There was a porch over the front entrance of the bungalow, the horizontal ceiling of which was covered by a pointed mini-roof. The tiny space underneath this roof could be entered by crawling in from inside the attic. As mentioned, we had no proper building materials. However, by placing a few sheets of available cardboard in line with the main roof, the little tent-shaped room above the porch was shielded from a not over-keen pursuer. The idea was that anybody who came up the stairs would see an empty attic, and mother and sister would be saved to face the next hurdle in this bizarre game of survival. It turned out differently.

On 22 August, the workforce was told that, on the next day, we would not be returning to Bochnia, but would be staying at some newly built barracks in the ammunition camp. The *Wehrmacht* must have been told the date of the next transport and tried to save us. Some of us went to plead for our families to be allowed to accompany

57

us – but this was refused. We did not know if this was a case of 'would not' or 'could not' – or even 'dared not'. On the 23rd, I went into the attic to try to improve the cardboard camouflage. I looked at it and was not at all happy – it could best be described as 'better than nothing'. A cursory glance would not reveal the hiding-place but a search could not miss it.

Father and I packed our suitcases. The time had come to say goodbye. I looked at my parents – they had known each other longest, they had created the family. Perhaps I expected the elders, whom we also looked up to as teachers, to come up with a magic formula, a solution that we children could not think of? Then I turned aside – there was no solution. 'Promise me that you will go into the secret place,' I urged my mother and sister and they both did so. We did not kiss or hug unduly as we would not allow ourselves to feel that this was a final goodbye. We left, heavily laden with our luggage, we turned round, they waved. Then I turned once more, my heart suddenly heavy with foreboding, and looked once again – as if to print their image beyond fading – then they were gone.

On 24 August the evacuation took place of the majority of the people in Bochnia ghetto. One trainload was sufficient. We only learned about this a few days later and none of the inmates of our camp knew whether any member of their families had been taken or left behind. One week later, we were allowed to march the 10 km to Bochnia – it was a much-appreciated gesture by the military as they were not obliged to do this. Father and I did not speak much, nor did we dare to speculate on what would await us. Because we had been told that there were quite a few hundred people left behind after the train had gone, we held on to the spark of hope that our loved ones would be among them – after all, they had a hiding place, which was more than most of the others had.

After one or two kilometres, my shoes began to give me trouble. Many were walking barefoot, why shouldn't I? But I was a city-dweller, with feet not hardened like many of the others, and, at the end of the journey, I could neither walk nor put on my shoes.

Arriving home we found the house empty. The mental anguish of realising my mother and sister had gone largely obliterated the physical agony of my swollen, blistered feet.

Worse was to come. Apparently, there had been so many at the station that the houses were not even searched. Then why had they

3 Little sister Hanna, aged about seven – one of the few happy moments in her
   short life

4 The ill-prepared hiding-place in the triangular loft above the porch

volunteered to go? The answer, as I had feared before, probably lay in the fact that the hiding-place was at the front of the house and, therefore, everything that was going on in the street outside could be observed through the crevices between the boards. Possibly, they might have seen the Rubinsteins and other familiar faces going and it would be typical of my mother to think that if other people, including intellectuals, were going, it must be better than staying behind. If the report was true that the SS went through the streets with loudspeakers, warning people that if they did not assemble at the station they would be shot, then the explanation as to why they left their hiding-place becomes clear. They were not physically forced to go but psychological intimidation and subsequent wrong decisions led them to make the wrong and fatal choice. 'Had they been doing nothing, or even just sitting at a table playing cards, nothing would have happened to them,' I cried to my father. 'After all, nobody entered the house.'

We went to the hiding-place to find out if it had been used at all – it had. Two postcard-sized photographs showing my mother and my sister on the famous Wawel in Kraków, where they had been taken during an outing in 1938, had been left. On the back of each picture, in a pitifully trembling hand, an identical goodbye message had been written – one for me and one for my father.

There was worse still to come. As I could not walk, my father went across to our Christian blacksmith and came back with a report that was like a knife turning in our wounds. The blacksmith told my father that my little sister had gone to him and begged: *'Prowadz mnie do tatusia, prosze, ja chce zyc. Prowadz mnie do stacji'* – 'Take me to my Daddy, please, I want to live. Take me to the station.' He hadn't – he was afraid. What else could we do but hammer our fists in anguish – on the table, the walls and our heads?

Whenever I calculated the chances of at least one member of our family surviving, Hanna always came first – her young features could blend easily with any European race, and her Polish was excellent. Oh you unfortunate, luckless little girl! Why didn't you try to find us by yourself? We would have been able to hide you and to feed you – for a goodly period at least – until further plans, to submerge perhaps, could be developed. You had the will to live, and the initiative, but the most important factor in survival – luck – deserted you at this very first major hurdle.

The pain was too deep to express. We sat still for a long time, my father with a pallid face and I with a labouring heart. Now and then, as if to show the thoughts which were most poignant, he muttered 'Gone, gone.' It was the first, and only, time that I saw my father cry.

* * *

Looking back, I believe that the possibility that our lost ones were most probably already dead did not occur either to my father or to myself. The unspoken 'gone for ever' prophecy was the result of the sufferings that we had already endured and, if the war did not end quickly, that were to lie ahead of us – all of us. We clung to the 'Resettlement' idea, incredible as it sounded, and so, at the time, did all the others who had missed these transports so far – the traumatic events inside these cattle-trains were not widely known then. We could not grasp the idea that our two lost ones had packed their bags, gone to a train and then taken a journey straight to death. Even after the war, for many years I somehow clung to, and carried forward almost to the present day, the illusion of their journey taking place in an ordinary passenger train. It was a vision, perhaps subconsciously never altered, that I had conceived at the time of their departure.

What haunted us was a picture of them enduring misery and hardship in their new surroundings. Even in later visions I saw my clever little sister alive in non-Jewish surroundings – having escaped the terrible workcamp-settlements – whereas my mother, with her weaker constitution, would have ... I never allowed myself to finish this train of thought. I now face the fact, which I could not face at the time, that, even if they survived the day of their departure (24 August 1942), it is most unlikely that they survived the next. New transports would always be arriving and German efficiency did not permit any backlog of 'work' to accumulate. 'Hurry up, get undressed! *Schnell, schnell,* we haven't got all day to waste!'

* * *

The two hours allowed to us before re-assembling were nearly up when our minds were suddenly confronted with a new problem. The white blisters on my feet had grown in size again and the pain, hitherto suppressed by other emotions, was acute but bearable – as long as I did not stand on my feet. To walk the 10 km back to the camp was obviously out of the question – I had to stay put in Bochnia.

My father hesitated, not wanting to leave me, and it was easy to fathom why.

'Please leave now, Papa,' I said to him reassuringly. 'I will get there somehow.'

We both knew that he had to return with the group in case any explanation was demanded for my absence and also because if both of us had stayed we would be regarded as escapees. With these dramatic events filling his head, he can easily be forgiven for leaving behind, somewhere in the house, his jacket (which was subsequently pilfered) and with it, in an inside pocket, one of the two photographs with their poignant messages – the only tangible legacy left to him. Unfortunately, I did not notice it either. However, he did leave what was left of his bread ration and also a small piece of margarine.

After a lengthy soak in a bowl of water, prepared by my father before he left, I could manage to walk on the outer edges of my feet, by now heavily bandaged with torn old sheets, to the back of the house. There I found the sizeable stack of firewood gathered at risk of life and limb on numerous previous trips. This had been intended to ease the burden of winter for my family, and would soon be used and enjoyed by other people who, most probably, would not give it a second thought. Selecting a suitable piece to support me, I hobbled to the front of the house, where I sat down.

The sun was shining. Everything was very quiet and peaceful, as on a tranquil summer evening when one is full of awe and admiration for the beautiful world which God has created.

To my right, six to eight minutes' walk distant, was the railway station, the venue of departure for perhaps more than 80 per cent of the inhabitants of Bochnia's ghetto, only just over a week ago. There was no barbed wire, no stench of burning bodies as in Auschwitz, to remind one of the unreality and artificial nature of one's present existence. There were no soldiers, no uniforms and no people. Perhaps I was dreaming that there was no war and no killings – just a late siesta that was keeping people indoors. The houses showed no outward signs of the unceasing tragedy taking place.

Ours was a corner house and directly to my left was a sandy country lane leading probably to the next village – where I had never been, although Hanna had. On one occasion, she had taken our landlord's only cow for grazing in the fields. If only she had gone that way on that fateful day of 24 August 1942.

61

On the other side of the road, which started wide but soon narrowed, there was a white building, quite well known in the community because of its inhabitants. The God-fearing parents, having produced seven daughters, naturally hoped for a son. I can only imagine the joy when, finally, child number eight was a boy. I cannot imagine the anguish when this boy turned out to be a little retarded, though he was, so I was told, loved by his parents and sisters no less than if he had been normal. From this rather large house a small figure emerged – it was the little boy. I waved and he came closer. I called out to him 'Good evening, Mendele, how is everybody?' trying to make my question sound casual. 'All gone,' he replied, but when I asked if there was anyone left he named two of his sisters.

For some reason, it had been decided that he should stay at home and two of his sisters had chosen to stay behind and look after him. Soon these two lovely young girls came out looking for him. When they saw me they asked the obvious questions. They invited me to stay with them, but I told them that I had to join my father at the earliest opportunity, although, in different circumstances, I would gladly have accepted their invitation. In fact, I intended to take the earliest train leaving for Klaj in the morning. In retrospect, I would have liked to have asked them so many questions, but I did not, and I never saw them again.

Early the next morning, with new bandages and a stick to help me walk, I left, never to return. For better or worse, and for well over a year, this had been our home, the last home of my complete family. I did not look back this time as there was no one to wave goodbye to.

The bundle we had prepared, together with my shoes, I slung over my shoulder, with part of the weight to the front and part to the back in order to leave both my hands free to grasp my supporting stick. Perhaps I caused a smile, or curious glances, because of my giant bandages and the way I walked but nevertheless I reached my new 'home' without incident – one lady on the train even offered me her seat. Had I been stopped, I would have had to try to bluff my way through, because I did not, as on previous travels, have any documentation to show that I was working for the *Wehrmacht* in Klaj.

*   *   *

The head offices of the camp, just inside the edge of a wood, were not far from the station. They were made up of several buildings. One of them was the residence and office of the *Oberleutnant* – the big wheel in the ammunition camp. Another, larger one, was the sleeping quarters of the German staff – all of them soldiers in uniform. Other buildings included canteens, recreation rooms and more offices.

The main camp itself was perhaps a mile away and deep inside the wood. It was surrounded by barbed wire – a very extensive operation, taking into account the previously described arrangement of the irregularly placed buildings, which consisted of arsenals of various types of ammunition and the newly erected barracks, inhabited by 150 male Jewish workers.

* * *

My father acquired a position as a sign writer. He had his own workroom and, at a later stage, requested and was granted, a helpmate – me. Although the officers did not let on, it must have helped that we spoke German. All the time I had the nagging feeling that if only we had started there a few weeks earlier we might have persuaded the management to take on my mother and sister, for kitchen work or cleaning. For years and even today I was filled with the 'ifs' of the unnecessary departure of our loved ones – always followed, however, by the awareness that they most probably would not have survived the many dangerous stages yet to come.

My sister, so the reasoning went, was a bit young; whereas, my mother, then 44, was a bit old. Yet in 1946 I met a Mrs Krautwirth, a friend of ours from before the war. She was of a similar age to my mother and had survived, with a daughter of a similar age to my sister. The useless self-torture never stops.

5

Klaj

I reported to the officer in charge and told him my story. He gave me a lift to the barracks and asked me to rest and present myself to him when the blisters had healed. He also promised to tell my father, who would be unable to see me before evening, that I had arrived safely. This almost sounds like a cosy set-up; truly, the contrast to what happened here, and elsewhere, could not be greater. Also the fact that I was lying in bed (a two-tier bunk, one person to a bed), and doing no work for several weeks, was unthinkable in most of the later camps.

Father came to see me in the evening. The first thing we asked each other was 'What might "they" be doing now?' We supported one another with all conceivable hypotheses why they should be alive, adding all probable and improbable visions of what they might be doing now. In the end, I believe, the sorrowful pair of us really managed to raise our hopes that there was a chance of seeing them again one day. The fact that our present working conditions were bearable, though tough at times, and that the behaviour of our masters in this camp was strict but not inhuman, helped to lull two grief-stricken individuals into imagining that perhaps we should not give up hope completely. Psychologically, we *could* not give up. To do so would be tantamount, we felt, to abandoning these two wretched souls.

After recuperation I worked with my father in the main offices at headquarters. The first job given to me was to make a giant graph – more than 4 feet wide and about 6 or 7 feet long. A peculiar little device, such as I had never seen before, about 2½ inches long, looking like a bird's beak which could only touch at its point, had to be filled with ink and once it touched the paper it had to be moved at a certain speed to make an even-looking line. Too slow and it blotched; a little too fast and the line of about one millimetre became too thin; a little faster again and the damned device would spill its content from its open sides. The large sheet was spread over four canteen tables put together. Perching, kneeling and crawling all over it I ruined quite a few before I acquired the dexterity needed for the job. I sweated profusely in fear of failing and being sent back to loading and unloading wagons of heavy ammunition and, of course, not working near my father any more. The soldier who instructed me had to be patient indeed – especially since both my father and myself had claimed that this was the type of work in which we were proficient.

However, it was not kindness that made him let me carry on until I got it right. In a few choice words he let me know that he didn't give a toss about the Nazis, about being in uniform and everything connected therewith. His name was Bonatz and I actually met him after the war. It was just a chance meeting at a kiosk on the Konstabler Wache in Frankfurt. There was only a short exchange of words and he seemed uneasy and as if his conscience was troubled – yet there was no reason that I knew. On the contrary, while in Klaj, he occasionally provided me with extra food and some cigarettes for my father.

There were three of us working in this somewhat exalted position away from the main camp, the third being a painter in his fifties. Next to the large room where I struggled with my graphs was a longish corridor. On the blank walls, off-white in colour, he painted war scenes which were nothing less than fantastic. The most impressive of these were the lifelike soldiers (Germans, of course), leaping on to an enemy tank and hurling hand-grenades into the open turret. The *Oberleutnant* took a special interest in these murals, and frequently came to inspect progress. 'He is going to show them off to his visiting superiors,' I told myself. Somehow I felt that our job gave us security. Inexplicable, foolish, yes – I know now; but that's how I felt.

There was a limit as to how many of these giant graphs were required and, by the time I had become an expert, no more were wanted. There was a 'lull' and nobody bothered to offer me any work. It was just the sort of oversight when everybody else thought that somebody else was responsible for me. Whenever somebody saw me, I looked busy – and that was enough.

65

One day there was more than the usual commotion; more soldiers appeared on the scene; something was in the air. Then came the whispers. First, somebody very important was going to pass by train tomorrow morning to visit the Eastern Front. Second, it was the Führer himself. I was eager to know who was coming but could not possibly ask. I looked for Bonatz, he was nowhere to be seen. I had 'the run of the place' – the Germans were used to see me working on the graph and probably assumed that I did some other similar job.

Several times I had been in the *Oberleutnant*'s office – even on my own. I have to confess that in a moment of boyish bravado I put on his uniform jacket and his hat and looked in the mirror. Both were too large for me but it gave me an idea of how the possession of a uniform of an ordinary soldier – my face was much too young for a higher rank – could come in useful one day. From now on I was on the lookout. If only I had contact with a spying or underground organisation, I am sure that I could have been useful to them. Rather than playing about, I could have studied his books and would have been told what to look for – such as the arrival or departure of ammunition trains, for example. The only time that I opened his diary was when I wanted to know if it was really Adolf Schickelgruber himself who would be passing by the next day. I found no corroboration to quench my curiosity. What if it really was? I could do nothing about it, I had no rifle, no grenades, and if I'd managed to steal any, I wouldn't know how to use them.

That evening I discussed these rumours with my father. He too had heard that the Führer was to visit the Eastern Front and would be passing a few stonethrows away from where we were. Stones? No, but what about wood? There was plenty of that around and thick enough to derail a train.

'How can one be sure that it is Schickelgruber who is coming – maybe it's just a general?' father deliberated. 'In any case it is too dangerous.'

'Rumours that it is him were getting stronger throughout the day, you have seen all the commotion, this is not just a general, we had one visiting here before – there is no comparison,' I argued.

'It is still hare-brained – there are too many ifs, too many unknown factors,' he continued. 'Besides, the increased activity around here shows that they are on their guard – they are patrolling the area for sure.'

66

'That's just what I mean – there were no such patrols when the general was here, so it must be a bigger thing still – who else but Schickelgruber?'

We carried on discussing and weighing the pros and cons of my idea. We enthused about the thought of ridding the world of a fanatical monster and, who knows, maybe we could end this war and save the lives of thousands or even millions of people, including – dare we think it – our loved ones.

Not from faintheartedness, but with the balanced reasoning and wisdom of his age, my father finally curbed my impetuosity. I had to agree: an attempt like this needed planning, attention to detail and preparation to have the slightest chance of success.

That night I could not sleep. Visions gripped me as if in a fever. I was convinced that it was Schickelgruber, the embodiment of all evil, who would come this way tomorrow. With him gone, everything would return to normal. Only a short while ago I had been scared that dropping one of the branches which I had collected for firewood might cause a derailment. Why not play it for real? Father was right, it should all have been prepared.

The episode of the dancing wood on the buffers invaded my mind, again and again. I grew restless. It was after midnight when I stole out of the quarters where the three of us who worked at the head-office compounds slept during the week. Straight on would lead to the station, where I had noticed most of the comings and goings during the previous day. Knowing the terrain well, I turned left – towards the main camp. I soon reached the denser part of the wood and kept off the road to avoid unwanted encounters. My footsteps were almost inaudible and, except for the occasional distant barking of dogs (guard dogs?), there was eerie silence.

I could not help thinking of the favourite author of my school years – Karl May, and of the adventures of Old Shatterhand and Winnetou, the Red Indian chief. What would they have done in this situation? They would have crawled to the enemy's camp-fire, listened to their plans, which were always conveniently discussed just when my heroes were in position, and then thwarted them – preferably after capturing their opponent's chief alive.

How exciting to read these adventures, how different and frightening the reality. After about five minutes, I reached the place where I knew that piles of wood of all sizes would be stacked. I selected the largest piece that I thought I could carry, put it on my shoulders and turned right, at an angle of 45 degrees and still in an easterly direction, veering off to complete my fateful mission.

I had to find out if there were any patrols on the whole stretch of the line or just, as I had seen yesterday, in the vicinity of the station. Cautiously, I went quite a distance further eastwards, listening all the while for any sounds which would betray the presence of any other living beings in the area. There was nothing – no noise at all, not even the sound of whispering leaves.

When I reached the rails, at a point which I estimated to be about 2 km from the station, I lowered my burden to the ground. After searching the surroundings, to satisfy myself that there was more material suitable for my purpose, I sat down on a log which was much larger than the one which I had brought. In fact, there had been no need to drag along the heavy piece which I had carried there on my shoulders. Then I did what I should have done much earlier, I did some serious thinking and evaluated the situation in earnest.

Balancing all the pros and cons put forward by my father, I had to agree that my chances of success were very small indeed. Although the train was due to arrive early in the morning, there might be an earlier one. I was, of course, hoping that the line would be cleared for the Führer to pass through the station at full speed. If the train did slow down, or stop, would it have gathered enough speed for it to be derailed and, even if derailed, would this necessarily kill the passengers? I grew faint-hearted. However, to go back without having even tried just did not equate with my nature and, besides, it would be forever gnawing at my conscience. It would have appeared to me in later life as a missed opportunity – one which could well have saved my mother and sister, whom I imagined to be languishing in a camp somewhere in the Ukraine. It could have also preserved the lives of innumerable others as well as possibly changing the course of history.

Suddenly, it occurred to me that placing a few logs across the line might not be sufficient to throw a giant steam locomotive off balance – I was not exactly experienced. It boiled down to the fact that I was here on the spot and certainly could not leave without doing something. There I sat, a lonely figure, in the early hours of what could be a fateful day. I hesitated, waiting for inspiration but felt indecisive and miserably inept.

After about half an hour of just sitting and staring into the darkness, I heard some faint noises. Slowly, these sounds, coming from an easterly direction, became discernible as voices – speaking in German. I withdrew deeper into the wood, taking great care to avoid making any sound. Were they patrolling the line? Did they have guard dogs?

More by the sounds of their conversation than by actually seeing them, I made out two Germans, strolling leisurely on the far side of the rails, towards the station. I listened very carefully, maybe I could hear something of value – no such luck. One of them, in a voice that could have wakened the dead, was talking, in a Bavarian dialect, about one lucky fellow who had broken a leg in a motorbike accident just as he was about to be sent to the front. If they were on patrol, would there be others? If so, what would be the use of putting anything on the rails? I would be endangering the local population, or ourselves, to absolutely no purpose at all. I decided to wait.

Daylight was breaking, and no soul had appeared – I could delay no longer. There were plenty of smaller stones about, which I heaped on opposite sides of the rails. Then, embedding a larger log into the two heaps, I wedged two sturdy stumps at an angle of 90° behind it, and against a sleeper. Then, using decreasing sizes of branches, I tapered this hasty construction in the direction of the expected train – ending with two more heaps of stones. A final look and, more running than walking, I made my way back.

I had no watch but I felt that it was still too early for anybody to be up yet. Unseen, I managed to reach our sleeping quarters. Father was wide awake; I did not have to tell him what I had done. I looked at him, feeling exultant and uneasy in equal measure.

'A move that is badly thought out, immature and downright stupid' was his verdict, perhaps not unexpected but nevertheless devastating. He then went on to explain that in life, as in the game of chess, it is your opponent's possibilities and likely actions that you have to study before attempting your own move and, by this criterion, I had committed a most foolish, unbalanced and extremely ill-conceived deed.

'If,' he continued in a whisper, 'by the remotest of all chances, you were to succeed, what guarantee have you that any one of his henchmen will not simply take over and carry on where he had left off? What's more, do you remember that they burned down all the synagogues in Germany under the pretext that it was the people's revenge for just one German who was shot dead in Paris?' This was a reference to the '*Kristalnacht*'. 'Such a move, in order to have the desired result – an end to this government and to the war – can only succeed if it comes from inside the German people. It is a well-known fact that the *Wehrmacht*, although they will do all in their power to win the war for their country, are in fact at loggerheads with the SS – and vice versa.

'Whenever there is an encounter with the military, the SS faction, who are indoctrinated as being the elite of the master race, behave in a most condescending manner towards their equals in rank in the *Wehrmacht*. This arrogance between proud but unequal rivals will, sooner or later, explode into a showdown. This "showdown", or the speedy end of the war, is our only hope.'

'How can you pin your hope on an early cessation of war,' I protested, 'presuming that you are envisaging a German defeat – when, according to everything we hear and see, they are succeeding on every front?' The slogan '*Deutschland siegt an allen Fronten*' could be seen everywhere. 'Besides, if what I did turns out to be successful, would it not be an opportunity for Schickelgruber's opponents to take over?'

'Only one thing is sure now, whatever happens, our lives are in greater danger than ever; as for the Germans winning in Russia – no chance, no one ever did. She is too vast and too cold and the prolonged winters are demoralising for any army. A Blitzkrieg cannot succeed there and the supply route is too long, and growing longer still, as the Germans push further and further into that country.'

'Why do the Germans not see what seems so obvious to us?' I continued the conversation, grateful that it was veering away from my night's adventure.

'They are intoxicated with their initial successes, just as in the First World War, and now they can't stop.'

'Yes, but how many people have to die before that happens? What are they waiting for?'

'At present, Germans are fed with news of glorious deeds of their armies,' father replied. 'In this euphoric climate an assassinated Führer would be revered as a martyr. He would be mourned as a would-be saviour whose untimely death caused the loss of the war and any ensuing misery for Germany. The killing of a few thousand Jews would certainly not cause a rebellion. Schickelgruber, in time, will be seen by his people for what he really is, as a man possessed, an irrational fanatic and a megalomaniac.'

'The killing of a few thousand Jews!' What did my father have in mind when he said that – 10, 20, 50 thousand? Neither of us knew that, at the time of this discussion, the machinery for mass-destruction was already in full swing. Treblinka, Chelmno, Sobibor, Maidanek, Belzec – they were already working with Germanic precision. These camps had been built for no other purpose than the destruction of Jews. During the last 40 years I have learned that there were a handful of survivors from some of these places but none from Belzec where, so rumour had it, the transports from Bochnia went. Belzec is generally not as well-known as some of the other extermination camps, probably because its reported death-toll was a 'mere' 250,000.

After a pregnant pause, full of very mixed thoughts, my father suggested catching some sleep during the hour or so before we had to get up. I was wondering if we shouldn't run away now. 'No, not yet, I have to arrange for some provisions. Let's wait and see what happens.' With these pragmatic words he turned away.

Sleep – that, of course, was easier said than done. Eventually nature took its course. Not unexpectedly, my slumber was disturbed by fitful dreams. A racing steam-engine shot up high into the air after hitting the contraption I had built. I had succeeded and the Hydra was beheaded – but then everybody stared at me and I knew I was going to be arrested any minute now. I saw myself running through wheatfields followed by a pack of dogs. I woke up in a sweat. The others had already gone to work, leaving me asleep. Nobody would miss me as I wasn't working under anybody in particular and, in any case, there was no more work for me here at the head office.

The fear in my dream seemed real enough. I hurried to my father and prevailed on him to be ready for a hasty departure. He had thought of that already and had prepared food to last for a few days. His reasoning went thus: success or no success there would be an enquiry. In the first case there was hope that major changes would occur and, during the resulting interregnum, upheavals and mass-escapes would take place everywhere and, in a few days' time, there would, we hoped, be no more reason to hide. The latter case, 'no success', looked bleak indeed – we did not discuss or contemplate the deadly reality. For the moment we could do nothing but wait.

Restlessness and curiosity drove me towards the station. Again I kept off the road and entered the forest which, at this point, was not very thickly wooded. Then I saw it. A train, stationary, with no more than a few carriages. As I drew stealthily closer, the locomotive belched some hefty puffs of steam and it started to roll. I desperately wanted to see more and, as I drew nearer still, I saw a uniformed but hatless man sitting at a window in the middle wagon, facing east and studying a sheet of paper. The train and the man in the window were real enough and the features, haircut and moustache were unmistakably those of Adolf Hitler. The vision was impeded by trees (now I saw it – now I didn't), and the expectation of soon hearing the sound of the crash of the derailed train, nailed me to the ground.

There I stood, waiting, listening – mesmerised in anticipation. Then, with the train disappearing unhindered in the distance, the tantalising realisation that a supreme moment, when history could have changed its course – had passed.

What had happened? Why had the train stopped here in the first place? I ran back to my father and told him what I had seen. 'Somebody has cleared the line,' he confirmed the obvious ... but who?

After a short silence, we both started with 'Perhaps ...'. I gave way and father continued, 'Perhaps there was no one of importance, perhaps it was an ordinary train, perhaps your contraption was inadequate – no real obstacle for a ten-ton engine; it was probably just swept aside.'

'No, no, no,' I said agitatedly, disagreeing with all three assumptions, and putting forth my own theories. 'Perhaps a local farmer saw the obstruction and simply removed it – possibly fearing consequences for himself; perhaps a German patrol cleared the line and police or Gestapo are already making enquiries.'

'Perhaps,' my father interjected, 'they will cover up the whole thing. An assassination attempt on their beloved Führer would give succour to the enemy and might invite imitation.'

'Could be,' I concurred, 'but we could go on guessing like this forever. What are we to do next?'

'Act normal, look, listen and be prepared!' With this laconic answer, we parted.

The failure of my plan and the subsequent conversation with my father rooted themselves deeply in my mind. The mass-destruction of my people might have been cut down by two-thirds, if only ... Seldom have so many lives depended on those two enigmatic little words. How often did I go over it all in my mind; could I have done better? Once or twice later on it even occurred to me that, if I had succeeded in assassinating Hitler and the *Churban* had been continued by his successors, blame might have attached itself to me and my 'foul deed' could have gone down in history as having caused it. This helped me to get over the various complexes which befell me after my unsuccessful attempt to eliminate the Führer.

Meanwhile, not knowing what really had happened to the stones and logs which I had heaped on to the rails, I feared for our lives. Nervousness increased by the hour. I would have asked Bonatz some sly questions, but Bonatz was nowhere to be seen. In the long corridor I saw the old Jewish painter at work.

'You are looking pale today – are you unwell?' he greeted me with unaccustomed friendliness.

'I feel fine,' I lied bravely. 'This mural is going to be a masterpiece.' With this genuine compliment I redirected his attention back to his work. His 'I need your help if you are not doing anything urgent', made me wonder if this was the reason for his friendly greeting.

'Nothing very urgent,' I replied, pleased to be occupied. 'How can I help you?'

Producing a pail, half-filled with paint, he handed me a coarse, unused floor cloth and asked me to dip it into the bucket. 'Now wring it out until it doesn't drip any more,' he said. I had never seen anybody put both hands into liquid paint before and, were it not for the situation I found myself in, I would have suspected a practical joke. Curiosity overcame my scruples and I did what he asked. He now took over the twisted cloth which I had doubled over for a better 'wring' and, using both hands, rolled it diagonally across the off-white wall. Gently at first, then with gradually increasing pressure, he squeezed the remaining paint on to the wall, thus creating an interesting and artful pattern. It didn't look very difficult. I asked if he would let me have a go. After some hesitation, and with a peculiar grin on his face, he nodded. Prudently, I chose another part of the corridor and set to work with enthusiasm.

What a mess! When I wrung out the rough fabric, I squeezed too forcefully and too fast – my trousers and my shirt, not the wall, received a generous splattering of paint. When I introduced the rag to the wall, I pressed much too hard and all it produced were smears and smudges. The rest of the morning was taken up with cleaning, accompanied by disparaging remarks from my instructor.

At lunchtime I met my father. Neither of us had any news and we decided to wait, at least until the evening, before raising our hopes of personal safety. When I told him of my calamitous attempt as a mural painter, a flicker of a smile crossed his drawn face. To my surprise, he asked to see the mural. He then explained to me, step by step, the proper procedure for making a pattern. I regained my confidence, and with it my enthusiasm. Within half an hour, before my erstwhile teacher had reappeared, a sizeable portion of the wall had been decorated, with a pattern at least as effective as his. With the right teacher, it was not difficult. After seeing my satisfactory progress, my father left. When the little painter returned, he saw me working assiduously with my newly acquired skill. 'Ambitious!' he said. Whether this was a compliment or not, it did not diminish my fervour.

Evening was approaching fast and there was still no news. 'If only we knew which of our theories was right,' I said to my father.

'If we do not hear anything by tomorrow, it boils down to only two possibilities. Either, as you suggested, the line was cleared, or, as I suspect, there has been a cover-up,' he replied.

The only news we had in the next few days was that the visit by the Führer to the Eastern Front had in fact taken place.

With the painter's consent, I was allowed to finish what I had started. After only a few days, the job was completed and again I had to move about trying to look busy.

Looking for work, I was given a few exercise books and told to write their purpose on their soft covers, all in connection with the graphs that I had made earlier. Knowing German fussiness for detail, I was on my way to ask father's advice when I saw the new *Oberleutnant*, a tall man who looked more like an actor than a soldier. I don't know what possessed me as I stepped right into his path and stood to attention. He stopped, with a quizzical look. '*Herr Oberleutnant*,' I began, 'where on this cover would you like me to put the inscription, right at the top or more in the middle?' He raised his eyebrows. 'Is that all you have to do?' With these few words he left me standing. By then, of course, I had already realised my folly in trying to appear to be busy.

My father shook his head and with a touch of sarcasm, unusual for him, he said: 'What a boy. A week ago he tried to change the course of history and now he behaves like the greatest ass who ever lived.'

Retribution was swift. Before the day was out I had to report at the main camp where, from now on, I was going to work and stay. Every action has its consequences – and not always what they seemed to be at first. Bad turns out to be good and, sometimes, vice versa. Initially, I felt cause bitterly to regret my action which could best be described as a mixture of youthful *chutzpah* (cheek) and immaturity. Hardly appropriate behaviour for a young man of 19 who, not so long ago, had conceitedly vowed: 'If only one Jew is to survive – it will be me.'

*   *   *

With a group of other young men I had to load, or unload as the case might be, wagons of ammunition. Each of these bullet-shaped, heavy artillery projectiles weighed 50 or more kilograms (about 1 cwt.). Carrying these on my shoulders for several hours at a time was not the worst of it; lifting them up and putting them down, gently, was the agonisingly arduous task.

Why did I seem to suffer more than most of the others? Was I such a weakling? I knew little in those days about 'workouts' or muscle-building. All I knew was that my body was aching beyond endurance, and I cursed the stupidity which had caused my transfer into this back-breaking situation. When the news broke that our *Oberleutnant* had been made a *Hauptmann* (captain), I thought with chagrin that he had achieved his promotion on my aching back.

Sometimes these shells arrived in specially constructed baskets and, peculiarly, they seemed lighter – or at least easier to carry. Whereas I took great pains to lift and lower these dangerous objects for fear of a gigantic explosion, others, probably more experienced, knew that these shells did not go off easily and practically threw them off their shoulders on to the stack and positioned them afterwards. Judging by the relaxed attitude of the German guard, I had to conclude that what we were handling may not have been the finished article. I therefore followed the others and unburdened myself the same way until a new and inexperienced soldier took over and he, visibly shaken, screamed at us for wanting to blow ourselves to pieces. I never asked, and never found out, the truth about the nature of the ammunition that we handled.

Our rations, although far from adequate for a young and hard-working body, were not actually, in this camp, a starvation diet. In addition, my father now and again obtained some extra rations, which he shared with me. The result was that, after about one and a half weeks, I grew noticeably stronger and decided to test my strength. When the guard was not looking, I took one shell on each shoulder and found it much easier than when I had started, with just one.

After about three weeks, I joined a couple of show-offs who actually managed to carry three and we did this when, as quite often happened, we were not being guarded at all. It would not have been at all difficult to sabotage all the storage places and to blow up the entire arsenal yet I am sure that no one seriously considered such a deed because along with the shells, we would have destroyed all the inmates in the camp.

Escape would also have been easy but for the vital question of where to go. The population outside was, to a large extent, either greedy or hostile. The greedy came in two sections: the scavengers, who enriched themselves with the belongings which Jews had been forced to leave behind; and the informers who would betray anyone for any reward. There were plenty of decent folk but they were nearly all afraid of the consequences of harbouring the enemy – Jews – and if there were any willing to run this risk, we did not know where or how to find them. In all the stories I heard after the war, there were more Jews helped by the Germans, in Germany itself, than by Poles – this, of course, may be because I lived in Germany for several years after the war. In short, escaping at this stage was a gamble with the wrong odds. Here we felt almost secure as the work we did was an important contribution to the war effort, food was adequate and nobody was unduly ill-treated, let alone killed.

The only casualty came about by accident. Very often we had to shunt wagons from one line to another, or just push one along to the next building, and since the whole group of 18 or 20 was engaged in this operation, it was an easy job. It was also another opportunity for a few show-offs – me included – to push one of the wagons all by himself. When pushing in groups, I always placed myself between the two buffers, where I felt safest. Within the camp, to shift goods from one place to another, we sometimes used flatbed wagons and with these one could see where one was going and when to stop, without any shouted commands to do so being necessary.

One day we were pushing such an open wagon, with me, as usual, between the buffers, and drawing near to one of the buildings, which were all equipped with ramps for loading and unloading. Those who were pushing on the side of the ramp would let go, walk up the steps and help from there, if necessary, to position the wagon correctly outside the entrance. One of these flank-pushers failed to let go at the right moment and, accompanied by the screams of all the onlookers as well as his own, was crushed between the ramp and the moving wagon.

I was bending down at the time but, roused by the screams, I looked across. What I saw chilled my blood. His body, which I did not see, must have been dragged under, but part of his arm and his hand were left sticking up from the narrow gap between wagon and ramp – in the manner of a drowning man trying to reach out or summon help. The vision of that arm and hand has stayed in my memory.

Although I felt stronger, loading and unloading ammunition was hard work and very tiring – especially compared with signwriting, graphmaking or painting. I asked my father to be on the lookout for something that I could do, and, as it happened, the little old painter had a job which he thought would be more suited to a younger man. Every storage building had a number, made of wood, placed at the end of a rafter which protruded, horizontally, from the side of the building, like a kind of gibbet. These numbers, in roman numerals, had to be protected from the weather with a coat of oil-based paint.

'Use a colour which will not be conspicuous, in case we have an air-attack,' he told me. Nothing easier, I thought, and so I started working at my new task which, I hoped, would help me to return to my previous employment. Searching for a suitable ladder, I looked up at these numerals to try to decide what colour would be best. It was a lovely cloudless day and I decided that, if painted in sky-blue, they would be indistinguishable from their background above – and so I did just that.

When the old misery-guts painter inspected my work, I thought that he would have a fit. 'Do you want us all to be shot for sabotage?' he thundered. He did not have to explain that, of course, aeroplanes would be looking down, not up, if they intended to bomb the arsenals. At the back of my mind, I wondered if the Germans would have taken any notice of what he was complaining about, as these 18-inch-high numbers could hardly have served as a beacon to any high-flying plane. Yet I still felt ashamed of the 'logic' that I had applied – the type of decision which, had it been taken by somebody else, would normally have drawn my mercilessly mocking remarks.

* * *

There was a new development which, even today, I do not fully comprehend. Every American, or anybody with American connections, had to come forward. As was customary with any pronouncements coming from the Germans, no explanation was given. Speculation was rife. Was it an exchange of nationals? It couldn't be an exchange of prisoners – or could it? Was it some sort of trick? Was there a softening of American or, for that matter, German attitudes? Well, we were not Americans but we still had letters showing that we had been waiting since before the war for the necessary entry visa to emigrate to the United States. We decided to give it a try. I am sure that every one of our campmates would have liked to be in our place when we packed our few belongings and departed on our 'journey to America'.

What a turnaround from being, as Nazi indoctrination would have it, subhuman, to being a free man – an American citizen – well, quasi. Enduring the master race ideology had made me ask myself if I really was subhuman; now, at a stroke, to be transformed into a potential member of the most advanced society on Earth – no wonder I felt confused. Parallel with this unreality was the down-to-earth fear that somewhere, somehow, there was a muddle – a mistake which would land us back where we were.

Meanwhile there was hope. The first stage of our long journey to the shores of liberty ended in Montelupich, the renowned prison of Kraków. There we joined about 150 other potential emigrants. Men and women were separated. Seventy-three males, plus our luggage, were to share a room of no more (maybe less) than 30 square yards. Adjoining, there was a large cubicle-sized space containing a single lavatory and washing facilities. Not quite the Ritz. Not quite what real Americans would put up with. Expectations were high and low at the same time.

We had handed in our papers, the aforementioned letters – and we waited. What was our status now, we wondered – were we prisoners or internees? These questions were constantly asked and debated among ourselves. There was little else to do but talk, sit and wait.

With every day that passed, I grew more despondent. It just could not be true. They were probably looking for real Americans and some official had widened the issue. Maybe the Germans hoped to obtain something from the Americans in exchange for as many of us as possible. Pure conjecture, we knew absolutely nothing.

We were now being guarded by silent, stern-looking, black-clad and fully armed SS men in steel helmets. Quite a change from our guards at the ammunition camp, with whom you dared exchange a word now and again. These black uniforms, with their skull-and-crossbone markings – together with the reputation of the wearers – exuded an aura of cruelty and fear which, even if they were just passing by, made our hearts tremble.

About a week later we were told to assemble in the large forecourt of the prison. As we were all standing and waiting for the verdict, we felt that the Last Judgement had come. Suddenly, a contingent of about 40 SS guards marched in and positioned themselves in a line across the yard, at a distance of about 70 feet from us. Mesmerised, I saw, and listened to the sound of 40 rifles being cocked with one big click.

What now? Had they found out that we were not even potential Americans? Had the Americans declined to take us as immigrants, so that we were now back to being mere Jews – people without a state and without protection – a kind of species of wild game which could be hunted down and shot at will, and for which there was always open season?

My brain started to work feverishly. Should we wait until the command 'Fire!' came, or should we rush them, as death was almost certain anyway? The odds were nearly four to one in our favour if we were to cross the few yards that separated us ... but then what? Whatever the outcome, it would be better than waiting like lambs to be slaughtered – but who would give the command and who would follow? This type of situation must have occurred thousands of times. Without organisation, if someone were to give a command the others would not know how to act, vital seconds would then be lost and enough time given for the guns to do their job.

However, the gates were opened and we were marched out. The

next thing I remember is lying down on straw in a truck. There was plenty of daylight – even sunshine. We were obviously not going to America but back to where we came from and, again, we were told nothing.

Next to me lay a very lovely girl. We began talking and, in no time at all, my whole heart and soul was aflame with love. She came from what remained of the Bochnia ghetto. Not unnaturally, we talked about two subjects. First, whether any of the group had been lucky enough to have the necessary papers to qualify for the journey to America. She thought that two or three might have. Second, the fate of our families. She had heard that the trains, with our loved ones inside – she too had lost all her family – had been sent to a place called Belzec. Somebody had escaped when the train stopped and brought back the news.

'Belzec? Never heard of it. Well, I hope they don't have to work too hard,' I continued the conversation.

'If they are still alive,' she replied, putting the unspeakable into words.

'We mustn't give up hope,' I told her. I did not know until after the war that Belzec was one of the extermination camps. It was newly built and, so the rumours went, without the gas chambers normally in operation at that time. I was therefore left with the choice of imagining whether my mother, Ida Wermuth, or my sister, Hanna Wermuth, were shot – or gassed by some other means. Perhaps they were ordered, as so many were ordered, to dig their own graves, undress, and then, after neatly folding their belongings, were shot – either individually, one by one in the back of the neck, or machine-gunned all together in a group. Or perhaps they died in a 'mobile gas chamber' – a specially adapted truck, hermetically sealed, where the exhaust pipe choked the life out of people – slowly. Death from carbon monoxide took at least twenty minutes in these vehicles, as against the later used 'merciful' Zyklon B gas, which took 'only' three minutes. Methods varied, so I have heard, and so the choice is left to my imagination – forever. These are the 'best' choices, the others I do not wish to think about, or to describe.

*   *   *

Back at Klaj, was there any glee or satisfaction at our return? Possibly. It would have been an entirely human reaction, balanced by the good side of human nature which would have wanted us to have got away safely. We took up where we had left off and I managed, through Bonatz, to get some more painting jobs. Once, he invited me into the barracks, where he had cooked a special meal. While I was munching away, at what I thought to be chicken, I ventured to ask him: 'How far, do you think, will the German army advance into Russia?' He shrugged his shoulders; he didn't know and, true to his character, he didn't care. It was the last time I saw him until that chance encounter after the war, when I referred to the lovely chicken, only to find out that it was rabbit.

The next day, we were told to pack and assemble. Unceremoniously, and without any warning or explanation, we found ourselves in a train – destination unknown. The first thing I noticed was that we were not going east. Some instinct, recognising danger in that direction, made me feel a sense of relief. On the other hand, as I said to my father, there might have been a chance of finding mother and sister there. Above all, we hoped that our next workplace or camp would not be under SS management.

The journey was short. We arrived at the *Zwangsarbeitslager* (forced labour camp) named Kraków-Plaszów. We did not yet know of its infamous reputation. Infamous reputation? Although it looms large in my mind as, possibly, the worst camp of the nine that I went through, I found that, with the exception of its survivors and the readers of *Schindler's Ark*, comparatively few people have heard of it. The word 'Plaszów' does not easily stay in the memory as it is really only a suburb of Kraków.

6

Plaszów

There is still confusion, if not ignorance, among the public in distinguishing between a 'working' camp and an 'extermination' camp. As in almost anything else, there are degrees and variations. *Zwangsarbeitslager*, or forced labour camps, were those which used slave labour to further the war effort. Extermination camps were built for no other reason than the liquidation, en masse, of the almost daily trainloads of Jews, and, after completing their gruesome task, were razed to the ground. Auschwitz, with the dubious fame of killing more than all the other camps put together, also retained a 'stock' of people for all sorts of purposes.

The full name of Plaszów (pronounced Plushoov) was *Zwangsarbeitslager* Kraków-Plaszów, and it was a slave-labour camp, run by the SS. Its commandant, so I learned on the first day there, bragged that he was the 'greatest murderer of all time' and that he had actually killed 80,000 people with his own hands. Not, as many claimed after the war, by obeying orders – no, with him it was a task he relished. He derived pleasure from destroying as many as he could. Killing was a sport for him. Luckily, for me, I never knew him to 'waste' more than one bullet on a person, as his pride and reputation might suffer. This was a man obsessed with his power, he was a god in his own right – the sole master of the life and death of his 'slaves'. Death was a punishment for his every whim or displeasure.

We entered the camp and, just inside, were made to stand in line – all of us with our few belongings. We stood and waited, apprehensively, not knowing what to expect. Instinctively, I felt that our 'good' times were over. Four Ukrainian guards positioned themselves about ten feet in front of our group. One of them strolled along the line. My mind was busy evaluating the position. Four men with rifles. They actually looked a bit bored – probably a routine job. No, they would not open fire but … what were we waiting for? The strolling guard came closer. I took out one of our last three items of value, a pocket-watch – neither silver nor gold, but still in those days a prized possession. I swung it on its chain – my mind not clear as to what purpose. Perhaps, in the manner of clutching at a straw, I was hoping for a favour, either for now or for the future. My brain, too muddled to think straight, let alone logically, was unable to assess whether this man was in a position to be of any help. All I felt was that I had to act – I had to do something.

'What are they going to do with us – why are we waiting?' I mumbled as he came close enough to hear. In a split second the watch had disappeared into his pocket. 'Delousing – not ready yet,' he snorted as he went by. I looked at my father to see if he was going to admonish me for this foolish attempt at futile bribery – which had left us with less to offer should a situation of real need present itself. He said nothing.

It turned out that there was work in progress to repair the 'delousing' installation. It was winter and the hot-water system had broken down. ... This, apparently, was the normal procedure then, whether needed or not. When, in the spring of 1945, during those infamous train journeys, I was practically eaten alive by lice, no such procedure was available. In this case, German thoroughness fell short of its objective because, when we came out of the wash-house, all our luggage was still piled up outside – undeloused. The armed guards had gone – I never saw the new owner of our pocket-watch again.

To my horror and amazement, two Jewish camp inmates, armed with buckets of paint and a brush, proceeded to make red lines on our suits. Two vertical and several horizontal lines – a short, two- or three-runged ladder – front and back. Then the trousers. On each leg they made a line starting from the belt, stopping above the knee and then continuing below, all the way down. Then, and this little extra incident committed this episode to my memory, they made a big, round, yellow spot on each knee. I felt like a clown, wilfully humiliated and ridiculed. I wondered whether this final piece of artistry was their own idea or whether it had been ordered. This action was part of our dehumanisation process – and would also make escape more difficult. I consoled myself with the thought that my two better suits in our 'undeloused' luggage had not been painted and thus escape, which was always at the back of my mind, was still possible – at least in theory.

We marched on to our sleeping quarters. On the way, we first saw a *bagger* in action. *Bagger* is the German word for a dredging or earthmoving machine. Our guide told us that, quite often, the machine dug up skeletons. I was no sooner told this than I seemed to notice bones sticking out with every scoop. It may have just been imagination but it made my flesh creep. I imagined that these bones could be thousands of years old until I learned that part of the camp had been built on a Jewish cemetery of fairly recent date and that the tombstones had been used to pave the newly built street. For a macabre moment I imagined that this machine would, before long, scoop up my bones too.

The 'beds' were like giant wooden shelves – three tiers high. Father chose our places at the top, probably thinking it would be safer, up there, two metres above the ground and, perhaps, a bit out of the way and out of sight.

As newcomers, we were assigned to the hardest jobs going. In this camp, as in some others of the future, we started with roadbuilding. We were soon told by others that not only did we have the toughest work and the longest hours (minimum 12) but that, most of all, we were also working at the most perilous spot in the whole camp. The most dangerous times were in the early hours of the morning when the commandant, Amon Goeth – may he roast in eternal damnation – felt like some sport.

We all used to call him 'Get', as most inmates, Polish Jews, were unable to pronounce his German name correctly. I myself thought of it as spelt that way until I saw the proper spelling in Keneally's *Schindler's Ark*. The very mention of his name still sends a shiver down my spine – even today.

Apparently he could spot us from his villa. Using a high-powered pair of binoculars, he would select a victim – usually someone resting – taking a 'breather'. One well-aimed shot and he had achieved what was, by now, the policy of his superiors – either to kill the Jews or work them to death. From then on nobody dared to take a moment's rest and people worked until they literally dropped. In an instant, all that had been hitherto rumours and hearsay had become cruel reality.

Now was the time when I passed abruptly from boyhood to manhood. Now was the time when all dreaming had to end. Everything now had to focus on one aim: survival.

It was then that I first developed the art of scanning the surrounding terrain and assessing what a potential assassin would, or would not, be able to observe. From any distance the lurking murderer could see whether a body was in motion – working – but I doubted if the amount on the spade or shovel could be focused on. The casualties were mostly those who, from sheer exhaustion, took the risk of leaning, for a few moments only, at rest on their shovel or pickaxe. The ploy I adopted was simple. Since it was the weight and the lifting which drained a person's energy, rather than the actual movement, I went through the motions of lowering the tool and lifting it – empty. By only simulating the action of digging and displacing the soil, I conserved my strength – which served me well when my diligently scouting eyes spotted approaching danger. When observed, I was probably the hardest worker of the group!

One evening, shortly after arrival at this camp, I suggested to my father that we should be on the look-out among the thousands of inmates for someone, perhaps in an 'elevated' position, to help us better our situation – either by changing our place of work or by adding to our food ration – preferably both.

Prominente was the name for those survivor types who, by some means or other, had managed to put themselves in a position above the masses. They were to be recognised by their authoritative behaviour and by looking better fed and better dressed than the rest of us. In Auschwitz and thereafter, these were the often notorious '*Kapos*'. In this camp we also had the OD (short for *Ordnungsdienst*), the Jewish police, who were dressed in a black uniform and military-style cap identical, or almost identical, to their Polish counterparts. They were even graded in ranks. The study of how these ranks were obtained would, I am sure, reveal a most disturbing aspect of the depths to which man can be made to descend.

Like the men of the Jewish Council which I have already described – who, as ordinary people, would not dream of betraying their brethren out of the most basic instinct of preserving the lives of their families, as well as their own – the OD fell into the same trap. Whereas I have understanding for their all-too-human reaction during the most terrible situations, some of their numbers were zealous over and above the call of 'duty'. Their motivation and incomprehensible, despicable actions, I cannot even attempt to analyse.

Ranks were indicated by stripes on their shoulder-straps and, if I recall rightly, somewhere on their sleeves. There was only one OD with three stripes – the Chief of them all, Chilowicz. There were very few with two stripes, more with only one and the majority, of course, were just ordinary policemen. Ordinary? For a start they were the only inmates who had sleeping quarters where they could keep their wife and family – if they still had any. Many ODs, in spite of having served their masters in one way or another, had only a reduced part of their family left.

Couples who had lost some or all of their children must have nightly embraced in tears rather than in joy. During the day, however, they were the people with the power – the extended arm of the commandant and his henchmen by whose indulgence they retained their elevated position. I can remember the names of only four of these OD men – Chilowicz, Finkelstein, Salz and Sigmund Rosenblum, my father's cousin. Finkelstein, though he had no gun, was the cruellest of these.

I had met Sigmund Rosenblum's father and mother and wife (then his girlfriend) not long before on a visit with my father. The elder Rosenblums were my father's uncle and aunt. The five of us, without my mother and sister, were having a Sabbath meal. I remember that the meal was accompanied by many jokes, one of which involved Sigmund getting up during grace, after the meal, and, having previously spoken of the lameness of the German Propaganda Minister (Goebbels), proceeding to imitate his limping walk, in time to the tune of 'Ken yevorech'.

The girlfriend (later wife) of Sigmund Rosenblum was exceptionally beautiful. In those days, it did not take a lot for me to fall in love and when I first saw this woman, as she was collecting Sigmund after the meal, it was love at first sight. She had one peculiarity which I specially remember – she pronounced the letter 's' in a way that I never heard before, nor since. It was not a lisp but rather a slight sibilance, and it added enormously to her charms. The second, and last, time that I saw her was in the camp, still beautiful but with lines of great anxiety showing in her face. After the following incident, I had never met her again – even though I remained in that camp for a further ten months.

About two weeks after we entered the camp, word went out that

Get wanted 150 men to be shot. No reason was given. We could only speculate as to what had displeased this self-styled demi-god. Rounding up had already started and people were fleeing in all directions – many prepared and with a hiding-place in mind. We, the unskilled who worked in the open, were perhaps the most likely target. My mind worked thus: as it was likely that the Jewish police would have to help in this rounding-up process what better place to hide than in the police barracks itself? So we more or less tricked our way into this shelter. It was Sigmund's wife who was instrumental in ensuring that we were not thrown out until the raid was over – by which time 150 inmates were no more.

Sigmund must have been the one who arranged, probably after talking with my father, to have us transferred to the *Metalver-arbeitung* – the metal workshops, positioned in a different part of the camp. It was a camp within a camp – partitioned off by barbed wire, as were several other sections in the camp (see map, p. 110).

Our job was to create something out of the huge amount of odd bits of metal of all sizes and descriptions, heaped just outside our workshop, a large barracks at the end of a row of others destined for various types of work. Because our life revolved around work, food and rest, as well as keeping out of harm's way, we had little knowledge of what went on in those other workshops.

I have hazy recollections of obtaining lots of carrots and some potatoes which were stored by the ton in a kind of underground silo – a welcome addition to our food ration. It was only much later that I learned of a case where the finding of one potato led to the flogging of a whole hut, 20 or 25 strokes a person, the victims having to call out the numbers. Even hazier are the memories of one or two occasions when I obtained extra food directly from the kitchen which, by the way, was also surrounded by barbed wire, though not marked on the sketch map. The kitchen barracks must have been on the left of the garage (as we called the workshops for the camp's vehicles) and, according to my memory, also surrounded by barbed-wire fencing. An OD with two stripes, by the name of Salz, handed me some extra rations.

The arrangement was probably made through Sigmund Rosen-blum who apparently tried to do what he could for us, and I was just the messenger boy. This Jewish policeman, Salz, was shortly to be involved in an act of great drama.

So now we worked in the slightly privileged metal workshop. By no stretch of my imagination could what we produced here aid the German war effort. But we were unpaid labour, producing something out of nothing – discarded and otherwise useless pieces of sheet metal – and the results, when resold on the hungry black market, lined somebody's pocket, most likely Goeth's.

There were products of all kinds. My assignment was to select, from the vast heap outside, such pieces which, by size and gauge, were suitable, with the appropriate machinery, to be made into dustpans, hundreds, thousands of them which my father had to paint in various shades and colours. We worked in two 12-hour shifts; I preferred working at night. The reason for this was twofold. First, not many killings took place during those hours – the 'management' was too busy with whoring and drinking parties at which, so I heard later, prospective black-market clients were wined and dined.

The second reason was that I had acquired a new friend, Professor Springhut, a doyen of music, whose parents, back in Frankfurt, were acquainted with mine. Many a night passed in interesting conversation and invented games. One night in particular we tried to score by mentioning the first few words of a song, old or new, a current hit or an operatic aria, even in another language, and the other then had to continue the words or the tune and start another. Our astonishment grew by the hour as we managed to carry on until our shift ended. We both felt that we could have gone on for much longer. We arranged to do it again the next night. I never saw or heard of him again. Having observed his unusually severe cough, my father suspected that my friend had galloping consumption.

My father also had a companion, Siegfried Vogler, a real 'character' from Vienna. He mostly sat next to my father, helping to paint this workshop's products. They seemed to play another game. Every time I approached their workbench, one or the other was telling a joke. If I had to declare a winner it would be Siggi, as we called him, but then I should not be the judge, knowing most of my father's jokes already. Fourteen years my senior, Siggi survived and became my first business partner – in Rome.

Why, after the description of these cosy-sounding interludes, do I declare that, in my experience the *Zwangsarbeitslager* Kraków-Plaszów was worse than Auschwitz, a name I had not yet heard of at that time? Once you had survived the initial selection there –

whether to be gassed or detailed for work – the threat of death, although permanently present, was not quite on the same basis as it was here in Plaszów. Here we had to get used to the idea of being a possible target at any time for the commandant, whose daily sport and pleasure it was to notch up one or more killings; unless, of course, he had a 'real' reason. Rare were the days when no reports of killings were circulated.

Most people regard Auschwitz as synonymous with, and the epitome of, the most evil happenings of the *Churban*. By sheer numbers of lives cut off it was and will go down in the annals of history as such. Only another cataclysmic event such as a Third World War could dwarf the significance of this supreme hell. Atrocities and extremities of cruelty, however, have occurred in so many places that it would be pointless to nominate the 'worst'. We all know that Auschwitz meant death to more than 95 per cent of those arriving there. In this horrific notoriety Auschwitz was 'bettered' only by the other extermination camps whose record of killings was 100 per cent, discounting the handful of escapees from Treblinka and Sobibor. For those selected to escape the gas chambers, there was a *momentary* feeling of relief. The future looked just as grim as it had in Plaszów but at least there was no Amon Goeth – Get – stalking the camp in search of his 'quota' of victims. I felt just that little bit more sure of seeing the end of the week in the Buna-Works, Auschwitz, than I did in Plaszów, where the fear of being 'the next' was constantly with me. There will be those who will, understandably, disagree about my comparison; for this reason I stress this as my very own experience.

* * *

'Alles raus – auf den Appellplatz – schnell, schnell!'
Everybody out – on to the assembly place – on the double! My father and I looked at each other – whatever the reason for such a call, fear and terror strike deeply. Maybe somebody had escaped and Get needed his usual 50 victims in revenge.

We had no time to deliberate as we rushed to the assembly place to await what Get had in store. There we stood, line after line, in military precision – all 10,000 (*my* estimate). A long single line of steel-helmeted, black-uniformed Waffen-SS stood facing us, rifles cocked and at the ready.

89

My vision of the scene is as clear as if it had happened yesterday –
so is the recollection of my feelings and my thoughts. My terror
abated slowly when I noticed that there were no machine-guns in
position. Then Get and other SS officers walked on to the scene
towards a goalpost-like construction, right opposite me. It was only
2–2½ metres wide and about 3½ metres high, with two looped
metal hooks under its horizontal beam.

Two hangings! Must I feel ashamed that, when I saw the gallows,
my survival instinct signalled a message of relief through my system?
Two poor wretches were going to die – but it wasn't me.

Curiosity took over and then a flash of hot anger. Here we stood, in
a ratio of perhaps 100 to one against them, hopeless, helpless. My
eyes wandered. Was there not one of those classical heroes among us
who, by sheer personality, would unite us in an instant by moving
forward and giving the command – 'Attack!' We could crash into
them, take their weapons, kill them. I was almost willing it to happen
– I would certainly join. After a spontaneous move by a determined
smaller group, the rest would surely follow, if only because there was
no alternative – kill, or be killed.

Alas, there was no such person or organised group. Ten thousand
frightened people had to watch, in powerless misery, the hanging of
two of their brethren. Seething, but frightened like the rest, I stood
and watched in silence.

At first, I saw only one of the victims, a very young man whose
name I did not know – until recently when I read it in *Schindler's Ark*.
His crime, I was told by the fellow standing next to me, was whistling
'The Marseillaise'. (According to Keneally it was the Communist
'Internationale'.) The youngster stood on a raised platform – a chair
or a wooden box, maybe. My attention was fixed on his terror-
stricken eyes – and his mouth. *'Ich bin unschuldig'* – I am innocent,
he yelled, I am innocent. When the noose was put around his neck
his voice became a scream – repeating those three words over and
over again in the direction of Commandant Get. Nobody expected
this monster to be moved; he probably needed this little spectacle as
an ice-breaker for that night's party.

The drama took an unexpected turn. The platform was pushed
from under his feet, the rope broke and the boy, his hands tied
behind his back, fell to the ground. I remembered having heard of an
international law whereby such an incident would be regarded as

90

'Divine Judgement' and the condemned would be reprieved. No longer than two seconds did I delude myself that such a law would be applied here. The young man, now on his stomach, crawled towards Get, mingling his 'I am innocent' with other supplications. With an impatient shove of his right boot, the monster pushed the cumbersome worm back. Then he turned to the OD Saltz, who had to be his instrument in preparing the execution. In the especially hushed atmosphere of expectation, I could clearly hear Get's voice: 'If it happens again *you* will hang.' This time, the Jewish policeman with two stripes was seen to double the rope. To save his own life – what else could he have done?

A doubled rope, it occurred to me, would prolong the agony of dying: an added dimension to the tragedy of so young a life being extinguished by hanging – being hanged twice – for whistling.

Curiously, I did not see the other man until that moment. He was nearer middle age, lying on the ground, his hands tied behind his back and dead. He had cheated the hangman and Get by cutting his wrists. He was lifted into the noose next to the young man, now silenced, whose body, judging by its spasmodic convulsions, still showed signs of life.

An SS man of much smaller stature strutted forward. The upper part of his body leaning back to a degree that, in different circumstances, would raise a smile of derision, he was obviously posturing to appear taller and important. Slowly and nonchalantly, he drew his revolver and pumped several bullets under the chins of the two bodies. As the victims were certainly dead by then, it looked a superflous gesture. The jerking of the two heads, on the impact of the penetrating missiles, was a ghostly but suitably macabre end of the 'show'.

We were dismissed and went back to work as if nothing out of the ordinary had happened. The nightshift, roused to bear witness, went back to their quarters to continue their interrupted sleep. I am sure that some could – one does get hardened.

*   *   *

Again I was on day-shift when news came that someone from the garage-repairshop had escaped. Joy mingled with shock. Joy, because – so we hoped and prayed – somebody might stay alive to tell the outside world that hell is not a place for sinners in the world

91

beyond, but here on Earth. Joy also for those like us, who nurtured hope of escaping one day. Shock: for as certainly as night follows day, there would be a number of us who would pay for this brave young man's bid for his freedom and life with our own.

Speculation went thus: usually he, Get, would punish the group whence the 'culprit' came, but in this case we doubted that he would take his victims from the somewhat privileged body of people employed at the garage. It was well-known that he liked showing off 'his' car workshop to prominent visitors.

The courageous fellow who had escaped was an acquaintance of mine from the Bochnia ghetto. On several occasions we even discussed how easy it would be to escape from the ghetto, unfenced in our street. What's more, his was one of the few escapes that were successful, as I met him again in early summer 1945 in Modena, northern Italy.

Daniel, as I shall call him, was reported to have made his escape strapped under a lorry. As he originally came from Bochnia, we wondered if there was a contingent from this town here in this camp and whether they would fall victim. As we ourselves had come to this place via the *Munitionslager* Klaj, we hoped that our Bochnia origin would not be a consideration for Get when choosing those to be punished. Should there be a raid or manhunt while we were at work, there would be nothing at all we could do. It was different at our sleeping quarters.

We had changed barracks since our arrival here, and now, instead of shelves, we slept on bunk-beds. As opposed to later camps – Auschwitz and after – we 'enjoyed' the luxury of each having his own bunk and even some of our own bedding. Again I had managed to obtain an upper tier. There was also another important difference between our erstwhile dormitory and the present one. We now had a ceiling made of wooden planks about three or four feet above us which, by shifting a couple of loose planks, could provide a sort of hiding-place. This was far from ideal by any stretch of the imagination, especially if others had the same idea and, if slow, were caught in the act of disappearing before the boards were back in place. Although I know that this was one of the hiding-places used on several occasions, mercifully I never had to make use of it. A mistake by one would be the end of all. We did, however, make use of our ceiling to conceal illicitly obtained potatoes, carrots and some of our few remaining valuables.

According to my recollection, 49 paid with their lives for Daniel's escape. Actually 50 were taken up on to the famous, or rather infamous, 'Killing Hill'. It was late in the day and filling in the mass grave could wait till the next morning.

The night shift in the barracks near us had a surprise visitor – bleeding, naked, but alive. One of the massacred was wounded and left for dead; it goes without saying, he was looked after. This brings to mind the gruesome question of how many people, during these thousands of Nazi mass-killings all over Europe, were buried alive.

I also learned about the most horrific, the most unthinkable, unimaginable of all hiding-places, used especially when a hunt was made to eliminate the children who, by one means or another, were hidden by their parents or, if orphaned, by adult friends – in the latrines. Such was their terrific will to survive, or equally, their fear of death, that they squeezed themselves through the opening and submerged to the chin in human excrement. They were even heard to be fighting for such places. It seemed, however, that whenever there was a raid enough victims were found without the need to search in hiding-places; at least, not during my stay in this camp. There was a short spell when the 'grapevine' did not report or even rumour any killings. 'Get must be on leave, may he never return' was the assumption and the prayer of the inmates.

* * *

An order came through to every workshop and every other working group to contribute a certain number of people for a special task. I distrusted every new order. In this case, however, we had fore-knowledge that a train with building material had arrived which needed unloading. Although I felt apprehension when selected to leave my place of work, I was happy that my father, who had just had his 47th birthday, was allowed to stay behind. Work was already in progress when our small group joined in. Soon it became evident why so many were required for this job. Five building bricks were piled on to my shoulder; then, holding them in position with my right hand, I started on a mini-marathon which I shall never forget.

'*Schnell, schnell!*' bellowed the man in uniform at the wayside. With the whip in his raised hand, he was ready to rain blows on the sweating prisoners who, on this hot summer's day, each laden with five bricks on his shoulder, had to run past, at a fast trot, to unload them nearly half a kilometre further on. Such a sadist was placed every 50–100 metres and one could see the enjoyment in their faces, each performing his task with relish. They could have been Germans or they could have been Ukrainians – the 'schnell, schnell' was roared in voices free of any accent.

After unloading, an immediate about turn, schnell, schnell, past the torturers, back to the wagons, five more bricks. I tried to trick my way on to the wagon – loading on to other shoulders was easier than carrying the load oneself – but no luck, five more bricks. I considered taking four but was warned of the dire consequences which had befallen one who had done so. I didn't dare attempt it. I managed to get some broken ones in between – harder to balance but slightly lighter in weight. Schnell, schnell – the blows rained on my back – grit your teeth and don't lose your load whatever happens. Some did, and had to reshoulder their burden under a hail of constant verbal and physical abuse. The guards seemed to delight in hitting those with heavy burdens rather than those who were returning for another load.

The load, the rushing and the heat were soon too much for some. After two runs, and more so after three, they started falling and no amount of blows could make some of the wretches get up again. I fully expected them to be shot but, probably thanks to Get's absence, they were not – although some died from the blows or from pure exhaustion. I managed to avoid the worst by using my eyes. There was a gap of nearly a hundred metres between two guards, about halfway to the unloading point, and there was also a hill and a ditch which I had noticed on my first run. Passing that little hill, and bending down, I knew that I could not be seen from behind, while the one in front was fully occupied with another victim. Off came the load into the ditch. I turned around and hurried back to the train. However exhausted one might be, it was still better to run without the load on one's shoulder than with it.

Once again I escaped the worst and my awareness grew that it would take every ounce of wit and vigilance to survive – or to give fate a helping hand and seize any chance of survival. The train was duly unloaded – I never learned how many victims of death or injury there were.

When, in a state of utter exhaustion, I entered the *Metallver-arbeitung*, I heard Sigi Vogler giving a rendition of his favourite song – the lively 'Wiener Fiaker Lied'. What a thin dividing line between the groans of suffering that I had just left outside and the happiness and unawareness of the one not affected. This amazing 'thin dividing line' would be magnified a thousandfold between hunger and satiation, utter misery and short-lived elation and between life and death itself. Human nature has uncanny resilience and, with the slightest let up of pressure, it will try to compensate for its situation. How else can one explain the happy singing of our friend Sigi, the occasional outburst of laughter and the jesting remarks by my father or myself?

*   *   *

Whatever we manufactured in the *Metallverarbeitung*, the raw material for it had to be sorted out and collected from the vast heap of scrap outside the barracks. That day it was my turn to search for suitable sheetmetal, large enough to be made into dustpans. Two others were already climbing about on that metal mountain, which, as I only recently learned, came mostly from the Emallie Works of that amazing fellow Oskar Schindler.

We were not after the same pieces of metal but, more by fate and coincidence, we had heaped our collections in very close proximity at the bottom of the mound. At one stage, I saw my two comrades just standing there, deeply engrossed in conversation as if they had never heard of Get and his deadly sport of picking off anyone suspected of idling. Furtively, I scanned our surroundings and, since there was absolutely nobody in sight, I climbed down and joined them. It was my intention to warn them against continuing their talk but, when I reached the chatting pair, my purpose was diverted by listening to the story of the younger one, who had arrived in the camp only a few days ago.

It was the kind of tale which, although in this instance I was hearing for the first time, I was to hear repeated many times over in the coming years in different versions. He, together with his parents, an aunt and a younger brother, was in hiding and being looked after by a Polish family. For six months, they managed to pay, with their gold and jewellery, for every loaf of bread that they received. Anxiously, the trapped family calculated the day when their fortune would be spent and they would no longer be able to meet the exorbitant demands of their 'benefactors'.

Three weeks ago, they had had to leave their hiding-place and take to the woods. A few days later, he went in search of food. From a farmer he obtained a few eggs, some bread and a pork sausage. He knew that his father, who so far had not been able to bring himself to break the Jewish religious dietary laws, would just take an egg but would look the other way if his hungry family tucked into the forbidden food. Happy with his successful endeavour, he made his way back to the place in the woods. All he found was a couple of open suitcases and a few belongings, mostly his or his brother's, strewn all over the place – but no family.

He sat down, numb with shock, until, after a while, he decided to go and look for them – come what may. He packed up the few belongings and started off in the direction of the nearest town. Even if it meant capture, he was determined to address someone in authority and to raise the question of his family's disappearance.

With a pounding heart, he approached two Polish policemen, asking them if they knew anything of the happenings that afternoon in the nearby woods. Denying all knowledge of any such event, they handed him over to the Germans, where he received no reply at all to any of his questions and entreaties. After two days, he was taken to this camp.

Having finished his sorry tale he reached inside his pocket and produced a number of photographs, probably to show us his family. It was the last thing he did. We had drawn closer together, listening intently to this, unfortunately, quite common drama. The tall fellow on my right, bending to look at the photographs, was hit first. The bullet struck right in the middle of his forehead. Spurting blood all over me, he fell forward and landed across my feet. I did not even have time to panic as the second bullet came from behind and tore the collar of my jacket. My hands, already covered with the warm blood of the first victim, jerked up towards my neck and face leaving a liberal smear all over it. With knees buckling, I dropped on top of him. The youngster was last, his body covered my left arm and his head came to rest on my neck.

Why did I drop? Was it presence of mind, shock, instinct or just an automatic reaction? I do not know, and I cannot recall, but there can be no doubt that this reaction, coupled with the fact of being drenched in the blood of my comrades – whose names I did not even know – saved my life.

I am lying face down, mouth open. I dare not move. Footsteps are coming closer – they stop. Fear keeps me rigid. No prayer or, as on other occasions of facing death, no flashing past of one's life – just don't breathe – do not breathe ... One picture comes to mind – a contest: six of us, at school, who can hold his breath longest – I won – I must win now – even if it takes ... The footsteps move away.

The amount of blood must have convinced the murderer that his task was successfully accomplished. My life was saved – or was it? What is the procedure now; who will come – and when – to collect the 'three' corpses for burial? Should I get up and hide? What if those ordered to collect three bodies find only two? Nonsense, I have to leave this place, I can't just wait to be buried! No, I must not get up now ... the guards! The shots must have alerted the guards on, at least, the nearest watch tower. He, or they, were used to this scene which happened only too frequently in this camp; to see one of the dead wander off must be rarer. I decided to wait a bit longer.

* * *

Some of the details in this particular story were filled in afterwards by my father. The first shot created panic among the workers and everybody busied themselves as if their lives depended on it. Get would observe people who, quite naturally, worked with all the speed that they could muster. After a while, he would say: 'You have made so many items in ten minutes – what did you do all morning?' Quite often this resulted in death too.

All eyes were anxiously directed towards the door, although if it had opened, and the huge contours of the Commandant had appeared, they would have been studiously averted (in any case, if any uniformed German had entered, somebody, usually the foreman, would have shouted '*Achtung*' and we would have all stood to attention at our positions). In fact, by an incredible stroke of luck, or just plain coincidence, Get never actually entered the *Metallverarbeitung* while I was on shift.

Whereas the others, after hearing the first shot, concentrated diligently on their work, father, knowing that I was outside, went to the window to look out for me – reaching it just in time to see me fall. His first reaction was to rush out and help me; he became angry when people tried to hold him back. 'Your son is dead, he cannot be helped and it is suicide for you to go outside now.' They added that they were afraid to attract even more attention, which would endanger them all; he had to see reason.

He did not describe his feelings then – he did not have to as he aged ten years in as many minutes – he just sat there, motionless. Had Get entered now, he would certainly have been a target. Then somebody called out that Get had left, but nobody knew the correct procedure for removing corpses. This time, my father could not be stopped – he wanted to see his son once more.

He needed some cover and asked for volunteers to help bring in the material collected by the three of us. There was none. He then went straight to the heap nearest to where we lay and gathered what he could carry. He looked around – nobody in sight – nobody interfered. Noticing the profusion of blood on my clothes and my face, he started sobbing. I heard him but still did not dare open my eyes because I was not quite sure who it was. He put down what he had picked up and started to recite '*Yiskadal v' yiskadash* ...' – the beginning of the Kaddish, the Jewish prayer for the departed. It showed his state of shock and confusion as this prayer is not usually recited without a *minyian* – ten male adults.

I recognised his voice. '*Papa, ich bin nicht verletzt*' (I am not injured), I called out, quietly.

His prayer stopped and so, nearly, did his heart. He did not quite trust what he had heard. 'Heinz,' he answered, in a shaken and subdued voice, '... You are ...?'

I repeated that I was not hurt; then I went on: 'Don't come nearer, watch the guard towers, go inside and discuss what to do.'

As if in a dream he picked up a few pieces of scrap metal and – more staggering than walking – he went inside to tell the astonishing news.

Night and darkness were hours away and, knowing my father, I fervently relied on speedy action. Minutes seemed eternities and again I was contemplating whether simply to get up and walk away, when I first heard and then saw three people from the barracks approach. They asked me to wait a little longer, they were just assessing what could – or could not – be observed from the distant watch towers. Picking up a few pieces they returned to the barracks – a distance of 15 metres or less.

I did not move all this time but now I kept my eyes open. Shortly, a group of six approached, unceremoniously picking us up, and carried us around the corner of the building – out of sight of any prying eyes. One more look to see if it was safe, and I finally allowed myself to stand up. The stiffness of my limbs, from lying motionless for what felt like an eternity but was probably less than half an hour, lessened swiftly enough during an initial cleaning-up process to walk the few yards unaided behind four others into safety. My father, who could be considered as quite tough and very manly, was sitting there, white as a sheet and visibly shaken.

Was I safe now? Of course not. Nobody knew what to expect next, everybody ventured suggestions and advice. The questions I had asked myself before were repeated by others. Would Get send for three bodies to be picked up? What would happen if he received the report that there were only two?

I was thinking of the meticulous German bookkeeping. How many 'demised' people would they register? The danger was not over yet. I sat down next to my father, busying myself with painting dustpans. My plan to hide the bloodstains which I could not remove from my garments with red or brown paint were frustrated; these very common colours were not available – out of stock. Fortunately, there was no need for this disguise – nobody came and checked.

The end of our shift came: no sign of anybody to remove my two comrades. I thought of this as a good sign, for, if Get had ordered their removal, it would have been done hours ago. I gave a last glance as we passed the two unfortunates, whose names, as I said before, I did not know and whose blood, I have no doubt, had saved my life.

*   *   *

Tallith and *tefillin* – prayer shawl and phylacteries – the appurtenances of the religious Jew should, to all intents and purposes, be among the few possessions we still had. They were not. I had not seen any of these items since we entered the first camp. They had been left in Bochnia, the place I departed from minus mother, sister – and, probably, religion. Nor did I hear or see anybody else praying during my years in the camps. There must have been prayers – uncountable millions of them – unanswered, but for a derisory few. For precision's sake I must mention three exceptions: when my father had started the prayer for the departed, just mentioned and, later, in the

Buna Works, by Auschwitz, when a bomb dropped near us. The third exception was that night, when I asked my father for a suitable prayer for those two souls, whom, as I then felt strongly, I should have warned more decisively, instead of joining in with their careless chatter.

Were we still believers? We never talked about religion any more, so I can speak only for myself. Belief is as difficult to define now as it ever was. I was brought up with the knowledge of the relentless persecution of the Jews throughout all of history. So – what's new? In the late summer of 1943 when, perhaps, the majority of European Jews had already met their fate, and genocide proceeded at an average of between 10,000 and 20,000 killings every day, we were aware of only a part of the tragedy. On learning that I had been an inmate of Auschwitz, many people later assumed that I must have known of all the atrocities that occurred in those days in those places. Not so. Not till after the war did I discover, together with the rest of the world – but with less astonishment – the full extent of the unthinkable methods as well as the unimaginable number of people annihilated. I did not know then about the infamous extermination camps. Even at Auschwitz, nobody told me about the daily arrivals of trainloads of human beings who, with few exceptions, went straight into the gas chambers.

The knowledge of our mortality is with all of us throughout our lives; yet, we manage to avoid thinking about it most of the time. Similarly, in those days, when we were quite sure that we were destined to die a premature death, I did not let this fact enter my mind unless compelled to do so by stark circumstances. Curiously these circumstances occurred even more often in Plaszów than at Auschwitz.

It was as if God had nothing to do with the events – or vice versa. People with deeply held religious belief must have been bewildered indeed. Yet, given that they had the time to do so, I am sure they died with the '*Shema Yisrael*' (the Jewish confession of faith) on their lips. My own feelings were best expressed by Alfred, Lord Tennyson: '*I found Him in the shining of the stars,/ I marked Him in the flowering of His fields,/ But in His ways with men I find Him not.*'

I never consciously prayed – it seemed pointless – but I envied, I dreamt and I wished. I envied everything and everybody who lived outside those barbed-wire fences and without the perpetual threat of being annihilated. I dreamt of food. My wishes, ardently repeated and with increasing fervour as time went on, with conditions going from bad to worse, with no end but our own in sight, were expressed in one, ever-recurring sentence: '*Nor tzi iberleben abee mit a trik-kenem Kartoffel!*' (literally: 'Only to survive, be it with only a dry potato'). This contains both an element of prayer and an attempt to bribe or influence fate – or God. The 'bribery', offered to fate, God, or whoever might listen, was the pledge, should this wish to survive be granted, to live with just the basic minimum of sustenance needed to stay alive – a plain dry potato – and no more, no other aspirations.

*   *   *

The next day the sun was shining, the bodies were gone. I stamped out a few more dozen dust pans from the material gathered the previous day. Life went on as 'normal' and everybody asked the usual questions – about news in general and the exploits of 'our' commandant in particular. Towards evening I felt safer and after work I spoke to my father about the possibility of escape. It would have to take place when we were on night-shift. The *Metallver-arbeitung*, our workshop, was the nearest to the barbed-wire fence; there was talk that it was electrified but no one knew for sure.

At work we would find the necessary tools for cutting the wire. We would study how to avoid the floodlights; suddenly it seemed that breaking out would not be all that difficult. To escape meant a gamble of life and death; to stay seemed, especially after what happened to me, certain death, if not immediately, then, so our reasoning went, in the not-too-distant future. This commandant would not allow us to survive the war, whoever won it. As always, the question of where to go loomed as the apparently insoluble obstacle in our plan. 'Also', my father added gloomily, 'how many will they kill because of us?'

'I thought of that too,' I replied but, influenced by my close brush with death, I reminded him of our expressed conviction that it was only a matter of time and we would all die anyway. We remembered how we had envied and applauded the audacious escape of Daniel, hoping, of course, that we wouldn't have to pay for it with our lives. We were also convinced that such considerations would not deter others if they saw a way to make a dash for life.

That night, having balanced the pros and cons, we decided to work and plan for our freedom. My father, who was still suffering from yesterday's shock – even more than I – remarked that the decision itself had somewhat lifted the unbearable depression which had descended upon him. Night-shift was two weeks away. We did some reconnoitring, like soldiers who study a terrain in which they proposed a campaign. We knew the exact spot where we would make our break. Gathering provisions was next on the agenda, so was making two fearful-looking knives with pointed and well-honed blades, no less than 8 inches (20 cm) long. Unfortunately, among all that metal, there was no barbed wire to practise on. Sharing and evaluating our notes of the hours when the guards on the watch towers would change, we noted with some astonishment the absence of dog patrols, which we put down to our own inadequate observation – rather than believing that there was none.

We chose a Saturday night to make our bid for freedom; five days – or rather nights – to go. We felt that we were ready for it in all, except one, the most nagging aspect of our escape plan. The question that must have thwarted thousands of resolves – to which Hamlet in his famous soliloquy made the appropriate observation: 'and makes us rather bear those ills we have than fly to others that we know not of?' – after the breakout – where to?

We had worked out, so we thought, the only remotely feasible answer to that question. We would make our way to Switzerland. It was a sign of our unfaltering determination that, although we postponed the first arranged date, we doggedly continued to gather information on how to reach the nearest border. Unfortunately, this turned out to be Czechoslovakia which was, of course, under German occupation. We then would have to cross another country of equally unpalatable choice – Germany or Austria. At least we knew the language. It would never occur to us to go eastwards or even north. Great care had to be taken not to arouse suspicion, even among the inmates. Fear and self-preservation might make them betray us. We involved an elderly co-worker – in camp, a person of 50 was elderly – who knew his geography, in a mock game of escape and the routes we would take. My father, very knowledgeable himself, would greatly contribute to the facts we had to learn and the route we had to take. I just sat and regretted my lack of interest when this subject had come up in school.

The odds seemed insurmountable. In our favour we listed the fact that we each had suits and a coat which were not marked with painted-on stripes. Father still had his wedding ring and a pocket watch – both in gold. My Polish was far from perfect but good enough to get by and German was no problem. But the factor X, the unknown, was the people we would meet on this 600-mile journey.

Although I believed then, as I believe now, the majority of humanity, including Germans, to be basically decent, I was aware that it would only take one rotter on our projected route, be it out of spite, fear, panic or stupidity, to put the authorities on to us, in the belief that, as a civilian, he was just doing his duty, without a thought of what would happen to us. As we added each detail and evaluated our chances, our enthusiasm alternated between very high and dismally low.

We were on day-shift again when I stepped outside to sort out some more suitable pieces for us to work with. Longingly I glanced in the direction where the perimeter fence and the barbed-wire fence were, for a short stretch, running as one. A working party was busy spreading huge coils of barbed wire just a few yards outside the original fence. It would now be almost impossible to cut through all this in a reasonable time to avoid floodlights or patrols. A jinx, I thought. An unbelievable coincidence. 'Here goes our "weakest" breakthrough point,' I mumbled to myself. Adieu freedom, goodbye dreams; I rushed back to my father to report the disheartening news.

'It was not meant to be,' he said philosophically. And, who knows, maybe this point, evidently discovered, maybe by Get himself, to be no great obstacle for a would-be escaper, was better watched than we thought. We agreed that this calamitous interference in our plans could not have been the result of our observations as these took place very unobtrusively. But we were determined not to give up. Planning would take a little longer.

* * *

By now it was November or December 1943. Winter would make an escape harder – snow would make it impossible. One day, a number of us were again detailed for work outside our barracks. Not carrying bricks again, I hoped. It turned out to be road repairs – miles away from the camp. This would take a week; a splendid opportunity in the furtherance of our plans. In the evening I told my father about

103

this new opportunity. We were widely spread out, I told him, and the guards, for a change, grossly inadequate to supervise us all. The difficulty would be to get him to join me. It would have aroused immediate suspicion if he volunteered to exchange an easy indoor job with one that everybody tried to avoid.

The street through which we walked to and from work (partly paved with Jewish gravestones) was named by the Poles (long before the war), Jerozolimska (Jerusalem Street). It evoked an acute feeling of mockery.

When we entered the camp gates at dusk of the third day, there was an unusual amount of activity. Every happening in this camp which was not immediately apparent as harmless, created dread – mostly with good reason. There was shouting in the distance; not the shrieking of people in pain or fear but, by the sound of it, a number of voices bellowing commands, all at the same time. It was now too dark to see what was going on. I could make out lights and movement further on the right of Jerozolimska. At times we could discern commands to assemble. The *Appellplatz*, where the hangings took place, was much further and to the left. My worries of what lay ahead were soon superseded by a much greater shock. Our guards ignored the commotion and the commands and ordered us to line up in the usual rows of five; they obviously wanted to complete and finish their day's task. My thoughts were with my father: has anything happened to him – is he safe? My attention was brought back abruptly to our group.

'Forty-nine, one missing,' yelled one of the guards. My heart nearly stopped.

Panic – cold sweat. We all knew what it meant if one of us had absconded. It did not occur to me then that I had been planning the same thing. I saw myself being led with our whole group on to the infamous hill where all the mass killings took place. No escape, no hiding-place this time. The guards counted again and started for a third time when I shouted that one of us had obeyed the call to rush to the assembly place. Luckily, at this moment, a voice nearby (I could not see the caller) unwittingly aided me – or rather all of us – shouting in perfect German to hurry to the *Appellplatz* – *schnell, schnell.*

I took my two neighbours by their arm and, with a mighty pull, I roared in German, 'Didn't you hear – forward to the *Appellplatz* –

schnell, schnell.' Within seconds we were mixing with others heading in the same direction. As expected, the whole group followed us immediately. We had outwitted our three Ukrainian guards. I was sure that they would do no more than shrug their shoulders and call it a day. Perhaps they were even glad, not for humanitarian reasons – our death meant less than nothing to them – but they were saved from reporting a missing prisoner and thus prolonging their time of duty.

For a brief moment I felt the elation of having saved my life, nay the lives of our whole group. I felt ten feet tall – for a brief moment.

*   *   *

On the assembly place which, as mentioned, was not the same as the one where the hangings occurred, we found thousands of people asking each other questions. Nobody knew the reason for the gathering of such a large number of prisoners. Many were forced to leave their places of work. My first reaction, of course, was to find out whether anybody was taken from the *Metallverarbeitung*. 'No,' was the answer, 'nobody was taken from the metal workshop.' This relieved me from the task of looking for my father among this multitude and in this darkness.

Although, in common with everybody else, I could make no sense of all this, I reasoned that this assembly in the dark was not practical for the purpose of slaughter, but I could only wait and see. Forgotten was the escape from certain death only minutes ago, for now the worst part was the nagging fear that I would not see my father again. Whatever was going to happen, I was determined at least to try to rejoin my father.

The shouting we'd heard previously was that of the so-called *Prominente*, the 'elite' among the inmates who ordered everybody to get in line – five deep, as usual. Those already assembled marched towards Jerozolimska Street. It was all so confusing. This was not the pattern of mass execution, but surely they would not send these masses of people to work at this time of the day – or rather, night?

Before I could settle things in my mind, I was marching with the others. When I reached the street, matters became at the same time clearer and, if possible, more confusing. We turned to the right. About 15 yards in front of me stood Get, talking animatedly with other SS officers. Jewish police stood by. Once the column reached

105

that group, they turned left and, while being counted, they marched into another barbed-wire-surrounded area. Since I had not observed it before, I thought that it had been specially erected for whatever was going to happen tonight.

But why? When it came to murdering prisoners, Get had no need to resort to this type of action. No matter what reason, I must not join them. The thought of being parted from my father for ever was gripping me with no less panic than when I became aware that one of our number had vanished.

I must not join them! But how do I get out of this situation? My hand went down the side of my right boot where I carried the newly made well-wrapped knife. This movement was involuntary as I did not intend, at this moment, to use it. My body, my whole system, was tensed like a spring – ready for action at the slightest touch.

Slowly I was getting nearer to the lit-up area where our tormentors kept counting. I did not waste much thought whether Get would, by chance, recognise me – the boy he had 'killed' only a few weeks ago. Presently he seemed to hold a little conference with the others; I was still not near enough to make out what was being discussed. But then he, Get, raised his voice: 'Where is Chilowicz?' he called out (Chilowicz was the head of the Jewish police). These words were the trigger to release the tensed spring. Within a split second, certainly quicker than can be told, I shot like a bullet out of my line, pushing aside a few astonished people and – shouting the name 'Chilowicz, Chilowicz' – ran back 80 or 90 yards to the unlit assembly place where shadowy figures still commanded others to get in line. I looked back. It must have caused confusion and disarray for someone to break out of the lines of five – nobody had followed. If they had, I could have easily disappeared in the darkness. It was, however, not too dark and one could recognise faces up to two yards away. I stopped shouting and still remember the incredulous looks of those whom I suddenly commanded in perfect German to get in line. They couldn't make out why this young fellow, unlike the *Prominente*, very poorly dressed, was giving orders; nevertheless, probably impressed with my *Prominente*-like behaviour, they got into line.

My audacity could not last and, taking the first opportunity, I placed myself in line – at the very back.

Again I was on the march. I now knew what was going on in front. There was unlikely to be another chance to challenge fate and break out. The fact that people were being counted plus the knowledge that my father, together with the far greater prisoner population, was not present, gave me the idea, and the hope, that only a limited number was required. All I had to do was risk breaking out of my line in the dark – before we reached the lighted part in the street – and place myself at the back of the queue, hoping that there were more people than required.

Nobody had stopped me when I pretended to call Chilowicz, but I was afraid that this trick would not work twice. To step out of line could be fatal and, the nearer we came to the area where the SS were still counting, the greater the risk. In my determination to get back to my father, I was prepared to take that risk. With every step I took my heartbeat quickened and tension, once more, rose feverishly. Another few steps and I would be in the lit-up area and it would then be too late to act. Whereas the first run had been on impulse, this time I would brazenly walk away and trust my luck to think of something, if challenged.

Too late! I had stepped out of the darkness. In no more than seconds I would be counted into the compound. Then, just as in a film drama when salvation arrives at the last moment, somebody shouted: *'Genug'* – enough. The column stopped and, within less than a minute, the place had cleared, everyone hurrying to their respective barracks.

Never in my life did I feel so acutely the longing to be with my parent. Like a schoolboy who brings home better reports than had been expected, I was rushing back to see him. Not only for the obvious reasons but I was also dying to tell my father what had happened to me within less than one hour; about the incredible luck, my audacity in risking my life after escaping certain death because of the vanishing of one of our group, and about my determined effort to avoid being parted from him and, perhaps in so doing, glorifying a little in my success. I could hardly wait to see his face when he heard my story.

I had lost all sense of time and did not know whether my father would still be at work or back in the sleeping quarters. Poor man, I imagined how worried he must be about today's events and how happy he would be to see me again. On my way to the workshop I stopped at our barracks – he was not there. He was not at work either. Contrary to the information I had been given, he had been taken with some others into what I then called that 'camp within the camp'. I cannot describe my feelings on hearing this news.

*   *   *

That night, when it seemed that I had lost my father and only friend, and from now on I would be on my own, I shed the last vestige of protected childhood and crossed the last barrier of no return.

When, finally exhausted, I fell into a fitful sleep, all the questions to which I desperately tried to find a logical answer found their way into my equally fitful dreams. Again and again the same questions – all with the same negative result. This camp, so everybody believed, was our last; either to see the end of the war or, more likely, to die here.

The possibility of being sent elsewhere to be liquidated was, though it entered my mind, dismissed. From a camp like Klaj – yes; from Kraków-Plaszów it seemed as ludicrous as making a hole in a bucket to empty the water. It did not occur to me at the time that the Germans might have gone too far in their quest to kill all the Jews and were now running short of slave labour.

Morning approached and, having found no satisfactory answer, I decided that I would get my father out of this peculiar situation. Emboldened by last night's successes, I really believed I could do it. My plan was simple – its execution less so. Sigmund Rosenblum of the Jewish police, my father's cousin in whose wife's barracks we survived our first manhunt, was the lynch-pin of this plan. During our nine or ten months stay in this camp I had only met him twice. It would not be easy to see him, as Get had erected barbed-wire fences everywhere. Since starting work in the *Metallverarbeitung* our life had revolved between the working and the sleeping quarters – both separated by fences. I did not know how many fences there were between my place of work (where I had to start from) and the police post.

The idea was for Sigmund to find somebody to 'volunteer' to go into the mini-camp in exchange for my father. I was prepared, if need be, to hand over (as a bribe or otherwise) everything of value we had left. Father's ring and pocket watch were still where we had hidden them. He himself had been taken away without being allowed to take any belongings.

I would now go to work, show my face and somehow make my way to Sigmund through the internal unguarded fences. Shortly after starting work I found myself marching in a group to finish the outside job we had worked on for the last few days. We marched on the other main road of the camp and soon found ourselves passing at the rear of the compound with its inmates standing at the barbed wire, waving and shouting to us. Some of our group shouted a last goodbye when they recognised someone they knew.

What is shown on the sketch map of K.L. Plaszów (see page 110) as the Polish Compound, which I took as the one where my father was held, does not square now with my memory. The rear fence on this map bordered the street where we were marching. However, the distance between my father and myself was such that I had great difficulty in making him out among the multitude. We did not stop, nor did any of us dare to step out of line and go nearer to the fence. In a few seconds we would be past shouting range. Would this be the last vision I would have of my father? Straining my larynx to its utter capacity I tried to outscream the others, simultaneously gesticulating my intention to get him out of there. I could hear but not discern anything he shouted in reply. Then I saw and interpreted his gestures. He stretched out his arm – one finger pointing at me – then lowered it to point vigorously downwards. He must have understood what I said but was gesturing for me to join him.

I thought he might know something that I did not. As it turned out later, this was not so but, having asked himself the same questions, he acted on an intuitive feeling that people about to be killed would not be placed in better barracks or given a slightly better food ration. He concluded that, wherever they were going, it could not be worse. How could my father know that, in Auschwitz, better food rations were often given to inmates (not new arrivals) about to be gassed?

That day, besides physical labour, I also worked hard mentally. There was an added element which was very distracting. Our group was slightly larger than yesterday's, with only three Ukrainians guarding us. I found myself constantly observing all those in my sight, keeping watch that nobody should abscond. After last evening's experience I was very much afraid of such a possibility. Yesterday's lucky escape, perhaps the only bloodless one in the history of Get's camp, was unlikely to repeat itself.

The next morning I managed to avoid being detailed for outside work. The people in the compound were, so it appeared, not there to

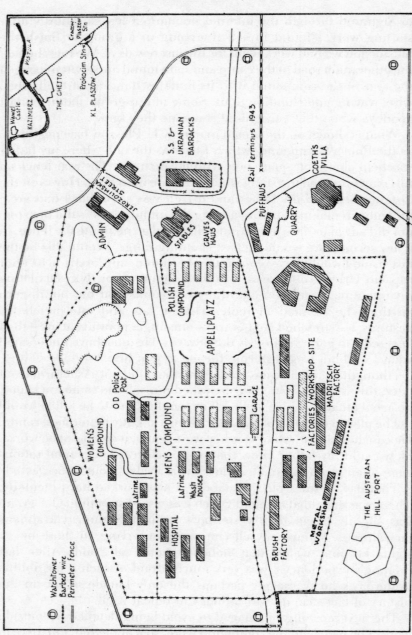

5 Sketch map of K.I. Plaszow (from Thomas Keneally, *Schindler's Ark*, reproduced by kind permission of Hodder & Stoughton).

be killed but to be transferred to another camp. But when? Suddenly I became frantic that I might not succeed – or not succeed in time. Also, whereas the recent dangerous situations were imposed upon me and my reactions had been immediate and without premeditation, today's planned adventure was my own doing. Wandering about in working time was challenging fate indeed. The conflict within me, fear of being caught (possibly by a roaming Get) versus the fear of being finally separated from my father, was brief indeed; there really was, as the saying goes, 'no contest'.

Rumours had it that departure would be in three days, but not a whisper about the destination. I had never been at the police post of the Jewish OD, although I knew, more or less, its position in the camp. As I have already mentioned, after seeing the sketch map of K.L. Plaszów I believe that the fenced-in place marked the 'Polish Compound' was what I used to describe as the 'mini-camp'. If it *was* the one and not one especially erected for the purpose just described, I would say with certainty that, at the time this event took place, the barracks and the fence as shown on that map did not reach the adjoining street. Also, the outer left of the four barracks at the bottom was the *Metallverarbeitung*. To my mind it was further to the left; in any case, since a dramatic part of my story took place in front of it – meaning towards the wire – there was a greater distance between the fence and the barracks than appears to be on this map. The larger of the two L-shaped buildings above the Brush Factory must have been the kitchen.

My first visit after leaving the *Metallverarbeitung* was to our sleeping quarters just past the garage, the repair workshop for the camp's vehicles. There I took a white featherbed cover into which I stuffed various items to make it look bulky. Putting it on my back and bending forward to make it look a heavier burden than it really was, I made my way back through the open gate in the fence, turned right and went along the fence until I came to a small opening just behind the kitchen. Looking at the map I suppose I could have gone straight there from our barracks but I must have felt safer to 'test the ground' and gain courage by first walking inside the working area.

Hoping to find the two-striped OD, Saltz – the one who had given us extra helpings on a couple of occasions in the beginning and who was ordered to perform the hangings a few months ago – I entered the kitchen from the rear. Had I met him I was reasonably sure that

111

he would have helped me with my plans. Going towards the front entrance I met no one at all. On the way I managed to swipe a chef's hat. Donning it soon after I left the kitchen, I gained confidence with every step, especially when nobody seemed to take the slightest notice of my outfit. I reached my destination unchallenged. Hiding my hat now I approached the OD on duty and asked for Sigmund Rosenblum. He did not know where Sigmund was nor where to find him.

After two hours' waiting, time was precious – every minute could be of importance. I engaged the man in conversation, asking questions about those in the compound. He knew absolutely nothing, not even the rumours that had reached my ears. The Jewish ODs were half expected by others (maybe suspected is the better word) to act as proper policemen and were thus viewed as being 'on the other side'. However, I could not wait any longer, I had to risk telling him the unofficial reason for leaving my work and coming here. I wished to be exchanged for somebody in the compound or, if somebody could be found who wished to go inside, I wished for my father to be exchanged for him. Would he please tell this to my father's cousin, Sigmund Rosenblum, and others who he thought might help?

The contrast between my feverish pleading and his apparent indifference could not be greater. This fellow certainly did not betray any sign of comprehending the urgency of my appeal. What did I expect at a time when torn-apart families were the norm? The niceties of normal life, neighbourliness, favours to one's friends, charity to fellow human beings, all had started to disappear when real hardship began and, with the oppressors' increasing cruelty vanished altogether. This man certainly knew my anguish; undoubtedly had experienced it himself, but the supposition that knowledge should evoke feelings for the plight of somebody else seemed to belong to a time so outdated that one could not imagine that it would ever become part of life again.

He then asked me to return to work and wait. He gave me no hope but warned me of the danger of 'idling' around here in case there was a visit by the SS. I told him that I was prepared to take that risk. I reasoned that there must be many clamouring to get out of that mini-camp, away from a fate so uncertain and back to 'normal' life.

My deliberations turned out to be correct and the risk I had taken was soon rewarded. An OD of the one-stripe variety made the necessary enquiry. After only 20 minutes he returned, telling me to be back here at eight o'clock the next evening when the exchange would take place. I was to join my father.

With a surge of happiness and exuberance I made my way back to work. Soon, however, fear of the unknown future I was voluntarily embarking upon crept in, changing my mood into sullenness and, instead of feeling pride in my achievement, I felt I had been duped, with my own help and connivance. That policeman was too friendly, looked too smug and the speed of his return was suspicious too. We had been in this camp for nearly ten months now – but for better or worse we were alive. I had the nagging feeling that whoever was to be released from the mini-camp in exchange for me had the patronage of one of the *prominente*, had possibly even paid for his 'freedom' and that I was the dupe.

During the next 30 hours my mood alternated between joy and hope at the thought of being re-united with my father, and misery in case I had made the wrong decision. The exchange took place the next evening. I entered the compound with two heavy suitcases, the only one among the many who had any luggage at all. The joy of my father who had given up hope of ever seeing me again may be imagined. I remember clearly my first question to him: 'Did I understand your gesture, did you really want me to join you rather than me taking you out of here?'

He looked at me somewhat in disbelief: 'You make it sound as if we had to decide the venue for our next picnic. I did not believe in either possibility but, in the few seconds I had to decide, it seemed that if there was any chance at all then it would be for you to join me rather than for me to get out of here.' I had to accept that, from his point, his conclusion was the logical one.

'Where do they think we are going?'

'Nobody knows anything, but the general mood is one of hope: could it be worse than under Get?'

I agreed to that too. Without being able to give tangible reasons my father affirmed his personal confidence that we had made the right decision. It was long after the war that I learned of transports to nearby Auschwitz from this camp.

We talked extensively that evening; not so much about our unknown future but just apprehending that, for the first time in our lives, we had been so close to losing each other. We touched on the subject which, out of fear of what the other would think or say, we had not mentioned for a long time: we wondered in what type of camp our loved ones were being held, uttering the hope that they were not suffering too much, knowing but not voicing the fact that, deep down, our hope was next to zero. We were well aware that we were lucky still to be together, in contrast to perhaps 99 per cent of our fellow inmates who had already lost all their family.

If ever a hunch has paid off, it was my father's when he asked me to join him. For 25 of us hell would soon be left behind and 'paradise' entered.

It was a short march to the train that would take us to our new destination – and destiny. Quite a long train but there were enough of us to fill it. Whether by coincidence or not we found ourselves mostly at the end of a queue or the end of the column whenever we were on the march. Sixteen months later our position at the end of a queue was to have dire – fatal – consequences; in this instance, however, it augured a lucky break.

Fifty of us at the end of the long column entered the last wagon. Immediately after the doors were shut, speculation began. Would the new camp be under the supervision of the SS or the *Wehrmacht*? We all knew the difference and we all had the same hopes. What we didn't know or expect was, that for the last two carriages, it would even be better than that. The fact that we were only 50 to a wagon and therefore not uncomfortable, did not occur to us as a privilege, as none of our group had yet experienced what inhumanity the Nazi beasts were capable of when they were overloading cattle wagons with human cargo meant for destruction; something yet in store for many of us.

We arrived at a town called Kielce, a place quite well known among most in our midst, yet completely unknown to me. That, of course, made no difference; no town was any longer as it used to be – for Jews. The last two wagons were opened and 100 prisoners alighted. It was immediately and with great satisfaction noted that the usual shouts of '*schnell, schnell*' were missing.

There we were, wondering, hoping. Except for the guards who accompanied the train no other uniforms were in sight. A large, rotund German in civilian clothes appeared to be the 'big shot' here. His face, anxiously studied by all of us, showed no visible sign of cruelty; in a different place, at a different time, I would have called it jovial. His manner I had come across many a time and, although I did not fully trust my judgement, he did not look murderous to me. He asked for those with skills or professions to step forward. Unhesitatingly, my father and I joined those who came forward claiming real or imaginary professions, 25 in all. I had no real idea what profession or skill to claim. All I remembered from past experience was that those with any skills were often detailed to less back-breaking work. There was also the faint hope of being needed and therefore having a better chance of survival. A delusion, of course. In retrospect, however, it may indeed have been one of the ingredients that contributed to my personal survival.

A small ingredient among many others. The lack of only one ingredient could, in this traumatic lottery, make the difference between life and death. Good health, sharpened wits, even supreme cunning, important as they were, would not have sufficed without the all important intangible element of luck.

7

Kielce

'What are we?' I whispered to my father. 'Signwriting got us easy jobs at Klaj. Here it might be the most unwanted thing.' Metal workers came next to mind, but what if we were really put to the test? Our German masters would not take kindly to deception. The large civilian came to us. '*Maler*' (painter) said my father – '*Metallarbeiter*' (metal worker) said I almost simultaneously, at once regretting it as I realised that with two different professions we could be parted. I opened my mouth to add that I was also a painter but the huge fellow had already moved on.

There were two camps, not very far from each other. The 75 unskilled were taken to the larger camp, a factory producing, of all things, horse-drawn carts. We, the 'skilled' ones, were taken to the smaller camp. Our job was mainly to load and unload trainloads of metal: metal of all sizes, mostly in long strips, tons and tons of it, looted from the Ukraine, sorted by us and, I imagined, forwarded to a German factory for the war effort. In fact, to my recollection, not a single wagon was reloaded by us and I learned from Zigmund Hocherman (a younger inmate of the camp who jogged my memory when I met him in London after the war), that Ludwików (the name of the place) was a foundry, though I have not the slightest idea what it produced, except for the horse-drawn carts of the other camp. Perhaps the foundry supplied the wheel-rims.

There were so few in our camp I could have counted them. Today I estimate that there were about 200 and probably twice that number in the larger one. Most of the inmates were first-timers. In other words, they were still in possession of most of their best and valuable belongings. There were even three or four married couples with children – a rarity.

I should explain in what way we had exchanged hell for paradise. On the one hand the work I was doing was probably the hardest I ever had to do, but on the other – and more important – we had all the food we could possibly eat. The inmates already here turned up their noses at the horsemeat offered in large quantities. They still had money and, through the Poles who also worked here but were free to go home every day, used to acquire food more to their liking from the black market. Even the hard work turned out a blessing in disguise. My slender rib-cage expanded and I developed strength and powerful muscles. Germans were rarely seen and, to my recollection, never in uniform. There were no beatings and, during the whole nine months in this camp, not a single death occurred.

But the stories I was told by the local inmates about what had happened to them before they came here were of a different kind. The fact that apart from a few couples, all these young men were on their own meant that they must have experienced a similar tragedy to mine when I had to part with mother and sister. I remember the names of three couples there: Otto Glattstein with his beautiful dark-haired wife and little son, the Hocherman family, and another called Drukarz.

Then there was an old fellow by the name of Sachs – between 60 and 70 years old, a former wrestling champion from Vienna. He may have been the oldest Jew left alive under the Nazis. I never saw him work. Otto Glattstein – the inmate in charge – probably let him do some perfunctory job to justify his existence.

Otto Glattstein, also formerly from Vienna, was, so the story went, not the real husband or else the second husband of that beautiful but unhappy woman who originally had two sons. She was allowed to take one with her into the camp, but the Nazis made her 'husband' (who they thought was the boy's father) hold up the other boy so that he might be shot and thrown on to a heap with other victims. Every time I saw Otto I imagined what it must have been like for him – even if he was not the child's father. What would I have done in such a situation: gone berserk? Thrown myself on to my tormentors? Would I have been able to think coolly and logically that by sacrificing one child I would save myself and the rest of the family?

I don't know if Otto had been the head of the Jewish police before the ghetto in Kielce was liquidated, but here he was in charge of the Jewish inmates of this camp. He was the only one in uniform, or at least wore a cap similar to the OD men in Kraków-Plaszów. He was

117

strict and he was correct. If he occasionally showed favouritism, who was I to blame him? Besides, at times, this privilege came my way too; especially when wagons arrived on a Sunday and he made the selection among the younger people to unload them. He never detailed my father on such occasions, for which of course I was grateful. Not having the SS as his direct superiors probably made all the difference to his behaviour.

* * *

What can compare with the resilience of youth? With juvenile exuberance I soon joined a band of show-offs. Before long I would challenge my fellow-boasters to lift a length of steel, about 3 feet long, round, flat on each end, between 6 to 8 inches in diameter and weighing, we all guessed, approximately 160 kg. Two of the strongest raised it off the ground and, with the help of a third, placed it on my shoulders. Triumph and pride in my achievement soon evaporated when my pleas to take it down again only met with amusement and laughter. I was afraid to move; any change of position could unbalance my load with disastrous consequences. Panic and fear must have given me the extra strength to rid myself of this fateful lump of metal.

'That's all we need; you to be sent away to a hospital with broken bones,' was my father's scolding reaction. I had not intended to tell him – somebody else did. He was, of course, right. All my acquired cunning, all my intentions of 'all systems geared for survival' and 'not to drop guard for a minute' were thrown to the wind by this momentary and immature urge to show off my newly attained strength.

Time went by. There was occasional news about the progress of the war, via the Polish workers in the camp, but hardly any news about other camps or what was happening to our fellow Jews. Whatever happened, happened elsewhere.

We heard nothing about the Wannsee Conference which took place early in 1942, where the decision was made to destroy a whole people under the name of the 'Final Solution', nor did we know of the existence of camps solely constructed for the mass annihilation of human beings. We were, of course, aware of our good fortune in having escaped Plaszów and landed in this place. The contrast could hardly be more extreme, but happiness is not the word to describe

our feelings. We knew enough to carry with us the nagging awareness that complacency with our situation would be but a dangerous
self-deception.

We had no letters, only occasional reports and rumours which, by
their imprecise nature, still left us with a glimmer of hope that
somehow, somewhere, there were camps, if not like Kielce, even as
bad as Plaszów, where people like us were working for the 'war
effort', among them, perhaps, our beloveds. All the reports said that
the trains went to the east – Ukraine, we assumed – part of which
contained one of the most fertile agricultural areas in the world, and
the world was in need of food more than anything else. Was it any
wonder that we still cherished the hope that our loved ones were still
alive? In this we were in the same position as our relatives abroad
when they first heard of the mass-killings. They too kept hoping and
praying that by a miracle, and with the help of God, their closest kin
were still alive.

Meanwhile we lived, we worked, we ate, we played cards and
even, at one time, football. There my father really came into his own
and showed the youngsters a thing or two. They could hardly believe
their eyes when a 48-year-old ran rings around them. I knew of his
ability but had never seen him play in a team. No mean player myself
(what boy thinks otherwise?), I felt an upsurge of pride. I remembered being told that, as a one-year-old, I was lifted up high and
carried on to the football pitch where my father was playing for Ivria
Frankfurt. 'Here comes the second king of football,' the one carrying
me called out. When father broke a leg, the club, apparently unable
to replace a player of his calibre, just folded up.

The Russians had finally taken Warsaw and were pushing forward
towards Radom, less than 80 kilometres away. It was almost unthinkable. Warsaw itself was only about 150 km away and, so I
learned after the war, while we were having a comparatively easy
time, the ghetto there was systematically cleared of its 500,000
inhabitants while the Russians were biding their time for the final
push into Poland's capital.

Sometimes I think that the liquidation of the Jewish people ranked
higher in the Nazis' resolve than winning the war. Why else did they
employ their military might against a remnant of ghetto-dwellers,
most of them half-starved, instead of using the self-same troops to
help keep the Russians at bay? Another example: the slogan *'Die*

Räder rollen für den Sieg' – the wheels are rolling for victory – was displayed in large and small letters everywhere: in trains, in stations. But, incredibly, while their logistics suffered from shortage of rolling-stock, there were always trains available for transporting people to their death.

Liberation was almost unimaginable. What would we do first? Go east, of course, towards the Ukraine to seek our beloveds. Oh, what a vision, what hugging and kissing, what a relief it would be to be reunited. Never again would I disobey my mother, never again would I quarrel with my sister ... Only with the greatest reluctance and with tears in my eyes did I drag myself back to reality. The Russians were not here yet, we were not free yet and, as for finding them alive! The ugliest doubts gnawed at our hearts.

'What do you think the Germans will do with us when the Russians come?' I asked my father.

'Unless we make our own bid for freedom at the right time, the Germans will not hand us over to the Russians – not alive anyway.'

'Do you – do you think they have survived?' I asked hesitantly, fearing his answer. I received none. 'But we are alive, aren't we?' I insisted stubbornly as if to prompt him to answer in the affirmative.

'Let us pray and hope' was his noncommittal answer, the only one he could really give.

* * *

How could I know that, by this time (July 1944), about two-thirds (maybe three-quarters) of the six million Jews finally killed were already dead?

The Russians continued to advance. There was a whisper that some of the inmates were prepared to escape into the nearby woods. I imagined that they would be joining the Polish partisans who would welcome this strengthening of their numbers. Long after the war I learned that some of these partisan groups actually killed the Jews who wanted to join them.

Now came a rumour that Hitler had been assassinated. The mixed feelings of incredulity, joy and scepticism are hard to describe. Each day brought conflicting rumours. Whatever the repercussions elsewhere of the assassination attempt of 20 July 1944 and its aftermath, for us it was no different from my own futile attempt back in autumn 1942 – it might just as well never have happened at all. Whatever we had expected, for better or for worse, however closely and suspiciously we studied any deviation in the attitude towards us of our masters, nothing, absolutely nothing, had changed. A major event for the world's press – a non-event for Europe's oppressed.

Rumours abounded about the progress of the Red Army in our direction. Again hope and fear alternated almost hourly. Further rumours, of the pending evacuation of our camp, quickly put paid to any hopes of rescue or release. Because of the imminence of one or other event – to be freed or to be evacuated to yet another camp – my father and I once again discussed and contemplated escape. This time we felt that the urgent need to come to a decision did not allow for any lengthy planning. As the younger I was more adventurous and daring but left responsible decisions to my more cautious father. I pointed out to him that most of our valid previous reasons for not trying to escape might not, owing to the approaching Russians, apply here – and he agreed.

Our chances would be greatly increased if we could join the unidentifiable (we could only guess), tough youngsters who, so the rumour went, had already determined to escape. I approached a couple of the known toughies who assured me that they knew nothing of such a plan. Someone indicated that they would probably regard my father as 'too old' for an adventure promising such hardship. No use telling anybody that he was strong, tough and more resilient than any of us.

The group that finally did escape on the day of, or the one before, our evacuation, must have formed long ago. I never knew how many but my guess was that there were between four and eight. The escape was easy. The guards were used to seeing prisoners shifting carts from one camp to the other and, since no one ever attempted to escape, they did not give a second glance when they saw one or two of these vehicles being pushed outside the camp gates.

Did they survive? Nobody I have met after the war had heard of them again and, judging by the stories I have heard, the answer is probably not.* After their escape, rumour already had it (knowledge came after the war) that many Polish partisan groups were hostile to Jewish newcomers, even to the extent of killing and robbing them. Others welcomed them to swell their numbers. Who knows whether my former co-prisoners were lucky or unlucky. I only know that I

*If any reader should know better, I am eager to hear about it.

121

envied them as a fatally ill person would envy one who was equally sick but recovered to full health.

'We should have been with them,' I reproached my father unjustly, knowing full well that he could not be blamed.

Evacuation Day was 31 July 1944. The word spread that our German civilian administration would look after us. Wishful thinking? Probably, but the thinking went thus: as a small, young, strong and healthy group we were a good workforce.

8

A Night to Remember

Eight and a half months of 'paradise' had come to an end. We were marched to a goods train stationed nearby and, herded and mixed together, we boarded the wagons. The larger contingent of prisoners came from the sister factory, all of them strangers to us, all of them as able-bodied as we were. Our numbers had now swelled to about 600. The roofless carriages were filled to capacity but not unbearably overloaded.

Instinctively I tried to get a place in a corner but somebody beat me to it. My father and I were sitting with our backs to the wall, but so were most of the others, with the middle taken up by people's luggage; a bucket filled with jam was within my reach.

It was a most beautiful day. I remember looking up – not a single cloud in the sky. We had enough food for a few days, partly given to us, partly saved by us for this anticipated occasion. We all had our own clothes and bundle of belongings – even some suitcases. Since the Ludwików factory had been the first camp for many of the local inmates, some of them were in possession of substantial amounts of money and valuables. Opposite me, a young woman had taken her place in a line of squatting males; someone attractive to look at during this dreary journey, I thought. If only I knew where we were going. Again and again people voiced their hope that we would go to a place, somehow similar to, or connected with, our former camp and, of course, managed by civilian administration.

The first few hours of our journey were uneventful. I was wedged between my father and another person. Suddenly I felt uneasy. What if I had to respond to nature's call? I looked across to the pretty girl. Our eyes met briefly, then I turned shyly away. Soon these lively eyes were to be dulled with worry and horror.

The train, for some reason, had stopped. The man next to the pretty girl stood on some luggage and looked out over the other side of our wagon. Others did the same. It appeared to be some minor station. There must have been someone in sight but not near enough to converse with. For obvious reasons, although there were no guards in sight, they did not want to shout. By gesticulation they tried to attract this person's attention and also to find out where our train was going to. In reply, so they reported, this man, by dress or insignia a railway official, drew his index finger across his throat, signifying what our destination would be.

We started rolling again. Perturbed faces looked at each other. The previously subdued but not unoptimistic conversations had stopped. Everybody was evaluating the reliability of this crushing message. Father and I talked it over too.

'Maybe he just wants to frighten us ...'

'Maybe he's just an antisemite.'

'Maybe he is mistaken – maybe he's heard of trains going to unknown destinations where rumour had it that people were killed.'

'There is a war on,' continued my father, who had fought (in German uniform) in the First World War. 'Rumours are flying thick and fast and, more often than not, are exaggerated – just think of the recent one about Hitler's assassination.'

Our toing and froing was subconsciously designed to calm each other's blackest thoughts; probably, it was also an exercise in self-delusion.

'What about the promises of our German civilian bosses, that we would go to another factory?'

'Maybe this too is just another rumour.'

After the unambiguous sign of the Polish railway official, a mood of heavy gloom and an atmosphere of despondency settled in. Voices, some of them previously quite spirited, were now silent, hushed, or continued in depressed murmur.

'What are we going to do?' I asked my father. 'We cannot just ...' I did not finish the sentence, I did not know how to. My father sat motionless; his eyes staring into the void as if to scour the future.

'Gleiwitz,' somebody said, 'we are going in the direction of Gleiwitz.'

'Gleiwitz? – it doesn't sound dangerous.' I turned again to my father. 'Do you know anything about Gleiwitz?'

124

'Gleiwitz is a well-known town – we are cut off from the outside world – what can we really know for sure.' Although his answer was neither encouraging nor discouraging, our spirits lifted somewhat.

'Isn't there a sister factory of Ludwików in that town?' somebody asked. 'Yes, I believe I have heard of that too,' came the reply from another corner. Suddenly we seemed to remember that a consignment had once gone to this place. There is no need for a powerful catalyst to jolt the human barometer from deep depression to new and cautious hope. Every new piece of information was analysed for its content of possible threat and peril.

The wheels below us were beating a rhythm to the pitiless passing of the hours. It appeared to me that the train was going extremely slowly. There was, of course, no reason for alarm in the slow pace. 'You will get there soon enough – wherever that will be,' said the voice of reason within me, while my subconscious mind attempted to quell the tension which had developed after the ominous sign given in response to our enquiry regarding our destination.

*   *   *

It was evening when we reached Gleiwitz. We were shunted on to a siding where we waited for several distressing hours for further developments. Locomotives passed us in both directions, hardly visible in the poorly lit station.

A single sentence, spoken by someone in our midst, etched itself indelibly into my memory. 'If the engine is attached to the front of our train, it will be all right; if to the rear, the train will go to Auschwitz!'

The gravity of this announcement had a swift effect on my entire nervous system. I started to my feet, shaking like an aspen leaf, my intestines signalling an urgent call for immediate action. Frantically I searched our luggage and found a dish-drying cloth, white with a red stripe on either side, which I spread on the tiny floor space which I occupied on this journey. Even Auschwitz was forgotten as, with the dexterity of a magician who skilfully manages to hide what he doesn't want the audience to see, I used my three-quarter length coat as a screen for this activity which, because of the dimly lit surroundings, went, so I hoped, unnoticed. The parcel went overboard.

This was a night I never forgot. Any passing engine, any changing light, threw me from hope to despair (and vice versa) in such rapid

125

and frequent succession that, had I not had the constitution of a strong young man, it would have left me, there and then, a nervous whimpering wreck.

I stared transfixed at the lights in front of the train, all showing red for stop. But so were the lights at the rear of the train. I listened: an engine passed by, a light in front changed to green, the engine went the 'wrong' way. I prayed for another to go to the front and get us out of here – in a safe direction. After another leaden-footed hour one actually did – but the light had changed to red. Please, please God, let it change again. We felt a gentle jerk, the locomotive had been attached to the 'good' side, the side of hope – the front. But the light still showed red. Please, please, please – my prayers were monosyllabic but intense; my whole being was concentrated on willing the accursed lights to change to green.

At long last, the light changed to green; with a few convulsive puffs the steam-locomotive pulled the train forward. But why, why did it not gather speed? Faster, faster, my prayers changed; faster, please God make it go faster before the lights change back to red. I could swear that my heart was working harder and louder than this wretched engine. The green beacon drew nearer, it was over my head – we had passed it. Saved. Thank you, God, for answering my prayers. I did not think about where we would be going next or how long we would be safe. All I could think was that we were not going to Auschwitz. At such times one lives only for the moment.

Actually, until that momentous night, memorable as it was, I cannot now, and could not then, recall having heard of Auschwitz before it was mentioned by one of my fellow passengers. Since there must be a reason why I was gripped by such terror and panic at the mere mention of a name which, only hours before did not command much, if any, of my attention, I must presume that knowledge or just the usual rumours of this place of death must have been subconsciously acquired and was lying dormant or reppressed until it was projected as our destination. I must also have been affected by the behaviour of my fellow passengers. For no discernible reason, conversations were now being held in whispers. The mere fact of this – and not being able to hear what was being discussed – intensified my already overstretched nerves. In this atmosphere laden with foreboding of impending peril, the word 'Auschwitz' was taking on a new, dreadful meaning.

The train rolled on at a very leisurely pace – menacingly slowly I thought – then it stopped. Another line of four red beacons in front of us did nothing to alleviate the gloom and darkness which engulfed us. Six hundred people and not a sound in the darkness pregnant with silent prayers and questions and images of one's own fate by this time tomorrow. Yet, still thinking of the 'promises' we were given and reminding ourselves what a strong workforce we were, we held on to a sort of hollow or truncated optimism.

We did not know of the millions before us who, in similar transports (or even worse because they had a roof), arrived at Auschwitz and within hours were reduced to ashes and smoke. Had we known all that, many if not all of us would have attempted to escape: at other times this might have appeared almost impossible but now it would have been unbelievably simple. True, we could not see where we were but, for the same reason, we could assume that any silent escaper would not be seen either. What's more, if there were only a few of us, we would probably not even be missed in the morning. But no one, to my knowledge, did take this apparently easy way out.

The short trip must have taken us somewhat away from the station. I had just begun to implore God anew when we started rolling again – backwards – but with the engine still in front. Maybe it was just a rearrangement on to another line. The train stopped again. Clanking sounds could be heard: the couplings between the wagons and the locomotive were being uncoupled. We were stationary again, on a different line maybe, but with a quick return of the feelings of panic and despair. The uncoupled engine came almost alongside us – it stopped. We could see very little, but the unmistakable sound of gushing water changed our mood once again. Of course! Every steam-locomotive needs topping up with water from time to time. How paranoid to be thrown into despair by every little change. I kept listening to this sound of hope until it finally stopped.

'Now, come on, let's get out of here,' I willed an urgent message to the unseen driver and in the direction where I could barely make out the contours of that engine, that merciless beast which, in my fevered imagination, held sway over our life and death …

Nothing. No sound, no movement; it was as if that noisy chunk of metal and steam, on whose movement I had pinned so much hope – and fear – had suddenly died. Then came the sound of footsteps slowly fading away into the distance. The driver too had left us; an eerie silence descended.

The guards! Where were the guards? By no stretch of imagination did I believe that we were left unguarded, yet the pulseless, noiseless night gave no indication of life outside our wagon. It was as if we were the only living beings in the vicinity. Here I was, worrying that this was my last night on Earth, whereas everybody else – so it appeared – was sound asleep.

'We've got to escape,' I whispered to my father. 'It won't be difficult to climb over the top and lose ourselves in the dark.' I heaped up some luggage and, stepping on it, I could look out into the inky blackness of the moonless night. Maybe the darkness appeared darker to me because my eyes had been trained for hours on those disconcerting red 'eyes' glowing ominously in the distance. I could not see the ground beneath me and, as we had arrived here after nightfall, had not the slightest idea about the terrain surrounding us. At one time I even had the foolish notion that we might be surrounded by water.

Once again there was an exchange of the same old questions and answers: 'What direction would we take, where would we go?' Even unseen, there must be a guard; what if he had a dog? A decision to escape, once undertaken, becomes, after only a few steps, irreversible, and lands the brave trier on a path of no return.

Our frame of mind was conditioned by the comparatively easy life we had had in Kielce. The absence of any visible guards had lulled us into a sense of false security. It would be so unlike the Germans to leave condemned prisoners unguarded.

Also, there were a lot of so-called 'tough guys' in our midst. Why didn't they make a move. We could have joined them. Perhaps they too believed in those promises of work in a sister factory – so why take risks? I was sure that they too balanced the pros and cons of the situation and were just as irresolute as I was. Once again it was 'taking a chance on tomorrow' rather than challenge and confront the peril now.

We had no sheets to tie together for me to go over and explore the territory outside. At the slightest hint of guard-dogs, or any other danger, I would quickly climb back. But however much we tried, we could not think of a way to make a rope. Had we known which direction the train would take in the morning, all the overriding negatives, which invariably put paid to any courageous enterprise, would surely this time have been swept aside.

The waiting and guessing game started to wear me out – my emotions were spent. Before long, my legs began to give way and I sank into a cowering position in my little place on the floor. I do not recall whether or how long I slept during the next few hours, only that, shortly after the train-driver had left us, my tortured and exhausted brain went into a kind of stupor.

*   *   *

A not-so-gentle jerk brought me swiftly back to my senses. The engine had been attached to the rear end of our train – which now became the front. We started rolling at a leisurely pace; after a short stretch we stopped. Uniformed armed guards were placing themselves in such a position that they could overlook us. They were sitting, so it appeared, on a protruding part at the end of every second or third carriage. The train soon took a slow bend to the right and suddenly gathered speed. Soon it went much faster than at any time during the previous day; in fact, I would say that the pace was the fastest I ever went in a train.

'This speed is meant to make it impossible to jump,' I whispered to my father.

I have the picture clear in my mind. Whereas the previous day, our place was on the right-hand side near the front, now, moving in the other direction, we were on the left near the rear part of the carriage. We were standing up while almost everybody else was sitting down.

'What now?' I asked. 'There is no more doubt in my mind as to where we are going.' My father nodded agreement.

Suddenly I felt no more panic. I can recall many times in my life when, in the face of danger, I would grow icy cold. No more nerves, no feverish befuddled thinking.

'We are going to jump,' I said to my father. 'You must step on to the shoulders and head of the next man to you – I will do the same on the other side.' Father nodded again.

We had both managed to obtain a pair of high boots inside which we carried a long, well-wrapped knife, which we had honed out of suitable pieces of available steel at Ludwików. We both knew that the chances of landing uninjured were remote but we were both convinced that the alternative was certain death. The surrounding

129

woods and the greenery we saw gave us the idea that alongside our train the ground might be grassy which we hoped would lessen the impact of our 'forced landing'. Methodically we put on extra clothing to soften the fall even further.

'Now safeguard your hands,' my father said, and we began putting on every scrap of cloth and socks we could find in our luggage. We were a sight to behold on this first day of August, a beautiful day which promised to be hot and gloriously sunny.

The neighbour, whose shoulders and head were to be the means for my father to help himself over the side, meanwhile stood up, eyeing our preparations with suspicious glances. I ignored him; father would have to step on someone else.

We arranged that, when I was ready, I would count 'one' and 'two', whereas my father's 'three' would be the signal for our simultaneous action. I looked across. The most convenient as well as the highest points which I was aiming for, and which were to be my 'stepping-stones', were the shoulders and lovely head of the very lady whose looks had so fascinated me at the beginning of this fateful journey. Chivalrous emotions were ditched in less than a second. 'One,' I started counting, 'two' ... I was ready for a tiger jump. The word, the triggering code, remained unsaid. I turned round and looked at my father. Did he hesitate or was he just waiting for the right moment? He told me later that, just like myself, he was hoping for a grassy ditch or slope and that looking out for such a terrain was the reason for his hesitation. The side-wall was too high for him to look over and ascertain with any degree of certainty what we would find outside. To step on something or somebody could alarm the guards, the nearest of whom was on the next wagon at the far end from where we stood.

We did not, of course, discount the fact that we would be shot at but a hit, at the pace this train was going, was most unlikely. If they stopped the train, our chances of escape, with the added handicap of being dressed the way we were, were almost nil. However, since this was not a passenger train with emergency cords, stopping the train was also only a remote possibility. The inherent danger of jumping at such an enormous speed was, at least, balanced by certainty that no guards would jump after us and, within minutes, they would be miles away.

All these thoughts went through my father's mind, hence the delay ·

in what was possibly the most fateful moment of his life, when by the utterance of one word – 'three' – he would have made the irreversible decision over our fate. Only our fate?

'If you don't stop that, you'll be getting us all killed.' These words came from the man now standing next to my father, the one on whose shoulders he had originally intended to step. 'Stop that or I am calling the guards,' he added threateningly.

'What would that matter – we're all dead,' I turned on him. He muttered something which I could not understand. I sat down. The supreme moment of decision – when both my father and I had agreed and determined to make this leap for life, or death, and which was only seconds away – had passed.

Moments before my whole system had been tensed like a drawn bow, ready to shoot its arrow. But as I sat down, I was actually relieved that we had been stopped, as it were, in our tracks. Was this not the typical 'I am alive now' syndrome – the explanation why so many, who could have escaped, delayed until it was too late? The instinct to stay alive is so strong that it celebrates reprieve of the smallest duration. Every breath becomes an awareness, even enjoyment, and minutes, even seconds, become noticeable. Maybe this 'I am alive now' syndrome could also explain, at least partially, why so many appeared to go like lambs to the slaughter.

The moment of relief passed quickly – reality returned with brutal swiftness. Alive, yet dead – only a few hours from now. Why was I to be slaughtered? What had I or my father done to the Germans (whom, ironically, I thought of as 'my' people up to the time when I learned that I was hated by them, or at least by those in power), to deserve being killed? Was there no way out?

To jump on my own was unthinkable – but so was the idea of just letting them kill me. At this stage I had no real perception as to the methods of our extermination.

'I am going to break loose and run,' I said to myself. 'No doubt somebody will send a bullet after me and that will be it.' I saw the whole drastic scene in my mind. 'But if I should only be wounded ...' The rest of the journey passed as in a dream. After, perhaps, half an hour, maybe only a few minutes – I had lost all sense of timing – the train started to slow down and came to a halt. The guards disappeared. I stood up and, perching on somebody's luggage, I could see, at some distance, a group of about 50 people, all dressed identically.

They were proceeding in an orderly fashion, like soldiers, but were obviously prisoners marching to work. It was then that I saw, for the first time, the pyjama-like striped uniform of the concentration camps.

'There are people alive – going to work,' I said to myself. Maybe as we were a group of mainly young and strong men, they would let us live and work. Maybe the administrators of Ludwików did put a word in for us. I would naturally cling to the smallest hope. Around me, some people became very active. My mind was too occupied to observe in detail what they were doing – probably trying new hiding-places for their most valuable belongings. I saw people throwing items into the large bucket of jam. Were they thinking of retrieving it later? Were they just getting rid of things? Valuables? What muddled thinking made them do this? How many other times before and after this had people found items of value hidden by others in the same plight, only to repeat the process by trying to hoard the items themselves? What a futile waste of energy.

Of the Jews who were thus engaged, hardly any survived; corrupt guards, however, except for the few who had to answer for their deeds, lived a life of luxury in this world where 'justice' had ceased to be administered from on high.

Was it at this point, was it later or was it just on our arrival, that I noticed the by now infamous sign over an entrance gate. The words were shaped in wrought iron letters: '*Arbeit macht frei*' (Work makes free), a cynical promise, meant to deceive. It was designed to raise people's hopes that all that was required of them was to work – and even I, knowing the German attitude to hard work, had my hopes raised for a brief moment.

For a very brief moment; then I felt deeply the insult this mocking sign presented. I don't think that there has ever been anything like this sign of cynicism elsewhere in the world. And this without my knowing that the bulk of 'work' for which this camp was built had already been accomplished.

Suddenly – though I still don't know what grapevine operated here – we all knew that we were going to be killed in gas chambers – that our last hour had come.

I have tried, throughout this narrative, to describe and define accurately my feelings and emotions at the exact moment. This time the assault of fear, the panic, an overpowering will to live, while

facing the crushing perception of inevitable doom and utter helpless-
ness released such a storm of emotions, and all at once, that it is
impossible to relate what was really going on inside me. I had
covered my head with a blanket, whether to shut out the world or to
keep others from seeing me, I don't know. Most likely I wanted to be
alone with myself for the last time as my life passed in front of me,
just as it is supposed to do before one's death.

Into this onslaught of unstoppable, alternating interplay of visions
and fear I heard my father's voice. He sounded so dispassionate, so
naturally cool as if he were offering me advice on how to behave at a
dinner table. He then uttered the unforgettable words which I have
chosen as the title to this book: 'Should we be gassed, breathe deeply,
my son, breathe deeply, to get it over with quickly.' What did I say,
how did I respond to this ultimate example of pragmatism? I could
not and did not react.

I did, however, ask myself questions, hoping perhaps they could be
heard by a higher authority. Why had my life so often been saved –
more by a miracle than by coincidence – only to have it all ended
here? I asked again and again, and almost had the feeling that I was
dreaming and that this situation was not true. Then, for the first time,
I felt something which I can only call 'a presence' hovering above me.
I could not then and cannot now explain this phenomenon but I
called it my Guardian Angel. (Very often, in later life, I felt that I had
such an angel watching over me.)

I took off my blanket and, as soon as my mind had cleared, it was
ready for scheming, and for split-second reaction, should there be
any opening whatever to delay the moment of my extinction.

9

Auschwitz

'Alles raus – schnell, schnell!'

We could hear these fearsome, soul-destroying shouts even before
our heavy sliding doors were opened. We were segregated. Women
and children to one side, men to the other. It was the first time I had
witnessed and participated in such a segregation and I knew it did
not augur well.

Hardened as I already was, I did feel a brief pang of sorrow for
those who, so they believed, saw their loved ones torn from them for
ever: a belief that was fulfilled almost every time such segregations
took place at this station. As I learned later, many of the 'lucky' ones,
who were chosen to live, were told by other inmates, who had
experienced these emotions before, that the smell of burning flesh
and the smoke they could see were all that was left of their families.
At this moment, I was glad that my mother and sister were not with
us.

In situations like these I was anxiously looking for points of
reference – for pluses or minuses. Segregation could mean – at best –
placing us in different barracks or camps; at worst that one group was
to be eliminated. Since ours was, obviously, a very fit group (first-
class slave material), my hopes were selfishly raised a little.

In reality we knew as much as before – nothing. Nagging doubts
and fear that this would be the end of my young life outweighed
heavily the little signs which I interpreted as hope.

I found myself walking in a column on a road, at the end of which
and at some distance I saw a few buildings. I did not concern myself
with these, although I should have done so, as we were marching
towards the gas chambers. I concentrated on some people whom I
saw working at the roadside; this was registered by me as another
plus point. If they needed people to work here, we should have a
chance too; so I tried hard to bolster my suffering spirits.

Our pace was not particularly fast as most of us carried some luggage and a few still had a lot. We were approaching a young man with a shovel. 'Is this our last ...?' I did not quite know how to finish the sentence. He looked at me with the briefest of glances, his silence more eloquent than words, then, as we passed by, he lowered his head. I took this as an affirmative nod. With this, albeit reluctant, confirmation of our impending doom, I walked with leaden legs towards my destiny.

We were let into what seemed to me a large wooden hut where we were left unattended for a while. A sort of anteroom I thought. Again I noticed the frantic activity of people who were trying to rearrange the hiding places of their valuables. In the midst of my own despair I remember feeling a sort of sarcasm: 'How stupid – dead people don't need these things.' But wait, perhaps they knew something I did not. I asked one of them whose hand was inside the lining of his jacket; he turned his back without replying.

Before long we were taken to another building. Nothing unusual about it – I didn't know what gas chambers looked like anyway. The process began: 'Get undressed!' was the command – and we did. By the time I'd finished, I saw the first ones already being shaved. Not a facial shave, but a complete head and body shave. Other prisoners were, of course, doing that job. Not with lather and a razor but with hair clippers. I turned to my father who stood beside me: 'I don't believe they would cut all that hair, if they intend to gas us.' I thought I saw a flicker of hope in his drawn face. My heroic father was resigned to his fate. The fact that I was not would, of course, have made no difference, except to extend the agony of dying.

What had happened to my resolve to make a run for it – regardless of the consequences? Standing there, naked and degraded, dis-spirited and confused, even if a moment for such a run had presented itself I do not know whether I would have been able to make use of it.

About 20 feet behind us a group of chattering, well-nourished, healthy-looking young women were going about their work. I did not look to see what this work was but I assumed sorting out our luggage. What did they do with their rich pickings? Hand them in? Share them? Hide them? The latter thoughts did, of course, only occur to me much later and I am sure that there are still millions of pounds worth of valuables buried there. They did not bother to look at us, they were obviously doing a routine job. Little did I then know how

135

right I was. Ours was an insignificant small 'consignment' against the 15 or 20-fold of victims who passed through here on a daily basis.

Presently I was busy tearing bits off the edges of the postcard-size photograph of my mother and sister to make it fit into my palm. In case of their not surviving this would be the last remnant, the last memento of what had been once, so long ago, a happy family. I was determined to keep this last possession I had on Earth, come what may.

Then we were ordered to go into the adjoining chamber. As we walked past an unusual door (like a safe, I thought), we were once more looked over to check whether we had hidden anything on our person. The inmate doing this job noticed my palmed treasure, and with a flicker of a smile he let me take it. I noted he had a kindly face: how could he do such a job? Well, we know now the strength of life's instinct – self-preservation. (On the other hand, what would he have done had he found a concealed diamond?)

We stepped into what I could immediately 'see' was a shower-room. The door shut with an ominous thud. Nothing I could perceive betrayed the fact that I was standing at the spot where the world's most momentous crime was still taking place. No square footage on this Earth has ever heard the same volume of screams which the sudden realisation that this was the end of life – not only of their own but that of their whole family – elicited from the tortured, labouring lungs and the suffocating throats of an unending stream of ordinary people: husbands, wives, parents, brothers, sisters, children, poor little babies.

After several eternal and infernal minutes, not fathomable by human imagination and never described by an actual witness, for there were no survivors, death finally claimed their lives.

How often, how many times did this take place?

With train loads arriving here almost daily for about two years, 8,000–12,000 a day during the 'high season', and several hundred pressed into a chamber at a time; this apocalyptic happening became so commonplace as to numb the emotions of those clearing up the mass of bodies and became a matter of monotonous routine to the unfeeling Germans.   What presented itself to them when the doors were opened must have been unforgettable. The chamber would have been filled to such capacity as to leave no more standing room –

small children, for reasons of 'productivity' were thrown on top of the masses. When the doors were opened the picture would have changed. The movement was away from the centre of the gas and, there being no space, the strongest would climb and the weakest would be trampled underfoot. The result: a weird conical shape of naked and distorted bodies. Then the workers' real task began: disentangle the bodies, remove spectacles and gold teeth or fillings, search inside their orifices for valuables, take them to the furnaces, the crematorium, burn them.   Some of these workers became insane, some committed suicide. Most of them, however, urged each other to carry on, to prevail and survive; if for no other reason than – to tell. 'Somebody must survive to tell the world' was their motto.

Groups of workers were usually called a 'commando'; those who did the grisly work just described were nicknamed the 'Canada Commando'. Probably the thought connection was Canada, the land of plenty and the only commando in Auschwitz who did not share the deprivations of the others would thereby be aptly described. However, their life of plenty was to be a short one. Every few months, it would be their turn to be liquidated. Each group, knowing what their end would be, hoped that the war would end before their turn would come. They lived by the day, day by day, and it is my assumption that they tried to find solace in the arms of the women, their workmates, who were, of course, to share their destiny. Except once. A few months after my arrival in Auschwitz, one group revolted. They blew up the crematorium and tried to escape. (It was many years later that I learned that there was more than one gas chamber and probably more than one crematorium.) Most of them, so the rumour went, were caught and, of course, suffered the inevitable consequences. That left a fortunate few who, to my mind, successfully escaped. Unfortunately, I never had any corroboration. Maybe escaping in autumn (1944), they did not survive the cruel winter that followed.

*   *   *

'The water isn't very warm' I intended to say to my father in a show of bravura, playing the cool hero. This reaction was no more than the discharge of tension after the realisation that we were not going to be killed. I actually had a smile on my face (if only of the briefest duration), quite realising the bizarreness of complaining about the water temperature at the very moment when I realised that this lukewarm water meant that we would live.

The exit was opposite the entrance door of this not extensive room. Still very suspicious of its true purpose, I left this harmless-looking place to receive my new outfit – a pyjama-like striped jacket and a pair of similar trousers. I do not remember what type of footwear we were given nor whether we received any shirts, socks or underwear. On such a glorious summer's day, these items would not have been my main concern.

What I do remember – and shall do so to the end of my days – was the moment I left the building and stepped out into the sunlight. Seeing the sun seemed – no, was – the epitome of LIFE, each letter written in giant capitals to express my emotions at a moment when my body seemed to want to soak up every available ray. Each year, on 1 August at 11 a.m. I make a point of looking out for the sun, my lifegiving friend.

'*Aufstellen!*' – get into line – '*Schnell, schnell,*' was the command which brought me back to reality. No matter, I took a deep breath, we were alive – what next?

We were marched to our new 'home': one of those barracks, as depicted so often in films and photographs, with the three tiers of shelves and filled, sardine-like, to capacity. But we were not to enter it for some time yet. We were left standing for about three hours before anybody bothered to address us. A new type of '*prominente*' appeared, called '*kapos*' – a word we learned to fear and hate. One such *kapo* arrived in the afternoon. On hearing our complaints about beeing left standing in the heat without food or drink, he sharply informed us: 'As newcomers you will be lucky if you receive anything for the next three days.' His voice full of his own importance, he told us that 4,000 gypsies had been gassed the day before to make room for us. We were suitably impressed. (Our previous German adminis-tration must have put a word in for us, if only to recommend us as a strong labour force – as good slave material. I was, of course, grateful, even for that.)

So it was true that they gassed people here. It was the first corroboration. For a minute or two, shock and renewed fear made me forget heat, hunger and thirst. I even felt a brief upsurge of pity for those poor wretches who had to forfeit their lives so that I should live.

Another *kapo* had joined the first. They also wore the striped garb, except that they looked almost smart. Their trousers displayed a sharp, ironed crease, their jackets looked tailor-made. Even the peculiar headgear one of them wore, made of the same material as their suits, had a distinct appearance. Although different in shape, it had a peak like an officer's cap but without the shield, and was obviously a poor attempt to imitate their SS masters' head-gear. The *kapos* also wore a number and a green triangle on their chests.

One of the first things I learned in Auschwitz was to distinguish the inmates by the triangles they displayed. Political prisoners and criminals had green triangles, the former pointing upwards, the latter pointing downwards. Black triangles denoted antisocial elements – mostly homosexuals, the work-shy and, if I am not mistaken, members of the clergy who criticised and did not bow down to the 'new order' in Germany. I am not sure whether gypsies had them too. (There was, I believe, also a purple triangle – rather rare – maybe this was for the clergy.) Jews of course wore the Star of David, the shape made up by a yellow triangle and a red triangle, one placed on top of the other.

As far as I know, the green triangles were all Germans and in no danger of being gassed. They had a better chance of surviving the war than the fighting soldiers or even the civilians inhabiting the big towns which were bombed by the Allies. They were all in some elevated position and, among them were the most cruel elements of the camp, imitating, and often outdoing, their jailers. On a day-to-day basis, the inmates, the vast majority of them Jewish, suffered more from their cruelty than from the SS.

*　　*　　*

Being in these camps does not, contrary to the assumptions of many, imply that I knew all and everything there was to know about them – much of which has been documented and testified to since the war. My overriding concern was to stay alive. The presence of my father was, without a doubt, a major factor of my survival; but it also meant that I did not have, nor was I in need of, any other social contacts. Of course, normal social life was non-existent; what I mean specifically, and for numerous reasons, was that it appeared best for us to have no other attachments and so I can probably present fewer details than some other survivors.

Unfortunately, many facets of these horrendous experiences will never be known. Many of the survivors have been unable to bring themselves to relive their sufferings by describing them. No matter how many accounts one hears or reads, they all contribute something in their story, unknown or unheard of before.

Making us stand in the hot August sun was just a perverse whim and, towards evening, we were finally let inside the barracks. After being told that we would get nothing for three days, even the watery bowl of soup we were eventually given was more than welcome. Then we sank down exhaustedly on to our 'beds', the bare-boarded shelves already described.

The next day we were tattooed on our forearms. My father's number was B 3406 and mine was (and still is) B 3407. For those in the know, seeing these numbers would tell them, more or less, where people came from, and when they arrived. Actually, we were the odd ones out, because most of the Polish Jewry was already liquidated and it was the turn of Eichmann's Hungarian transports. Then we were given small pieces of cloth, displaying our number, as well as the Jewish star, to be sewn on to our jackets. I had ceased to exist as a named person; from now on I was a number.

In the height of summer with the usual high atmospheric pressure, the stench of burning corpses was barely noticeable, as our barracks was at some distance from the crematorium. The story went around how the gypsies were given a special ration of white bread, butter and sausages the night before they were gassed. What on earth, or rather what in hell, was the purpose of this gesture? Was it meant to be a sign of humanity? Was it intended as a *Henkersmahl* – the last meal before execution? Who could fathom those twisted minds?

For the next few days my main worry was that I should not be given such a special meal. Then, one night, my father and I overpowered two SS guards, stripped them of their weapons and uniforms and made good our escape in their jeep. Even after waking up, I felt quite elated about this idea – except that neither my father nor I could drive a car. In my dream I had relied on my father to take the steering wheel; after all, he had once possessed a motorbike.

On the fifth or sixth day we had to assemble nearby. Again, a couple of *kapos*, with green triangles, were giving the orders.

'Any skilled labour?'

Now experienced and knowing the importance of possessing or pretending to possess a useful skill, father and I stepped briskly forward when they asked for painters. Were there too many? Didn't they like the way I pulled my father along? We were both rejected, which was better than only one being chosen. We were both shocked and panic-stricken at the thought of what being left behind as useless might mean. We went right to the rear of the still sizeable group. Other skills were called for but we did not dare to go forward again. There were now fewer than 30 of us left. 'Carpenters,' shouted the voice. We separated and approached the *kapo* within a small group but from different angles. It worked. Now we were specialists in a profession we knew nothing about. However, we were less worried about being found out. Anything seemed better than being left behind.

The following morning we assembled near the entrance gate. On my way there, it appeared to me that this huge camp was made up of many squares – all fenced in with barbed wire. In other words, penetrating through one of the fences, if successful, would just lead into another square. (I do not know if all the fences were electrified – the outer ones definitely were.)

We stood, several hundred of us, in one long, single line. An assembly of SS officers in their greenish-grey uniforms, some of them high-ranking, were there to 'inspect' us; maybe the Commandant himself among them, I thought.

Then – I could hardly believe my ears – an orchestra started to play Viennese waltzes. Not knowing then that this orchestra had often accompanied people marching into the gas chambers, I felt, nevertheless, the outrage, the extreme insult we were being subjected to.

About 15 metres to my right, from the nucleus of the SS which had gathered there, a very tall officer stepped out. Pointing at an inmate to come forward towards him, he made, judging from his gesturing, a complaint. I did not hear what was being said and it was probably irrelevant; the officer just wanted to show off to his comrades his latest party trick. Stepping on the prisoner's toes, he thumped the young man's forehead with the palm of his right hand. Only a short sharp jerk and the fellow, who could otherwise not move, fell backwards. Letting go at the right moment ensured that his body landed with the maximum impact to the back of the head. Meanwhile the orchestra played 'Tales of the Vienna Woods'.

In the by-now accustomed formation, five-a-line, we marched out of the camp. The musicians had changed to a lively march. I doubt whether the motionless body we left behind heard the beautiful music, any music – ever again.

We did not have very far to go. Only a few miles and we entered the 'Buna-Werke', a slave-labour camp also known as Monowitz. It was a subsidiary of the still existing I.G. Farben GmbH of Hoechst near Frankfurt, a giant company, equivalent perhaps to Britain's ICI. A large marquee was to be our initial home until we were allocated a place in one of the many barracks.

Almost immediately we started work. As carpenters? Of course not – it was digging and repairing roads. We had learned by now that newcomers were, almost automatically, given the hardest jobs going. The physical downhill path would start on the very first day. My father, having been spared those hard jobs in Kielce, found it especially exhausting. But he was tough. Tougher than I was, for sure.

We saw, for the first time, those skeletal types who were cruelly nicknamed '*Muselmänner*'. Anybody so dubbed was on their way out – finished. Their physical appearance betrayed the fact that a recuperation to normal was, under camp conditions, beyond hope. If they held on, if they did not die, they were certain to be picked for 'special treatment' at the next selection.

In the evening we found ourselves at the end of a long queue to receive our bowl of soup. It was watery and contained very little of any substance. If this was to be our daily intake of food, plus a piece of bread (of which four thin slices could be made), some margarine (the size of two sugar cubes) and some black, unsweetened coffee substitute, it would not take very long for us to join those marked for death. I expressed my astonishment to my father that we did not see more *Muselmänner*.

Whereas we ate our soup slowly to savour every drop, I saw many of the inmates gulping it down. Their reason soon became clear. There was some soup left and the queue started again. Now we started rushing to empty our bowl. Back to the queue. We were getting nearer and my heart pumped in anticipation like a racegoer who sees the horse he had put his last shirt on coming in for a win. Then the disappointment – the container was empty just before we reached it. During my time in the camps I regularly suffered the pangs of hunger. On this occasion, however, coupled with anger, frustration, as well as the fear that such rations must, inevitably, spell doom, I went back to my camp-bed, lay down and cried.

The next day we tried to make sure that we were among those who received a second helping. Unfortunately, our group was the last arriving so we went hungry again. This time I did not cry. I was gripped by a fierce determination that, come what may, our food and, if at all possible, our work situation had to change. Our determination to find somebody we knew, who would be in the position, and willing, to help us, needed a helping hand from fate. Around 10,000 prisoners were in this camp and we used our remaining energy after work to look out for such people. Days went by. Our stomachs got into the dangerous habit of accepting the feeling of permanent hunger. Our bodies began the process of losing weight. Our determination, however, if anything, increased.

Two weeks went by and still no change. 'We are registered as carpenters, aren't we?' I said to my father. 'Let's see if we can get such work.' Though I knew nothing about this profession I hoped that my father, being generally very handy, might pull us through. He did not share my confidence.

'There is no alternative. The hard work is getting us down even more than the lack of food. Maybe we will find somebody we know in the "administration"; there is no alternative, we are both going downhill fast.'

*　　*　　*

We were living in barracks again – 600 of us in 100 three-tier bunk-beds. Two to a bed but at least we had straw mattresses, which were an improvement. At least our bodies could get a proper night's rest after an arduous day. In the endeavour to survive, everything counts. Soon we had a second stroke of luck. We noticed that our new *kapo* would rather disappear somewhere than stand around, supervising us. As we were nearing our place of work he asked if any of us had ever been a work-foreman. Imitating his coarse Southern German dialect, I pointed to my father who was marching two rows in front of me: 'That one over there, he's been a foreman.' My father was promptly elevated.

My father, rather than harassing his poor, undernourished fellow-sufferers, stood on guard, watching to see if anybody in authority approached. When such a warning came, the grateful boys would work hard. They didn't mind at all when, on such occasions, their 'foreman' would shout some opprobrious German epithets. It helped to keep the job. I had the easiest time of all. I disappeared for hours and came back just in time before the *kapo* returned – in other words, just when we would break up for home.

This ruse was extremely important in slowing down the process of physical deterioration, but lighter work did not make up for insufficient nourishment; what's more, it couldn't last. Soon we got a new *kapo* and it was back to hard slogging.

* * *

Everyday we would queue for our morning rations. A small loaf of bread would be divided into four 'equal' pieces and then given out to four eagle-eyed people – eagle-eyed because the portions were, inevitably, not exactly of equal size. The difference could not be more than one or two bites but, magnified by hunger and instinct, it seemed to make all the difference to the length of your life, and probably did. Then there was the tiny piece of margarine and the unsweetened black coffee substitute. Whatever this substitute was made of, it must, I reasoned, be agreeable to the human stomach. So I scooped some of the sediment out of the container and ate it. The taste was of something roasted or burned, but otherwise indefinable.

Whether or not there was any calorific value in my 'extra ration', I felt sure that it alleviated or even cured the diarrhoea which had plagued me for several days; besides, it helped to fill me up a bit. Was it because, during the daytime, I was too engaged to preserve my energy, too much on my guard not to be found slacking when observed, that the hunger pains simply did not occur? Or, was it because nature, after a while, gives up and does not demand what it has no chance to get?

There were generally two groups of people: those who believed in satisfying their craving for food at least once a day and therefore devoured all their portions as soon as they were received. The second group divided their rations into two meagre meals. We belonged to the second group, except that, on my father's advice, we cut our piece of bread into four thin slices. It took enormous discipline not to nibble at the next slice and, more than once, I gave way to the temptation. This arrangement was more a pointer to my father's

144

pragmatic thinking than evidence that our method had any medical advantage over the other. Whatever, we thought it helped.

Three weeks had gone by and both of us had lost weight. Substantial though this loss was, our health was not yet affected, and we had quite a way to go to be categorised a *Muselmann*. The time would come, however – between one and two months was our gloomy prediction – that we would be down to that level.

We could not pin much hope on the fact that the war was going badly for the Germans and might end soon, for, as far as we were concerned, there was no change. But it was rumoured that fewer transports were arriving and, as one old-timer told us, selections became rarer.

'What are these selections?' we asked.

'It depends who is doing them,' he said. 'If the SS conducts a selection, they ask people to stand in line. They are then counted (or have to count themselves) and every tenth person has to step forward. To be gassed, of course. An SS doctor tells people to undress and those who are ill or visibly undernourished are separated for special treatment, meaning the same thing. It goes without saying that illness is diagnosed without bodily examination.'

The Russians had made their last big offensive in summer, just before we were evacuated from Kielce. 'What keeps them, why are they so slow?' I asked my father.

'Who knows what military considerations there are? One thing is certain, the liberation of concentration camps is not a part of their strategic thinking.'

'Why not?' I argued. 'They must have seen what happened in those camps they overrun. They are human beings, they must have a heart; besides, there must be many Jews in their ranks.'

He shrugged his shoulders. 'What do we know?'

I was reminded of this little exchange when, after the war, I met a Jew who fought in the Russian Army when they drove the Germans back from occupied Polish territory. After seeing what the German Nazis had done, he disregarded the white flag of surrender and mowed down anyone in German uniform. So, as he said, did many others. Many a young soldier paid with his life for the enthusiasm his parents had shown for the 'New Order'.

* * *

Another stroke of luck. My father found somebody he had known back in Frankfurt, a Mr Tiber (or Tieber), who was working in the *Schreibstube* – the administration. He promised to get us jobs as carpenters. Though we were a little apprehensive, it surely couldn't be worse or more back-breaking than road-building – the hardest job in the camp.

The promise alone helped our sagging spirits. After an impatient week, B 3406 and B 3407 were ordered to help in the building of a cooling-tower. I didn't know then and still don't know what a cooling-tower is or does – but I helped to build one, though not for very long.

With mixed feelings we joined the Zimmermann Commando and reported to our new job. From early childhood I regarded my father as 'the man who could do anything'. Whether this was justified or not, I was afraid, for the first time, less for him than for myself, the 'carpenter' who had never managed to hit a nail straight without bending it. What would happen if I was found out?

I need not have worried. What I was asked to do could have been done by anybody with a head for heights. However, after just half a day, I implored my father to try to get us transferred to another job. My new assignment was not back-breaking but downright dangerous.

Imagine a very tall tower, the structure of which was a steel framework. This skeleton had to be clad all around with wooden planks. When I started my new job, the ground and second levels were already completed and the third was in progress. Every level, being some 12 feet high, was supported by diagonal bars, erected in a zigzag fashion. Balancing on a 2-inch (5-cm) girder and holding on for dear life to such a steel beam, I had to heave up planks handed to me from the level below. I then had to hand them to the experienced carpenter who nailed or screwed them into position, each one tightly to the previous piece. This fellow's job was not as hazardous as mine, as he always had the choice of holding on to either the framework or the piece he had just secured.

At first I managed easily but, with every step along the 2-inch horizontal bar, the hand with which I had to hold on to the diagonal to keep me from falling, had to grip higher and higher until I could reach no further. I could not even stretch to my full height because I had to bend down to receive the next piece. More than once I let go for vital seconds to get a proper grip on the board I had just lifted.

146

Then my circus act, for which I had had no training at all, began in earnest. To reach the next hold (from the zig to the zag), I had to walk, tightrope-wise, about five or six feet – steadying myself with arms outstretched like wings – until I could reach my next hold. At this point I was only about 24 feet above the ground. Looking up, however, and seeing this five, six or even seven level construction, I feared for my life.

*　*　*

Almost every day, tired as I was after work, I went in search of somebody I knew and who might, I hoped, be in a position to improve our lot. Without such help, unless one had resigned oneself to one's fate and torpidly stopped thinking about it, the end could be calculated in weeks rather than in months.

On this particular day I decided to turn in early. My body was weakened and I could foresee that, before long, I would not be able to muster the energy to go out after a day's toil. By sheer chance, I met Adolf König, a former classmate. Though a *kapo* he would, before long, change my views that all *kapos* were rotten. I told him of my predicament and asked if I could join his commando. I also told him about my father's connection in the administration and he promised to help with whatever was needed. Then I asked the vital and inevitable question about some additional food. He told me that another classmate, Max Spira, was in charge of the camp's soup distribution!

I lost count how often the fear of impending death was relieved by a realisation that this time, it was not to be. Here was another reprieve. Max Spira, may he and his family be blessed forever, filled my bowl from the bottom of the container – not watery but lots of solid stuff, even two tiny pieces of meat. I took it to my father. Words cannot express our joy, our feeling that, once again, life had been given back to us.

Max could not continue to hand out extra rations without a good reason. He could lose his job, or worse, he could be punished. He gave me the task of looking round the camp for any *Essenträger* (soup canisters) which had not been returned to the kitchen. This meant getting up a few minutes earlier but I soon found out that this job was an invention – or almost. During the three weeks I was searching for this elusive item, I found only one. It looked to me more of an

oversight than a purposely abandoned container. But his idea saved
him as well as us.

Nothing is achieved without some sacrifices. I could not keep on
collecting my soup in a bowl; besides, it was not enough for the two of
us. We had to give up half a day's bread ration in order to have a
Menashka made – a small, elliptical-shaped food container with lid,
which held about one litre of soup. Even this extra litre of nourishment, although enough to slow down our bodily deterioration considerably, did not really satisfy us. It was certainly not greed nor
gluttony when I asked Max whether he would give me more if I could
bring a larger *Menashka*. He knew that I also had my father with me
and he agreed. We now had to give up part of our bread ration for
several days but, after that ... victory. For the moment we had
eliminated the greatest threat to our lives – starvation.

We knew of the orchestra of Auschwitz, we had heard about the
special food ration given to the gypsies before they were gassed, and I
must not forget to mention yet another anomaly in our unreal world.
When I had the one-litre *Menashka*, Max asked me once if I wanted
'diet' food. It sounded exciting, special, nourishing. I tried it, but I
had to agree with my father that the sweetened semolina – that's
what it was – tasted all right but somehow left one wanting something more solid and we did not ask for it again. The anomaly was
that, in such a place, where everything emphasised that our well-
being was the last thing anybody worried about, a diet ration was on
offer. Possibly it was meant only for people with bad stomachs or
diarrhoea (how considerate), but it was available just the same. Even
today, I cannot offer an explanation.

Our barracks were of the usual rectangular shape, the entrance of
which was in the middle of the longer side. There was a certain
advantage that our bunks were almost exactly opposite, facing the
other wall. Sitting at the bottom of the three tiers, we mostly
managed to eat our extra ration without too many envious eyes
watching us. One of our neighbours who did observe us offered half
of his bread ration for the contents of the smaller *Menashka*. Our
soup was an improvement on the watery ration given to the poor
wretches. Max made sure that we had the more solid stuff from the
bottom of the unstirred can. One litre of this brew, full of nourishing
substance, was of greater calorific value – and more filling – than two
thin slices of plain bread.

In retrospect, I feel a little bit ashamed of having accepted half of his bread (though it was the smaller half and getting smaller by the day). But that was not the time to have the luxury of a delicate conscience. The odd piece of meat which he or we would sometimes find in our soup, being specially scooped from the bottom of the large container, would provide us with an evening's conversation.

During our time in this camp we met other people whom we had known back at home. Hermann Rosenblum, my father's cousin, and the brother of Sigmund, was one of these. I rarely participated in his conversations with my father but I am sure that they did not discuss the present situation at length – curiously, very few did. Of course he wanted to know everything my father could tell him about his family whom he had last heard of in Kraków. My father probably told him that Sigmund, by becoming a policeman, had been able to save his newly-wed spouse – though not his parents. Hermann visited us a few times, shared some food with us, until suddenly he came no more. Father tried in vain to find out what had happened to him. He looked quite strong but perhaps he might have been the victim of a selection when every tenth person counted was eliminated.

Another was Josef Kampler, another classmate and former close friend of mine. He was well fed and it was obvious that Max Spira was helping him too.

* * *

Meanwhile, at work, we had completed yet another level. With sufficient food in my stomach and, having learned my balancing act, I had lost all my fear. I almost enjoyed my newly acquired profession and, at a height of about 50 feet, I had visions of a future high-life – not as a carpenter but as a celebrated tightrope walker in a circus. Then news reached me from my father who, fortunately, worked at ground level, that we were being transferred to my classmate's commando.

We met his group only in the morning while assembling and going out to work and in the evening coming back. I never learned what the others did. My father and I were detailed to lighter work, sometimes together, often apart. When marching with the others of his commando, I never heard an adverse word about Adolf König. How this decent and gentle fellow could ever have – let alone retain – such a job was beyond my comprehension. Maybe he was lucky that he was

149

not required to show toughness or cruelty to the other inmates. Maybe he acquired and kept his job through *protekcja* – patronage. I never asked, neither then nor after the war when I met him, and Max Spira, again in Frankfurt. True to the unexplained phenomenon among sufferers, the past was not discussed. So, Max Spira and Adolf König, more than four decades later, if, as I hope, you are still alive and should read this – please accept my belated thanks.

*   *   *

Thus, the second threat to our lives, excess fatigue from overwork had been, momentarily, averted. I was now working indoors, and not before time. It was late September, the days were getting shorter and much colder now. My task was to paint road signs. Something I had a talent for but was far from being experienced, especially to the professional standards expected from me after I had claimed suitability for that type of work.

I soon had some German civilian breathing down my neck. I didn't mind his sarcastic play on the similar-sounding German words *Maler* and *Mahler* (the former meaning painter, the latter, grinder). It was the fear of what he might do after his remarks that I was a *Mahler* of a mill, but not a *Maler* of signs or letters, that worried me. However, having off-loaded his wit, he gave me another chance and, seeing the vast improvement in my work, another. It worked. My father, though not working with me, had a similar job. He was more talented and had no trouble at all.

But good things don't last long. Soon we were working outside again, and although we had the advantage over the vast majority of our comrades of having sufficient food, we still suffered. It was bitterly cold and we were all flimsily dressed. What double misery the others must have gone through on their way to become *Muselmänner*. I remember the agony of the freezing temperature we endured, as well as the remedy my practical father came up with. One day he took me behind a hut where, hidden for a quick change, was our new underwear – empty cement bags. The bags were turned inside out and he had made the necessary openings for head and arms. We now had the luxury of thermal undergarments. Paper not only retained our body heat but proved a protective shield against autumn gales and, if drenched by rain, was easily replaced.

Then, we made a mistake, we developed a conscience. We told our secret to a *Muselmann* who was shivering more than most and was already unable to exert himself enough to create a little warmth by vigorous movement. Soon, more and more of our comrades were wearing protective paper under their striped suits.

One evening, as we were entering the camp gates, a random search revealed our hidden treasure. Once again we were lucky. Just before they reached us they had found enough victims to keep themselves busy. 'Theft', they called it, as they confiscated the 'stolen property'. The 'culprits' were beaten to deter other 'thieves'.

A beating saps a healthy person's strength. For a body emaciated from lack of nourishment, it is, more often than not, the last straw. The following day, our group had shrunk by at least eight members.

Fortunately, my father was given an indoor job again which would last him for a few weeks, whereas I, minus undergarment, went down with a bad cold. It is strange but true that whereas in normal times I was very prone to illnesses and often suffered from a sore throat, during the war years I recall only two such indispositions. The first was at the beginning of the occupation in Kraków when I had shovelled snow at −30°C. The second time was in late October 1944, the day after I had to stop wearing my paper underwear.

The camp hospital was one of the most dangerous places for a sick person. From time to time, at irregular intervals, an SS doctor would call. His unfailing prescription for those most in need of medical help would be a transfer to a special place of recuperation. We all know what that meant.

Blissfully unaware of my precarious predicament, I enjoyed the unaccustomed rest. On the second or third day, a male nurse approached me. It turned out that he also came from my home town, though I could not remember him from there.

The first thing I noticed was that he walked with a slight limp – it appeared to be permanent. This would normally not register as being of great importance but, at a time when the young, the old and the disabled were most likely to be selected for annihilation, it did strike me as a small miracle. He was kind and seemed genuinely concerned; showing it by bringing me extra food – including the previously mentioned so-called diet.

On the fourth day, after giving me double portions, he told me that he was on late duty and would visit me that night for a chat. When he called, he asked me to move over and placed himself beside me. As I was not exactly equipped for guests, I found nothing peculiar in his action except, perhaps, that he also covered himself with my blanket. When I replied to his questions about my personal tragedy he took hold of my right hand. I took this as a gesture of sympathy. Slowly, as if unintentionally, he moved my hand on to his body and my naïvety turned to sudden enlightenment. My unceremonious withdrawal was accompanied by the casual continuation of the conversation as I wanted to pretend that nothing had happened. (In those days one could not afford to make enemies.) He got up abruptly and I did not see him again until, more than two weeks later, he came to warn me of the forthcoming visit of an SS doctor. I was well by then and left the hospital immediately. My sore throat had soon healed, my temperature had gone and I should have been released after about a week. Not realising the danger of staying there and not relishing the idea of working again in the cold, I had been malingering.

* * *

The saying 'out of the frying pan into the fire' could hardly be more aptly applied than by my leaving the hospital to avoid the menacing visit of the SS doctor, only to be confronted by him in my barracks. When I arrived there, everybody was already undressed and ready for inspection. Needless to say, I had to join them. Regardless of their state of health or fitness, everybody weighed up their personal chances of surviving this selection. According to my memory and the pictures I saw after the war, the SS doctor could have been the notorious Josef Mengele. However, some people, who had survived selections before, spread it around that this doctor was not the worst. This, though, did very little to alleviate my personal fear.

There were basically three groups: those who knew that they would survive this selection – the *Blockältester* (the one in charge of the block) and his protégés, all well fed and not required to undress; those like us who were desperately hoping; and those who were certain that, by tonight or tomorrow, they would be no more.

We had to walk in single file past the uniformed god who, by a slight movement of his thumb, selected those who his medical wisdom told him were still fit enough to work and those who, ruined by systematic starvation, were fit only to be destroyed. His decision would not be interfered with by any other divine being. The one in attendance would certainly not respond to prayers.

152

This Angel of Death sometimes picked arbitrarily, and some whom I would have thought passable had to go to the 'wrong' side. Selection was not confined to those skeletal beings – the *Muselmänner*. Inmates marked by their harsh new lifestyle, worries about their families, greying hair and other signs of premature ageing, were also singled out to die. Father told me to push out my belly to increase my chances. In comparison with the vast majority of my terrified blockmates, I was really rounded; what's more, I had just had three weeks' rest.

I passed through the dividing door into the room where the selection took place. The doctor stood about five feet in front on my left, busy talking to the *Blockältester*; his thumb had just pointed to the right as he passed a fellow whose body was far inferior to mine, but the man behind him and just two in front of me was unlucky. As the doctor turned to the person he had addressed, his thumb veered to the left; a lively-looking young man, in much better shape than the one before him who had been passed, was hustled by those in attendance for this purpose to the group of the doomed.

Luckily he had finished his conversation when my turn came. I felt his eyes examining my physique. Looking away and trying to appear unconcerned, I visualised the direction of his thumb when one of the helpers pointed me to the right. I am sure they were not so gentle with those directed to the left.

I did not turn around in case my eyes met those of the doctor and he changed his mind. Feeling safe now, I was struck by a thought which kept me rigid for a few seconds which seemed like an eternity. Where was my father? He should have been right behind me. He had never had to pass a selection and although his body was still in good shape, his age was against him. What should I do if he failed? Join him or just wave goodbye? My brain virtually stopped thinking until I heard his voice next to me.

'What kept you?' I said, trying to make light of a far from humorous situation. I have a habit of making unfunny and unsuitable remarks after a catastrophe has been averted or a major worry has been resolved. This worry had not altogether been unfounded. There had been some hesitation, a minor discussion had taken place and, although we shall never know the truth, his strong body had probably swayed the decision. My father heard the words 'this time' – enough to make me fear that I might lose him at the next selection.

There was a minor commotion. The last few had to be forced into the line-up. The eyes of the SS and the *Blockältester* turned in that direction – only for seconds – but enough for the lively youngster, whose body I had thought was still in fair shape, to slip out of the doomed group and lose himself among us. This must have been noticed by some of the helpers, inmates themselves, who, realising that the escape had not been observed by the doctor, simply looked the other way. He has a rare story to tell – if he survived.

The selection over, we rushed back and dressed. Recovering from the traumatic experience, I began collecting my thoughts. Twenty-eight victims out of 600, a 'reasonable' percentage. This SS doctor must have been of a 'kinder' disposition to have picked so few. Another idea that occurred to me was whether the open secret that the war was lost for the Germans was beginning to influence some of these murderers. The mountains of corpses yet to emerge in the dying months of the *Churban* did not bear out my theory.

My father doubted whether the perpetrators of this unparalleled crime were likely to leave anyone alive to bear witness against them. Unknown to me at the time, one of the saddest things, since my family had been torn apart, must have happened during this period and because of the selection. My camp suit had an outer breast pocket in which I kept the only possession that connected me with a world that seemed gone for ever. I had lost the photograph of my mother and sister – the mutilated piece of paper, which I cropped to make it fit my palm when I entered the gas-cum-shower-chambers.

It was a dark autumn morning when, after the usual reveille, I discovered that I had lost this only link to my past, the only legacy and proof that once I had a real home and a real family. It was then that I felt for the first time, with brutal reality, that I had suffered a personal bereavement. Frantically, I began to search every nook and cranny in and around my bunk-bed. I then proceeded to the camp's refuse heap where I went through the rubbish like a man possessed. Running out of time and afraid of being late, I reluctantly gave up the search and hurried back to the assembly place.

Visibility there was so poor that I could only recognise faces up to three yards away. Finding my father in this milling crowd of many thousands was difficult. I resorted to what I often did in those circumstances: I whistled. Whistling our distinctive family tune was a re-uniter *par excellence*. My father's reply was unmistakable. Having lost the identical picture left to him, the one which was inside his jacket when it was stolen, he was anxious to know whether I was successful.

That day I wept more than on my return to the Bochnia ghetto when I realised that they had been deported; for then we had clung to the purposely disseminated rumours that they had been sent to the East to help with the harvesting. While I still had the photograph, with its shaky message on the back, I could still somehow feel their presence; when I looked at their faces, the part of me that said they were still alive was in some way supported, the best I could hope for in the circumstances. Having lost their picture I felt I had lost them now – for good. Irrationally, I now blamed myself for not having looked after them as well as I should. It was my fault that, now, they were lost.

*   *   *

Who would believe that, suddenly, there was a danger that we not only welcomed but actually yearned for. I cannot precisely recall whether it was a siren or the actual ominous humming of a bomber that sent slaves and masters, in one united purpose, scurrying for cover. Oh what a pleasing sight to behold; the SS, the masters of the glorious master race, forgetting all dignity as well as any care about their prisoners, running to save their rotten lives. In the ensuing panic, I had the impression that they would not have lifted a finger if somebody escaped during the confusion. I was just about to pass on this exhilarating observation to my father when the sonorous boom of the approaching bombers seemed directly above us. Everybody in sight threw themselves to the ground. Father and I landed in a ditch beside the road. A bomb fell nearby – near enough for my father to think that this was our last moment.

'*Shema Yisrael* ...' I heard him say the major confession of faith, the principles of belief, which should be the last words on the lips of a dying Jew. What's more, I found myself starting the prayers too, but stopped after the first two words, saying to myself, 'What am I doing? There is nothing or nobody to pray to ...'. Or was the realisation that the bomb had not dropped on us and that there was no more immediate danger my real reason for discontinuing the prayer?

The danger was over. The planes flew on unhindered, carrying their destructive load elsewhere. As far as I can recall, this was the only bomb dropped on Auschwitz during the entire war. This casual attack was rumoured to have damaged or destroyed the very cooling tower which I had helped to build and which had just been completed, killing one man in the process.*

* * *

Rumours circulated in the camp that the Russians were again on the offensive and were making steady progress. Hopes of liberation and survival managed to produce a tiny spark in our darkness and, notwithstanding the fact that I had given up believing that there was anyone who could hear me, I found myself repeating the fervent wish (or prayer?) which I had so often heard ever since we entered the ghetto: '*Nor tzi iberleben, abee mit a trikkenem Kartoffel*' – Oh to survive, be it with only a dry potato.

The question is, to whom did I direct my 'spur-of-the-moment' prayer?

Gradually it sank in that the tide had turned and the hitherto seemingly invincible Germans were being pushed back.

What did it mean to us? Very little. Our own situation was not affected. On the contrary, my father's and my worst tribulations were yet to come.

Meanwhile, however, in the closing days of 1944 and the beginning of 1945, when the weather was at its worst, and uncountable numbers died from the additional effects of winter, I had the cushiest job of my entire period in the concentration camps. I worked in a room, entirely on my own. This tiny chamber, measuring about 2.3 × 1.4 metres, contained fuse boxes, switches and other electrical terminals. I have no idea what the rest of the building was used for; I saw hardly any people working there. My task was to paint letters and numbers on every encasement. This indentification work could have been completed – even by me – in less than two days. I managed to stretch it to more than four weeks. I was under no supervision whatsoever. I had, next to my tools and my food container, a chair

---

* Any excuse that the Allies were unable to bomb Auschwitz has been disproved by this one occurrence. The question of the Allies' integrity in having failed to bomb the railway lines has been covered by many writings and is not a subject for this book.

AUSCHWITZ

and an electric heater. The contrast to other inmates could not be greater. I had warmth, I had food (which I could warm up), I was working as slowly as I possibly could and sitting down to do it.

I was very conscious of my extraordinary luck. The drawback was that I had too much time to think. Every day, when the hours of artificial idleness ticked slowly away, my thoughts – usually diverted when concentrating on my work, approaching *kapos* and other dangers – were painfully aware of the preposterousness of my existence. I was warm, fed and comfortable, but destined to die when worn out by the conditions, which were calculated to wear out an average human being within six to eight weeks. During these dragging hours I used to dream of the end of the war – which could not be very long now – of liberty and of seeing my whole family together again.

What would I do first? I would take a machine gun and start shooting indiscriminately into crowds of Germans. Germans would die – left, right and everywhere. I was carried away by these imaginings until, suddenly, I had small children in my sights. I stopped shooting and looked at their innocent faces. Innocent? So was my little sister – and she had had to die (this was probably the first time that I admitted the thought). With renewed and uncontrollable fury I continued shooting though, even during this fantasy, I aimed higher so as to avoid hitting the little ones.

Then I came across faces of German people I knew, friends of old, who would have helped us if they could. I stopped shooting and returned from daydreaming into the real world. How I hated that, for my first thought was always that it was just a dream – never to be fulfilled. I thought of the saying that every German had his Jew – including many of the top Nazis. I remembered that when my father came home from his travels, he reported to us how he was treated by some Germans who believed in the 'New Order'. 'We don't mean you – it's the "others" we are after.'*

Since I had no watch, my only concern was to be on time at the place where our commando would assemble before going back to the camp. On the way we met other groups, some not as lucky as ours;

*Even Hermann Goering, whom I always thought of as the deputy leader, as I'd never even heard of Martin Bormann till after the war, had his Jewish protégé: Erhard Milch, an air ace of the First World War. In a 'famous' declaration: *'Wer Jude ist und wer nicht – entscheide ich'* (Who is a Jew and who is not – I decide) he declared him non-Jewish.

157

some where every third or fourth was a *Muselmann* or showed signs of being well on the way to becoming one. These poor wretches, many barely able to walk but clinging with amazing tenacity to whatever life was left in them, I am sure all dreamt, hoped, that, perhaps soon, the war would end and their living nightmare would be over. Some looked as if they would not even survive the journey home.

What were my feelings when I met these boys whose impending end was written all over them? I must confess, not much. When it is drummed in to you that, sooner or later, it will be your turn, all you muster is a sense of satisfaction that your turn hasn't come yet. It was different, however, when, one day, we were passing a group which had momentarily stopped. The reason was a young man who had dropped to the ground, probably with exhaustion. An all-too-familiar sight which, because of its monotonous regularity failed to evoke little more than apathy. As I stepped nearer I saw the almost angelic face of a teenager. I was overcome with an unusual urge to help and offered him the piece of bread I had saved to eat with my soup. I shall never forget the expression of amazement, then gratitude in his eyes before they closed, never to open again, and before his mouth was able to accept what I had offered.

When I said 'I shall never forget,' I meant in the context of normal life after the war. When this incident actually happened, no sooner had I reached my barracks after collecting my special rations from Max Spira, than my toughened, conditioned mind had already forgotten it: a sure sign of my own advancing dehumanisation. In this, however, I was no better or worse than most of my co-prisoners. Egotistical, selfish; these words did not have the same meaning as in ordered society. We were ruled by the paramount drive of self-preservation – survival at all costs. 'At all costs' often meant at the expense of somebody else. The man who proudly told me how he managed to save himself by quickly changing position during a selection had no qualm, nor did he give a thought to the fact that the price for his 'success' was another person's life.

Having one's bread ration stolen was another thing to beware of. Stealing bread meant stealing someone's life. I have seen fights breaking out, not only when somebody was caught: often mere suspicion could cause a fight which, in one case I witnessed, ended in the death of the thief or alleged thief. Nobody lifted a finger to intervene, nobody regretted the result. When once, before the time of our extra soup, my father's bread was stolen, I remember only too well the anguish it caused us. After a day's hard building work on the road, it was like a physical pain.

*   *   *

The Russians had made further advances, and we expected to be evacuated any time now. Tension grew as there was always the possibility that orders would be issued for our liquidation. Why should they burden themselves with people for whom there was surely less and less work? It must have been clear to the most stupid German that the war was lost. Few now believed in the miracle weapon which their Führer promised would win the war – but neither could they envisage defeat. To us, the *Untermenschen*, the sub-humans, they behaved as if nothing had changed.

The most vicious of them, and those who knew that they were responsible for the heinous crimes perpetrated on their orders, must have initiated their getaway plans. The machinery of destruction, however, although slowing down somewhat, was still following its own momentum, destroying hundreds of thousands of lives in its now automatic path, before coming to a final halt, not in gas chambers but by the final death-throes of a dying, giant evil, by diminishing rations, by the now infamous death marches, by over-crowded trains, being shunted for weeks from one place to another, without any food or drink at all. Never before in history had the adage 'the survival of the fittest' been so aptly proved.

*   *   *

One morning, I believe it was early in, or about the middle of, January 1945, the order to assemble was given. Without any further ado we started marching, leaving behind the fateful camp of Buna-Monowitz. I was wondering if any of the prisoners had had any forewarning and gone into hiding. Most of the Germans had left as well and there might be nobody left or interested in searching for them.

I never learned the answer to that question. As so often before, I thought we could have risked slipping away and hiding for just a few days. (The Russians liberated Auschwitz a few days after we were evacuated.) If only we had done so, we might have saved ourselves four months of steadily increasing hardship and even greater misery than we had hitherto experienced.

I cannot recall how long we marched that day but we spent the night at a place which may well have been another camp. Josef Kampler joined us as we discussed the situation. When I bemoaned the loss of my extra ration, father warned me that I had better learn to do without it. 'How soon before we'll be *Muselmänner*,' I sighed with prophetic despondency. I did not expect a consoling answer but he put into words what we all longed for – an end to hostilities and the crushing destruction of the SS State.

Every time this hope came to mind I had to ward off the accompanying thought: 'They simply cannot let us survive.' Hope for an end to war barely outbalanced the wish for yet a slight delay of that day, which I expected to be my last. An unimaginable, an uncanny predicament.

'We just have to hope and pray – what else can we do?' was my father's reply when hearing of my fears. 'There may, in the end, be no other alternative than to make a dash for it – let's hope that we shall know the right moment.'

Auschwitz was behind us in name only. The guards were the same, so were the *kapos*, this additional bane of our miserable life. Any sufferings would not affect them, only us worthless outcasts.

We waited at this new place a few days at most, until the arrival of our transport. We had to assemble into several groups. Obviously this was intended to split us up for dispatch into different camps. Having learnt the hard way how different these could be, I anxiously looked for any sign that would give me a clue – but there was none. I looked out for Max Spira or Adolf König, in vain; they were nowhere to be seen.

Suddenly, Josef Kampler, who was with us at the time, darted across and joined another group. I cast about for a reason for him to do this, or for us to follow, I saw none. Neither did he wave or even glance in our direction. If there was an advantage, why did he not tell us? I had the feeling, probably unwarranted, of being betrayed by a friend. When, after the war, I had not heard of him, I remembered this little episode and I was even more angry. Had he stayed with us, I thought, he might have had a better chance of survival. About 25 years later, he paid me a surprise visit. He had survived and joined other surviving members of his family in Boston, Massachusetts. He is happily married and has adopted two children.

Did we discuss this episode? True to the peculiar and, as yet, unexplained characteristic common to most ex-prisoners, we did not mention camp life at all; except in answer to my only question as to the names of camps he had been sent to, after Auschwitz.*

We walked towards the station. This was precisely the situation when my instinct for survival was at its sharpest. Just as we were getting on board, I saw several of the *kapos* going to the front of the train; some carrying mattresses, others blankets and other parcels which I assumed to be provisions for whatever lay ahead. With an unfilial jerk, I pulled my father out again and, with no explanation, we followed them. Entering the first car we helped to lay out the mattresses which, eventually, covered the whole floor space. For the moment the *kapos* were too busy to take any notice of us. No prisoner in his right mind would have mingled with these sadists; yet how lucky we were to have done so.

Why was I drawn to follow them? I thought mixing with them might improve our plight. The sight of mattresses told me that these people knew how to take advantage of a situation, but mainly I thought that there might be special arrangements for *kapos* and other *prominente* of the camp and that I might find one of my classmates among them for further protection.

Other prisoners were trying to get into this grossly 'underfilled' wagon, but they were shooed away by those already inside who, on account of their strength and authority, as well as being used to having things their own way, were forcibly preserving their comforts. No doubt, had they noticed us earlier, we would have been thrown out too.

The doors had been shut, we were inside the lion's den. Some of the 38 passengers (including ourselves) were still settling down when, next to me, I heard an angry voice bellowing: 'What are you doing here – get out at once!' The posture of the tall and hefty fellow, whose visage betrayed a ruthless nature, was more than a little threatening. With a courage probably emanating from despair and

---

* Since then I have spoken to him on the telephone. His explanation was that an order came through a loudspeaker: 'Jews to one side, Belgians to another', and that he had slipped over to the Belgian group. I did not hear this order, and it had not occurred to me that there were other groups.

utterly alien to my usual diplomatic approach, I roared back: 'We are staying, if you want us out you'll have to kill us first.' Would he and his mate next to him grab me and throw me over the side of the open wagon? Without turning round I was sure that my father, by far the braver of the two of us, stood behind me. I saw the second German *kapo* give a sign to the one who had threatened me. He turned away and began busying himself. My bluff had worked, I had won.

The clash, brief as it was, had not gone completely unnoticed. Although most of our prospective fellow travellers, being too occupied with themselves, took no stance one way or another, at the far end of the wagon, a pair of eyes were winking at me approvingly.

Judging by the amount of parcels and boxes (presumably food), we were certainly in the privileged part of the train. There was ample room for at least ten more and nobody could complain about not having enough space. Every inch of floor space was covered with mattresses – and there were plenty of blankets too. Comfort *par excellence*. The only snag was that ours, as far as I could see, was the only open car in the whole line of a very long train. After all, we were in the depths of winter. However, it soon become evident that it had both advantages and disadvantages.

Neither we nor the *kapos* had any inkling of our destination. I did not look over the side of the wagon and therefore the only station we stopped at where I could read the name was when it was on a name-plate high above us – Praha.

My first melancholy thought was 'Well, now I can truthfully tell my children that, on my extensive travels, I also visited Prague.' How on Earth had we got to Czechoslovakia? It is beyond reason why the SS, with their track record for mass anihilation, did not simply finish us off. It was more and more apparent that there was no more use for us and the train, ferrying useless cargo, was surely needed elsewhere.

We had been travelling for two weeks and by now it was probably February. As expected and hoped for, we had enough food and, most important, water – and hot water at that. Being next to the engine had the advantage that the driver gave us the water we needed. Not for washing but nobody cared and it would have been too cold to undress anyway. The *kapo* who had winked at me before was one of the two who liaised with the driver and we had no trouble receiving our ration.

At night we slept with our heads beneath the blankets, of which we all had several. One morning I was the first to wake up and I had the eerie experience of seeing a thick white sheet of snow covering my 37 co-travellers. No movements, no human sounds were to be heard; it was as if I were the only living soul. The little mounds of the bodies, with valleys between them, heightened the impression of a mini-cemetery with a large white shroud spread over its surface. My position was at the end of the wagon, farthest from the engine. I lifted the blanket on my left and, with a sense of relief, I saw my father peacefully asleep.

Slowly, after a one-by-one 'resurrection', the usual scene developed. Some prisoner put a substance into the hot water which we called coffee – but was nothing of the sort. Having brought our *Menashkas* made us popular with some of the *kapos* who had brought all sorts of things – except a container for holding liquid. I must say here that, during the whole of this journey, not only were we not molested, but we were treated with a kind of 'respect'. In different circumstances, they would surely have deprived us of our two receptacles. Perhaps my tough stand helped. Perhaps they were feeling uneasy about their own future.

That day, however, we all started by throwing overboard as much snow as we could. Did I give a thought to the rest of the transport? Just fleetingly, barely enough even to appreciate that, once again, my guardian angel had looked after me.

What an understatement. Unbeknown to me only a few feet away, divided by two walls and two pairs of buffers, a drama was taking place, matched in horror and tragedy only by similar transports of prisoners during this period of inhuman cruelty. While we were ridding ourselves of the bothersome white blanket, less than six feet away people were dying of hunger and thirst. The tiny bit of snow, which found its way through some crevices, was fought over, often with deadly results. With their fingers and tongues they tried to reach ledges where some of it had settled. If we had had a roof over our head, a fact which, initially, made me envy the rest of the prisoners, the driver could not have passed the hot water – any water – to us, with a result I dare not think about.

Strangely, during this journey, escape did not even occur to us. Guards were not seen, and heard only when the train was stationary. We had warmth, plenty of food and our co-travellers largely ignored us. Actually there was not much conversation going on altogether. When we were not eating or sleeping (which we did copiously) we were reflecting on our future. I am sure this was also true of the ex-*kapos*. We nourished our secret hope that the war might end suddenly, as we felt it soon must. Many more would issue their last breath before it became true.

Finally, in Nordhausen, we stepped again on terra firma. The train emptied itself of its human cargo, who almost to a man, threw themselves on to the snow, gulping it down to save their lives. By overdoing it, some of them lost it. They died with a mouthful of snow. 'Some of them', meaning some of the 2,500 survivors of the 5,000 who began this journey.

10

Finale – The Living Dead

Nordhausen, a town somewhere in the middle of Germany was, as we soon found out, a place where special weapons were being manufactured or assembled. Long after the war I learned that these were the famous V-1 rockets and (or) V-2 flying bombs, also nick-named 'Doodlebugs'.

'All right,' I said to my father, 'they need people here for important work, perhaps we have been lucky again.' Little did I know at the time that this camp was one of the most notorious for 'wasting' slave labour. Between 20,000 and 40,000 were simply worked to death here. No wonder, with this kind of a turnover, they found room for us, when other camps refused to accept the living cargo. Not knowing these facts, we regretted it when, after only eight days, during which we had to do no work whatsoever, we were again on the move. Apparently, there was no need for all of us.

During our short stay at Nordhausen, I met a young fellow to whom I had spoken a few times back at the Buna Works in Auschwitz.

'I am glad you survived that terrible journey,' I greeted him. 'What have you done with your glasses?'

He replied laconically. 'I dropped them, somebody stepped on them, I killed him.'

'But why? Surely he didn't do it on purpose?'

'Without my glasses I am dead anyway,' he told me. He continued to describe how angry he was when it happened, so angry that he took off his shoe and started raining blows on the unfortunate breaker of his spectacles, until he himself was exhausted – and the culprit was dead. This nice, unassuming young man who, in normal circumstances, would go out of his way to help, rather than hurt people, had sunk, in a flare of uncontrollable anger, down to the level of his oppressors. He showed no remorse – and nor did I expect him to. After all, a single dead person is a tragedy, one among 2,500 is scarcely even a statistic.

I met other survivors of that fateful journey but I did not ask them how they had managed to be among the 50 per cent who outlived the other half, nor how it had felt to start by travelling like upright sardines and end by sleeping on 'mattresses' made of dead comrades. Luckily for them it was winter, thus delaying decomposition. Needless to say, I did not tell any of them that, while they were crazed with hunger and thirst, suffering with cold and fear, I was travelling in comparative comfort.

When it came to the next train journey, we were even more on the lookout for any friends, classmates or, possibly, some of the *kapos* we had travelled with from Auschwitz. No such luck. We could only hope that this journey would not end with such high losses of life. We were greatly comforted by the fact that there were two of us and that we could support each other if necessary.

To our relief we found that we could at least sit down. No stretching out, though: it was too crowded. We were worried about how long this journey might take and whether we would receive any food on the way. We had one advantage over all the others: our two *menashkas* were filled with four litres of drinking water.

My neighbour, a talkative, scholarly young man, began a conversation. Unlike most inmates, he told me about some of the experiences he had had in Auschwitz. To be honest, I only listened halfheartedly, my mind occupied with crevices in the wall, loose floorboards, and other possible escape routes. He rambled on about experiments on Jewish twins, the attitude by doctors when these experiments ended in the death of the victims. 'There are plenty more in stock,' he heard them say. His tale included names which, unfortunately, I have forgotten – except for one, a man called Boger. I don't remember what rank or in what capacity he was working there. His method of torture was unique. His device, appropriately nicknamed 'Boger-Swing', was a contraption hanging from the ceiling, a kind of swing to which a victim would be strapped, naked, arms and legs spread. The 'game' was to make the unfortunate victim spin round in circles by pushing him with sticks aimed at his genitals. My train companion told me about one particular case where, when his ordeal was over, the poor man could neither stand

166

up nor move. 'I am finished,' he told those who tried to help him. 'Tell the world what they have done to me.' Unfortunately, my informant had already forgotten the name of the poor wretch, who died shortly afterwards.

My companion was still talking when the train came to a halt. The journey had ended in, what seemed to me, no time at all.

Although I do remember about our work and other details connected with the new working area, I have completely forgotten either the name of the place or where we lived, where we slept and what we ate. All I can recall is that we were working somewhere inside the Harz Mountains.

We must have been split up. I only counted about 150 prisoners; the rest of the transport must have gone elsewhere. We were marched into a long tunnel, at the end of which we had to spend our first night. It was bitterly cold and we huddled closely together to keep warm. On the side, and at a height of only 1.5 metres, a strong electric bulb provided the light. Subconsciously I gravitated towards it. That night I learned two elementary and obvious things. The lamp provided me with a previously unthought-of source of warmth and, secondly, as I held my hands above that source, the heat not only warmed my hands but, via the bloodstream, the whole body; sufficiently to withstand the freezing temperature which must have been well below zero.

My father, myself and a few others stood around this lamp all night and, in proper camp fashion, we, the stronger ones, kept our position. Some of the weaker ones fell asleep with exhaustion and some of them, especially at the periphery of our densely clustered crowd which was thronging together for a bit of warmth, did not wake up in the morning. They were carried out – frozen to death. Among them, I saw the young man who had killed his mate because he inadvertently stepped on his spectacles. His demise, although not the result of his bad eyesight, had come faster than he imagined when, just over one week ago, he prophesied his own death.

Nevertheless, our group was lucky. We learned of another, I do not know how large in number, who were kept, as we were, inside a tunnel. A large fire was lit at the entrance, mainly to keep them from escaping. They suffocated to a man.

Every story we heard took hold of our minds. In moments of despondency, and these were almost continuous, we imagined which of the methods of killing would be applied to us when the Allies were coming closer and there was no more transport available or nowhere to send us to. Again and again I was gripped by the nagging thought that the Germans could not possibly allow us to live and bear witness to the ineradicable shame, the blot that will forever be connected with their history.

The next day we learned that we were really needed here. About the purpose of the tunnel, which we helped to lengthen, I can only speculate. It must have been an operation of great priority as I saw a number of German workmen who, judging by their age, should have been in uniform, defending their fatherland against the encircling enemy. It was certainly bomb-proof. Deep inside the tunnel there were small passages branching off in which we were not allowed to set foot. I did, once, though, and I noticed that there were steps leading upwards. I did not go any further but the idea formed in my mind of the perfect wartime living accommodation. It was, at present, unoccupied but had probably been built as an impenetrable bomb shelter for the upper echelons of the Third Reich.

The method of tunnel drilling was primitive. At first we were loading stones and rocks of every size on to small mine wagons. My father was detailed to a group who pushed them on rails and unloaded them outside the tunnel. Forever anxious to avoid heavy work as it would tax our strength above our food or energy intake, I was seeking some way out for him as well as for myself. I asked one of the German workers whether he could do with some help and, to my great joy, he thought of something. For the next few days I helped him by doing – nothing. All I had to do was sit back to back with him, thus, as he told me, steadying him while he used a compressed-air drill to bore, horizontally, into the granite. The idea caught on. Two more people were required to do exactly the same. Unfortunately, my father was somewhere else when these were chosen.

However, after an hour or so sitting under the envious glances of the loaders, I was no longer quite so sure that my position was such a desirable one. The discomfort of sitting on hard rock was soon diverted by the feeling that my insides were being shaken up and I feared that my bones would come out of their sockets, while my organs jumbled about like dice in a dice-box. Only the thought that I received these vibrations (more like tremors, really) secondhand muted my apprehensions of a total collapse of my earthly frame.

Also, looking at the alternative such as clearing the debris, some of it quite heavy, made me decide to sit it out.

Slowly I became used to this condition, especially when the German worker took frequent breaks – and even offered me some of his sandwiches. I managed to secrete some away which I later gave to my father.

* * *

Were the Allied armies closing in? There was a faint, thunderous sound of gunfire in the distance but we could not be sure. For whatever reason, one morning on our way to work, we were simply redirected and put on a train. Even the *menashkas*, our only possession, were now lost to us. Our stay at this camp had been only about three weeks.

Again I have no memory of the journey but I think the new place was Helmstett. That's what I shall call it, anyway. We had been apprehensive because newcomers were always detailed to the most arduous jobs, but it soon became apparent that we were not expected nor wanted here and there was no work for us. Except for the Harz Mountains this new camp was the smallest I had been in. The inmates, according to my estimate between 400 and 500, were mostly Russian, with maybe some Poles and quite a few Germans. They were working in the attached brown-coal mine, a fact which I learned only later.

Why they did not send us down with the resident inmates, I have no way of knowing, but leaving us idle would not do either. Work had to be found for us, even if it had to be invented. So it was.

But first a description of the camp itself. It was more or less square, measuring about 80 × 80 metres. There were six or seven barracks and the inevitable assembly-ground. There were no Jewish prisoners and no gas chambers, but there were, as we soon found out, a few *kapos* and other ordinary inmates, cold-blooded sadists, who made us newcomers the victims of the viciousness, pent-up anger and frustration which dehumanising imprisonment brings out and magnifies in such people.

* * *

They found work for us. We had to walk for twenty minutes downhill to what looked like a dumping place for old machinery, furniture and all sorts of other waste. This we had to shift to a nearby spot which looked just as suitable – or unsuitable – as the previous one. In other words, we worked for the sake of working.

That, in itself, taking into account German mentality, would be understandable. The unnecessary harshness, the whipping to make us pick up heavier loads, the cries of *schneller* which, with apparent delight in our discomfiture, accompanied this toil came from either a personal pleasure in inflicting pain or an order to finish us off by subjecting our weakened bodies to extra hard work – or both. They surpassed by far any cruelties we had suffered from Auschwitz's *kapos*.

There was no let-up, no friendly face to turn to for additional food or an easier job. A phenomenon, possibly unique to this camp, was that the sigh of relief which usually accompanied the order to stop work was immediately followed by a groan when, without a moment's pause, we had to climb back to our camp. Twenty minutes' downhill walk in the morning became thirty minutes of dragging our bodies uphill at dusk. But for the threat of being whipped and, perhaps, the fact that the foremen and *kapos* were also tired (from the hard work of whipping us), our way home would have taken much longer.

The expected soon happened, the strong became weaker and the weak collapsed and, not being helped, soon died. The mortality rate here surpassed anything I had hitherto experienced. We saw our end in days rather than weeks and, in desperation, we decided to take risks, gambling with our lives rather than continuing to weaken our bodies by backbreaking work under the threat of the whip.

Father found a place where we could take turns hiding behind and underneath a large pile of wooden boxes: a hazardous venture which, if discovered, would surely result in being beaten to death. With one of us enduring the hard labour and the thrashings and being on the lookout for any danger, the other would hide and preserve a little of our fast diminishing strength. I would swear that the one on the lookout was fortified by the knowledge that the other was resting.

The small building, or rather shed, where we concealed ourselves was, literally, only a stone's throw away from where our group worked. To get there, I would pretend to follow nature's call; then, if unnoticed, I would slip inside, climb the stacked containers and, after lowering myself to the bottom behind the stack, pull one of the boxes across, on top of two others, thus creating a tiny but fully enclosed cubicle.

The contents of these containers were not known to me but some were light and others heavy. A stone, thrown against the wall of the shed, signalled either danger or that our group was assembling to go home. Sometimes my father would find his way into the shed and would make himself known by softly whistling in the way only familiar to us. It would then be my turn to join the others and be vigilant.

Looking back on the unreality of the situation, I would, had I not known better, almost have joined those who would shake their heads, saying that risking one's life just to escape a few hours' work was surely not worth the gamble, even though more time in hiding meant fewer beatings. The chances for a weakening body to survive, for any length of time, what was more a sustained ordeal than actual work were almost nil.

On the third day, I had fallen asleep in my cramped cubicle when I was awoken with a start by nearby voices. Knocking my head against the box covering me, I became almost numb with shock and fear of immediate discovery. By the flow of their conversation I soon realised that the intruders were two prisoners who either ignored or did not hear the noise I had made. They were obviously relieved to be here, taking a rest. Two more prisoners disappearing must increase the danger. Moreover, had they made sure that they had not been noticed? There was nothing I could do and I kept quite still. Apparently it did not even occur to them that under these boxes could be a hiding place. This pleased me and made me feel much safer – safer but also uncomfortable. I did not want to share my secret and I was worried about giving myself away by a cough, a sneeze or movement.

An hour or so passed by, I could hear every word of their conversation. 'The Allies are winning, they are closing in and it must soon be all over,' said one. 'That may be so,' answered the second voice, 'but, if they don't hurry up, we will not live to see them.' A sigh from the first speaker: 'I am the only survivor of my family – I had six younger brothers and two older sisters – it would be terrible to die now, just before seeing our tormentors trodden into the ground – it cannot take much longer.'

'That's what we said six months ago. No, we won't make it, not in this camp, not with this work and not with these sadistic foremen or *kapos* or whatever they are. They must be exhausted just from beating us.'

'How long do you think we can stay here?'

'Well, nobody saw us leave, we might as well stay a little longer. Perhaps we could come here regularly. It would be a great help – we could take it in turns.'

'Can you still imagine being free and leading a normal life?'

'Not really – only in my dreams and only with my family.'

'Do you still believe in God?'

'No – or, at least, I don't think so. Sometimes, though, I still pray, then I get angry and I stop.'

The other fellow started to reply when a German voice roared: 'What are you doing here? Hiding from work – eh? – *Raus, aber schnell*, you lazy dogs.'

They must have received a most vicious beating. I could hear them scream, being beaten while running back to their group. The screaming continued in the distance until finally, it stopped. That evening the prisoners had to push the cart up the hill with an extra load; two careless young men who were now barely alive.

Later that evening, I stepped out of my barracks and saw a small crowd gathering outside another. Drawing nearer and looking through an open door I could see an open bathroom opposite a hallway. Inside, next to a bathtub which was filled to the brim with water, were two of our German *kapos*. They were holding down the heads of two youngsters, still fully clothed, and I recognised them as the poor wretches whom we had had to transport back to the camp. They were being drowned, finished off; they were too weak to offer even the slightest resistance.

This new experience shook me more than I would have expected after being hardened by seeing so many others die. It was probably the thought that it could have been my father or myself in this bathtub; after all, they suffered for being caught in the same hiding place that we were using.

This cold-blooded murder, as if they were just doing a job, added a new dimension to that part of my mind which still refused to accept the measureless extent of a world gone mad. Worse, I caught myself thinking their way. What else could be done with such irreparably damaged people?

Our small group was shrinking by the day. I could not accept the visible proof that our turn for destruction was only a matter of time: weeks rather than months, possibly days rather than weeks. I discussed this in whispers with my father as we were preparing for the night. What measures – drastic measures – any measures, could we take to improve our chances? I even suggested the hitherto unthinkable: breaking our now useless rule of inconspicuousness by talking to the camp commandant, so far unseen by us. I was able to speak in several German dialects and the gamble I suggested taking was to imitate, I hoped, his idiom; maybe, just maybe, it would strike a favourable chord in his vile soul.

'And maybe it will achieve the opposite,' was his pessimistic but not unreasonable answer.

I became quite excited by an idea. 'Perhaps I should tell him straight out: the war is lost, if you look after us, we will look after you – I shall even offer him half of our buried fortune in gold!'

After a couple of seconds, a faint smile appeared on his startled face. 'Yes, either it will work or you will be shot on the spot.'

In every camp before this one, news had seeped through to us. Here, the Jewish inmates were in the minority and here, unlike previous camps, none of us had any position or contacts. For all we knew, the Allies might have already crossed the German borders and be on their way to rescue us.

'Escape! Surely this, of all times, must be the right time to escape.'

A deep sigh was his response. What an agonising decision to make. The chances of staying alive for long in this camp were virtually nil. The chances of successfully escaping looked equally grim. What a choice to be confronted with: which of the options had a less than 99 per cent chance of resulting in death?

'Maybe you are right; looking at our chances for survival, your idea, grotesque as it is, has certainly greater merit than attempting to escape – or being killed. The commandant must know that the game is over and he must surely be worried about his own life. Let me think about it, just a few more days but then, if such a drastic step should be taken – I will do it. Besides,' the rare smile appeared again briefly, 'the story of a buried fortune comes better from an older person – good night.'

'Good night.' To this day I do not know if he really meant what he said or if it was an attempt to ease my heavy thoughts, at least for that night. Also that night, I dreamt that we were helped by being made *kapos*. We had to hit our comrades to make them work even harder. I was glad when I woke up. Suddenly my idea, which I had thought to be our best chance of survival yet, had an ugly tinge. 'Nonsense,' still half asleep, I said to myself. 'One can always shout louder and feign hitting; maybe one could even help.'

The following day, on the way to work, I looked at my comrades. It must have been the most miserable group I had ever seen. There was always the odd *Muselmann* marching in an Auschwitz group; our shrinking bunch showed more than seven in ten to be on the way out. Hitting these poor wretches to work harder was outright murder. Although father and I had both lost strength and weight to a dangerous degree, we were still among the strongest of the Jewish inmates.

A sunny morning after a rainy night had produced a glut of fat and clean-looking earthworms – we could hardly avoid stepping on them. Gnawing hunger helped my imagination to regard their pinkish colour and their slightly larger than usual size as meaty and desirable. With just a little encouragement I would have picked them up for food. I looked to my right where my father was marching, then to the others. They seemed oblivious to what busied my mind. Did they not see these potential stomach-fillers? Were they too frightened to bend down during marching, giving the *kapos* the pretext for lashing out at them? However, in the struggle between hunger and the natural disinclination to eat worms – the latter won through. About a month later, it might not have.

This was the last day when I worked with my father.

Curiously, the viciousness of the foremen and *kapos* had somewhat lessened. The novelty of having Jews in the camp, driving and hitting them for the sheer lust of it, must have worn thin. It was this lessening of sadism which made me decide not to use our hiding-place. We also noted that our present job was coming to an end. Would they now make us take everything back from place B to place A? Would they finish us off because there was no more work?

Another discussion took place that evening. Since there was no chance that our previous luck in getting help or additional food could be hoped for, we judged that we had a maximum of five weeks to live – that is, if we were not killed before. We estimated that during our short stay here we had lost one in four of those who arrived with us.

'We are now in the position of the many thousands who had

assessed their chances of a successful escape as practically nil and have now perished without having taken that chance,' I said sorrowfully. 'Soon we will be too weak even to attempt it.'

'But we are alive today,' replied my father, 'and, from what we know, we would have been hanged, or shot, had we escaped as planned. Besides, we don't even know where we are.'

It did not need this discussion to convince us of our hopelessness, and it ended, as it was bound to do, in further postponement of a final decision. My father rightly observed: 'Tonight we are alive, the chances of being alive next week, even tomorrow, at this time are just that little bit better than escaping without a proper plan.'

*　　*　　*

The next day something unbelievable happened. As we were assembling in the usual manner of five abreast and ready to march out, somebody announced that only half of us would go to work – the others would stay behind. Immediate chaos. Those at the front were trying to re-assemble at the back, those at the rear were not going to let that happen and fell back further. The *kapos*, not without working 'hard', managed to whip us back into position. By 'us' I meant all those finding themselves in the front half, including myself. My father managed to be among those who could stay.

Of course I was happy for my father but we all envied their day of rest. Even if some work would be found for them in the camp, at least they would miss that terrible and exhausting climb back after a murderous day of toil.

It also meant that I could not go to our secret resting place. Or so I thought, but in the event I did. In the afternoon, when all of us were worn out and started dragging our feet, one of the nastier *kapos* took over. Fear is a strong motivater, it brings out unknown reserves. In my case it produced a courage born of despair. Of the three hours still left to work, I disappeared for about two and a half. Needless to say, I wasn't discovered or I would not be here to tell the tale. After a rest, I could work that much harder to avoid being whipped.

Back in the barracks I found my father in a good mood. He had been resting all day with nobody bothering him, or the others, at all. Unbelievable.

Fatal.

How could we have assumed, or even trusted, that such a situation could continue in this camp which seemed to contain the most vicious German criminals? One might have thought that, as prisoners themselves, they would hate and sabotage those who incarcerated them. Instead, they were all too willing tools and imitators of their jailers, and their methods of torment were, if it was conceivable, even cruder.

Perhaps it would not be too far-fetched to compare our situation with those wretches in an ancient Roman arena, except that gladiators were sometimes given weapons to defend themselves – and, should they still be alive after combat, after the applause had died down and the entertainment was over, they would be separated from the bloodthirsty beasts and reprieved. No such respite for us; we were caged in with these animals for 24 hours a day – every day.

We did not ask, nor were we informed, who actually was in charge. Our tormentors were our fellow inmates and, to us, it seemed that they were running the camp. I could have established the fact that we were under SS management by looking at the insignia of the uniformed guards but, curiously, these kept well back and, on the whole, were not much in evidence. Also, I was really not too interested, as the one who is whipped does not really care whose hand is doing the whipping – the pain is the same. Maybe the fact that the war was in its final stages and Germany already partly occupied (a fact that, even had we known it, would have been of little consolation to us at the time) meant that they were thinking of their own safety.

Thinking about their own safety, hiding when the war came to an end – why, they had done no wrong, they 'only obeyed orders', so they claimed when called to account for their deeds. Not one, to my knowledge, pleaded guilty. Why then make elaborate plans to disappear if their conscience was clear? I wonder whether any of the war crimes judges asked that question when given the stock excuse: 'I only obeyed orders.'

* * *

The next day was a day never to be forgotten. It started like the previous one, with the announcement that only half of our group would be going out to work. Already, in anticipation of this, every single person aimed to be in the last rows. Can anyone imagine the following spectacle: there was no fighting, only some jostling and constant manoeuvring. A silent, eerie scene, in the dim light of an early April morning (who knows, it could well have been on my birthday, 4 April). We were wearing ourselves out to get into the longed-for position that would give us a day's rest. In the melée of grotesquely moving men, father and I lost contact. In any case, we could not stand by one another. Being inside the swarm I can only imagine the picture which presented itself to the amused *kapos*. But not for long; with visible relish they started *their* day's work. Swinging their sticks, battering us aimlessly, they soon enforced order into our reluctant group.

Once again, my father 'succeeded' and I failed – tragically. Together we were a team and, if the word 'success' could be applied to the art of survival, our efforts merited an award. It was, or would have been, ours to claim. But we were not together when fate struck cruelly.

That day nothing memorable or out of the ordinary happened at work. When I returned to our barracks, I expected to be greeted by my father, well rested like yesterday and in hopeful mood, exchanging, as usual, the news of the day. He was not there.

The camp, as described, was very small and I wondered where I should be looking for him. Apart from the lavatories and the washroom, there was really nowhere for him to go. Everything seemed calm and normal; I could find no explanation for his disappearance without anybody knowing. Nobody in our quarters could help and I grew more despondent by the minute. A Polish or Russian inmate finally pointed in the direction of the 'medical barracks' which, until then, I had not known existed. Entering a sort of waiting room, I found a queue of five or six prisoners, waiting for treatment. Father was not among them.

I asked if there was a patient with the 'doctor' and began describing my father, when one of them pointed to a darkened spot at the other end of the room. With the sun already down, I had to step nearer in order to make out what, at first glance, looked like a hapless, indefinable heap. It was my father.

He was cowering in a corner, his legs drawn up to his chest, his head drooping lifelessly forward. I knelt down beside him. 'Papa, what's the matter?' The feeble groan I received in reply shook me deeply. The last time I had heard that sound was when we had to cart home the two unfortunate boys who were subsequently drowned.

177

The last thing my memory registered of that day was that I was not going to allow this to happen to my father.

Incredibly, he was permitted to stay in bed. In my thankfulness I gave no thought to the grotesqueness of the situation where one prisoner had the power to maim and kill, and another, a doctor perhaps, did his best, and had the authority, to redress the damage.

I looked after him as well as I could, outside working hours, of course. Amazingly, this Superman began to improve at a pace which would be hard to believe in normal conditions, let alone in our situation. After a few days he began to speak again. He told me that they had had a visit from the SS commandant who was enraged when he saw Jews 'idling' the day away. The whole remainder of our group was sent down the mine.

Their weakened bodies, not equal to the task as performed by other prisoners, provided a welcome reason for the mine *capo* or foreman to excel in sadism. I did not ask, I was not concerned about other casualties. Father, who was much the stronger of the two of us, was battered and kicked almost to a pulp. The conversation was sapping his strength and I kept it short. Many questions, left unasked at the time, were never asked again and so never answered, as other events put them into the background.

My main concern was how soon they would send him back to work which would certainly have killed him. How long it would have taken for my father to recover fully, I shall never know.

After six days, miraculously, he got up – and walked. Feebly at first but getting visibly stronger. In the evening of the seventh, we were told to rise earlier the next morning, as we were to be evacuated. When, during our last night in this murderous camp, we heard distant thunder, it did not evoke any euphoric emotions. We had heard it before in recent months and each time our situation had worsened. Lucky, I thought, that it did not happen a few days earlier, when it would have been impossible for my father to be moved – and we all knew what that would have entailed. I ought to have been overjoyed at the thought of leaving this place but I could not ward off the foreboding which dominated any other feeling.

It was still dark when we assembled in the morning. Prisoners were loading some items on to two or three lorries. Then a voice called out something which took us by surprise and would haunt me for many years. It was simple enough: 'Anybody sick or unable to march should get on to the truck!' We had to make up our minds there and then, within seconds. It was as if the offer was meant for us.

Feverishly fast we deliberated. How could we, from our past experience trust this, or any kindness offered. In the dark, we could not even make out whether this offer was made by a prisoner or someone in uniform. On the other hand this was not Auschwitz (not better but there were no gas chambers); could we both go, or would they only take my father – which would mean parting? We could not, or dared not, ask any questions. We (or was it I?) decided – as it turned out – wrongly. No time to make up our mind, so we decided to march.

This decision cost my father's life.

The weather was springlike, cool and sunny. For the first half hour, walking downhill was actually enjoyable. Guided probably by past experience, I was hoping for a short march to another camp or to a train. Right from the start I was supporting my still convalescent father. After less than an hour he noticeably began to weaken, and my support, initially only a gesture, become as time went on, more and more a necessity.

The marching column began to stretch further and further and the two of us fell back more and more until we made up the rear end of a file, a kilometre in length. The guard behind us made some impatient remark, urging us on to catch up with the others. This, of course, was plainly impossible – and the guard knew it.

Even if we had known then of the infamous death marches during the dying weeks of the war – hundreds of them all over retreating Germany – where people who had survived all that had been meted out to them were collapsing of exhaustion in their uncountable thousands and shot dead without quarter, even then, I do not believe that we could have walked any faster.

Another hour and my body was walking like an automaton. The lower part of my body, from the hips down, did not register as belonging to me any more. I could see my legs moving, step after step after step, incidentally carrying my body with them, separate entities which I could neither command to stop nor change their automatic even trot. And all the while, I was supporting, 'carrying', my father on my right. Impossible? Unbelievable? Certainly unimaginable, but what was the alternative?

How did my father feel? I did not ask. I probably took it for granted

179

that, as always, anything I could do he could do better. True, I supported him initially: later, though, it seemed that we were welded together and I could not say for sure who supported whom. His toughness, his resilience, were incredible.

After 4½–5 hours at a pace that was getting slower by the minute, long after having lost sight of the head of our procession, we saw them again. They were resting at the roadside. We saw them in the distance and although the sight of them, and the hope for a respite, invigorated any reserves we might have had, it took us more than ten minutes to join them.

There they were, well-nourished, strong-looking Poles, Russians, Germans, all in a good mood just after their meal. We were largely ignored. If I were to be asked the moment in my life when I was most envious – this was it. How I longed for a little rest. Despite having lost all feelings below my hips, I managed to sit down on a slope; all I had to do was just to drop.

'*Los weitergehen!*' The command to carry on marching was given less than two minutes after we arrived. Apparently, they had only waited for us to join them. There was only one snag, I could not rise. Neither, however, could I stay behind. Amazingly, father was up before me and, with his help and some contortionist manoeuvring, I found myself upright again.

Almost immediately, the distance between the front marchers and ourselves lengthened and soon, father and son, arm in arm, we were at the tail-end again. We were pacemakers in reverse and retarding the whole advance. Others, also tiring, slowed down but kept just ahead of us. It was a kind of shrewdness of theirs. It allowed them to slacken but, should the guards turn impatient with our snail-like pace, get violent or start shooting, we, the slowest and last, would be the first victims.

At one point, when it appeared that our new guard, a mere youngster, would really lose his temper and I had the feeling that, before long, he might use his rifle on the two who were holding back the whole camp of 500–600 people, I ventured to reply to his more and more threatening commands to move faster. With the courage of one who has nothing to lose, imitating his atrocious German dialect and with the calmest and most jovial voice I could muster, I said: '*Net mehr lang, dann sitze mer alle daheim bei Muttern*' (loosely translated: It will not be long now and we will all be at home with mother).

I did not observe his reaction, as I was purposely looking away, but I must have struck a chord, for he stopped urging us to move faster. After another half-hour, when we were not only the last but also out of earshot from the ones in front, he even spoke to us. Whereas I had always thought that the SS was made up of volunteers, with only the 'best' of German manhood being accepted, I now learned how his parents tried to keep him from being forced to join this so-called élite. He came from a small village and had never met a Jew personally. He knew that the Jews had been driven out of Germany. He asked me where I came from. I told him that I was born in Frankfurt am Main but recently came from Auschwitz. He knew Frankfurt but had never heard of Auschwitz. The incongruity of it all was almost too much for me. I had to believe him, he was still the master, and the time for the excuses of ignorance, heard so often from the guilty and innocent alike, was still months away.

This little interval, and not being driven to walk faster than our (and some other prisoners') strength permitted, may also have saved some lives. How lucky we were in comparison with other such evacuations. We were also aided by the fact that, by the afternoon, the front of the column began to slow down, shrinking the distance between us considerably. There were some more guards at the front but, curiously, none in the middle. For the other, stronger prisoners, there would have been little problem in escaping now. Nobody did. Everybody knew that the war was coming to an end; the German and other prisoners felt strong and safe; the Jews, having gone through incomparable deprivations, were, by now, too weak to contemplate any adventure.

That night we slept in a very large barn inside which there were several large pyramids of hay or straw. The Jews slept on one such stack, the other prisoners on other heaps; I did not observe if they had segregated themselves into nationalities. Somebody said that we had walked 26 kilometres, which in retrospect was a 'reasonable' stretch in comparison with other marches which lasted for days and, some-times, for weeks.

The stories I later heard of the various camps were less heinous by far in comparison with those of train journeys and those 'death marches' in the final weeks. One explanation as to why we and other slow ones were not shot could lie in the fact that this particular camp was probably established only to use foreign labour plus some

German criminals to man its mines. The guards were perhaps not used to killing their small labour force. We were the first Jews there. Within three weeks a large percentage of our group – which originally numbered 150 – if they had not been killed by the other inmates had finally yielded to the accumulated hardships and had died of hunger and exhaustion. Now, the 'fittest' were on the march and, as described, we all somehow made it to the barn.

The next morning we heard angry shouting; a German inmate claimed that his bread ration had been stolen. The *Lagerältester* (the head prisoner), a German criminal whom I had only seen once during our stay in Helmstett, ordered all the Jews to line up outside the open barn gate. That was when I noticed how pitiably our group had shrunk. He asked us one by one if we had stolen the bread.

Yes, of course, according to years of hate propaganda, who else but a Jew could have perpetrated this, the foulest of deeds among concentration camp inmates? The fact that we were well separated from the rest, and that any movement in the straw was accompanied by a rustle which would have woken up the others, was no proof of innocence to someone hell-bent on finding a Jewish scapegoat.

Several times in this book I have emphasised the imperative factors for survival – relentless vigilance and not taking chances. Not taking chances also meant never being conspicuous in any way, shape or form. We, father and I, had committed two cardinal sins, lapses in this crucial and unforgiving rule – with immediate and fatal consequences.

To have survived yesterday's marathon, so soon after his brutal beating, was not just a miracle but, for me, the surest sign of the phenomenal will power and physical durability of this extraordinary man – my father. I almost came to believe in his indestructibility. Nevertheless, and it was only natural, I put my arm under his, to give him support in his weakened state. Standing like this, in the line-up for questioning, certainly made us conspicuous. Our second mistake was to be, once again, at the end of the queue.

Questioning progressed quickly. The *Lagerältester* accepted (or so it seemed) everybody's denial of the theft and those questioned were allowed to go. As we drew nearer to him, we noticed his increasing anger as he received denial after denial. Feeling innocent and seeing him dismiss everybody after questioning, made me approach him without any foreboding of impending danger. He did not even ask us the usual question. With a face twisted by anger and hate, I heard him say: 'Of course, you haven't done it – nobody did.' With this he swung a stick, the size of a table leg, over his head and down towards mine. With a quick instinctive reaction, I bent forward and just managed to put my hand on my head, thus intercepting a fatal blow. The next blow felled my father. He was hit on the head and blood spurted out of a wound. I saw him sink to the ground. With my help he managed to crawl back into the barn.

The name of that *Lagerältester*, first heard back at the camp, is firmly engraved in my mind – Adolf Fernbacher.

My next memory is of being once again inside a train – with my ailing father by my side. He must have been suffering but not one word of complaint came from this heroic man. It was the usual cattle truck, this time with roof but very little space to move. Not sardine-like and standing room only as in the worst of these terror journeys, but neither did we manage to stretch our legs when sitting down.

I looked at my father's wound. On top but towards the back of his head I saw, in the sparse light reaching our part of the wagon, a round hole, about one inch in diameter. Inside I could see the hairy bit, missing from his skull, bathed in blood. Today, I reproach myself for not having tried to extricate the piece but at the time it did not even occur to me. He was so calm, he talked so normally, that I must have had the feeling that he could go on like this for a long time.

Of this journey, which again was to last for three weeks, only the last few days are recalled – but these are indelibly imprinted on my mind.

Whereas the will, and the spirit of survival that goes with it, were still undiminished, a certain lethargy had already set in. I did not even bother to enquire where we actually were. We heard no news and were unaware that the Americans and the Russians had already joined forces at the river Elbe. That means that a large, perhaps the greater, part of Germany had already been liberated. But we just went on and on.

Father started complaining of increasing pain. When our train next came to a halt, and the sliding doors were opened, I reported this fact to someone, probably to one of the German prisoners who to all appearances were actually running the camp. My father was taken to the *Krankenwagen*, two wagons away. I wonder whether ours was the only transport of this kind, which actually had a 'hospital' wagon attached to it. I had no alternative – I had to let him go. With the increasing suppuration, his pain became excruciating and he began to groan incessantly. This must have been Liberation Day minus twelve – 24 April 1945.

The next day, the first without my father, a minor incident occurred. We had not moved since yesterday. A young, round-faced Russian kicked me in the face because I refused to leave the wagon which, lately, was opened quite often when the train stopped in the middle of nowhere.

For the last two weeks I had had one overriding wish which became stronger every day. Because of lack of space, I had been sitting most of the time, by day and often by night, with my head resting on my arms which, in turn, were resting on my drawn-up knees. My wish was to be able to sleep, or just to sit, with my legs fully stretched out (we usually slept with our feet on other prisoners' heads and bodies and vice versa). This was probably the reason why I did not join those who stepped outside the wagon, a concession probably never before made to Jews during a transportation. I just wanted to lie down, my limbs fully extended, while I could.

Alarm! An air raid. Our doors were shut and the guards, so I heard, were hiding under the train or running to the nearby woods. I heard the 'enemy' bombers overhead. Surely I was not to be killed by those on whose actions our only hope depended? The pilots could not, of course, know that the freight of this transport was not helping any war effort. I heard explosions in the near distance.

We learned that there was a train nearby which had been bombed. All the prisoners except the Jews were allowed to visit the damaged train and to rummage in its crashed remains for anything useful they could find, preferably edible.

One small potato found its way to me. With the slightly honed handle of my spoon, which also served us as a knife, I peeled it, I cut it in slices and – I hesitated. Two things occurred to me: would the raw potato do harm to my intestines and how could I manage to give half to my father? I bit into a slice and waited for half an hour. No ill effects. A shorter wait, another bite; by nightfall, I had devoured all of it.

26 April. Our train was still stationary, we had not moved at all. Today, in what was probably an act of mockery by our tormentors, the Jewish inmates were allowed to search for and glean any unlikely

scraps that might have been overlooked by the previous party. We went, nevertheless. Oh, how we searched, how eager we were to find anything which would give our waning bodies another chance to carry on existing. I do not know what success, if any, the others had (except for one, of whom I shall speak in a minute), I had one of the completely demolished wagons all to myself; no one else even attempted to look here. I noticed then that my strength had almost gone. Trying to lift items which, normally, were not very heavy at all took all my efforts. Eventually I found an onion. Again I wondered if this raw food would do more harm than good to my starved body; I took a hearty bite and put the rest into my trouser pocket.

We were called to assemble and, with combined effort, to lift the blown-off roof of one of the carriages. With twenty or thirty of us on one side, we managed to hoist it high enough for our guards to see if there was anything worthwhile recovering. It crossed my mind that, if I did see anything, I couldn't bend down and pick it up. If more than one had the idea, letting go of the roof by just a few might bring it crashing down, killing those whose eagerness was greater than their good sense.

'Luckily' we found nothing. As we all lifted on one side of the roof, we had to move forward a step or two, in order to hold it up with outstretched arms. When the order came to let it down, some could not hold on any longer or were afraid that others might let go before them, and as we stepped back, the roof came crashing down, burying, maiming or killing four of us.

Actually, we could see only two. Their bodies were partly visible, the sheer weight must have killed them instantly. I can only specu-late on the fate of the others but I had the feeling that the guards had not seen them as they asked us immediately to return. Were the missing two killed on the spot? Were they hurt and condemned to a cruel and lingering death or did the curvature of the roof, which was also slightly raised by the bodies of their dead comrades, actually save them? Did they, after we left, manage to crawl out and celebrate their first day of freedom? A far-fetched piece of reasoning but entirely possible.

There was a fifth victim – myself. As the thing came down, only inches in front of us, something hit the back of my right hand which started bleeding profusely. The very faint scar is still there to remind me of yet another near escape, this time by millimetres.

With a kind of elation, I relished the fact that we did not have to line up and march in the usual way. It was an almost casual and totally disorderly group which made its way back. This lapse can only be explained by a 'couldn't-care-less' attitude of the guards. They must have known what we didn't – that, by then, their beloved fatherland was almost completely occupied by the Allies. Not till two days later did I know that we were not in Germany at all but near Mauthausen, in Austria.

Back at the train, the German guards left us. Suddenly we were stopped and made to line up. A few enterprising prisoners, Russians or Poles, I believe, began searching us. Oh, how I felt this mockery, this double humiliation. First, on German orders, we had not been allowed to join the first batch of searchers, and now the lower ranks of humanity were being allowed to pounce on the lowest. The weakest, the totally dispensable and worthless creatures of whom I was one, were to be deprived of anything that they themselves might have overlooked and that these poor creatures might have found. Not that I had anything to lose, unless anyone was interested in half a blood-soaked onion.

I noticed that my neighbour had become very fidgety. I saw a dented tin in his hand which, apparently, he was prepared to hand over. Was it out of fear or did he have more of the stuff on him? With the speed of a magician I took it off him and, in less than a second, this 500-gram tin went down my trousers. I had tucked my slightly overlong trouser legs into my ankle-high boots where they gave the appearance of overlong knickerbockers. Now the can could not fall out and, with its badly dented shape, it was half wrapped around my lower inside leg.

In no way was any of our group able to put up a physical fight any more with these much better nourished Slavs (by their appearance one could easily deduce that they had better food rations than the Jewish prisoners), and I just hoped that I would get away with it.

The one who approached me looked strong but not bright. My new acquisition, though fairly well hidden, would soon be discovered, when he bent down to search my trouser pockets. I held the piece of well-chewed, bloodstained onion above his head in order to divert his attention upwards. 'Here, take it, it's all I have.' As he looked up, a drop of blood fell on his face. With a Russian curse, he wiped it off, pushed me away and busied himself with the next fellow.

As I went to my carriage, quietly jubilant and eager to taste my booty, I passed the 'hospital' wagon. The doors were open, and I saw my father, sitting on a stool near the entrance. He was facing the other way with his head slightly bowed forward. A Russian 'doctor', with some instrument in his hand, was performing what I can only describe as an operation. I was sure that there were no anaesthetics but there was no sound from the patient. I could not just walk by. Standing just below them, I asked the foolish question as to his condition. Turning his head slightly towards me, father answered something which was almost drowned by the din made by those who were robbing my comrades. By the faint but encouraging smile he gave me, I took it that his words must have been equally hopeful. The round-faced medic also nodded with a friendly grin which pleased me very much, as it seemed that my father was at least in the hands of a kind man. I wondered whether he was the same man who had ordered bed-rest when, back in Helmstett less than a month ago, my incredible father was nearly battered to death.

I could not stand there and watch. Shouting encouragement and: 'I hope to see you soon,' I returned to my nearby place.

*　　*　　*

The rest of that day I felt comparatively cheerful. The unremitting misery of the last few months had lessened. The death of my two (or was it four) comrades earlier did not count – they had died accidentally. Neither did I waste a thought that, once again, I had missed death, this time by a mere hair's breadth. The laxity of the guards, the absence of routine beatings, outwitting that Russian and acquiring a tin of food, no hard work, no work at all, and sitting down with my legs stretched out while most of my other co-travellers were outside, had a cumulative effect on my state of mind. The fact that I had seen my father in an apparent, and again comparatively, good mood, created a subconscious certainty that I would soon be reunited with this indestructible man.

Somehow I managed to open that tin. It contained compressed meat with lots of fat, a substance which had not entered my body for a very long time. Had I followed my impulse to gulp it down like a famished dog, it would, if it did not kill me, certainly have made me very sick. Unnoticed by myself, I had become what was known among prisoners as the most dreaded category – a *Muselmann*. Not having undressed or washed for weeks, I had not noticed how thin I was, nor did I have a mirror to see my face. Back in Auschwitz, being weeded out by selections and sent to the gas chambers – if they did not collapse and die at work, to be almost immediately replaced by newcomers – meant that the *Muselmänner* were always in the minority. We, the Jewish prisoners of this transport (probably the only one of its kind with a Jewish contingent of not much more than 10 per cent), were, by now, all *Muselmänner* – or very close to it. Not having to work, on top of having a pitiful food ration, allowed people to last a little longer.

Was it my guardian angel that warned me to nibble not gobble my treasure? I took a morsel, no larger than a sweet, and swallowed it with equal care. The saddest statistic of all was the many thousands who died after liberation because of an uncontrolled intake of food.

Every now and again, I put a tiny amount of the life-giving substance into my mouth, kept it there for as long as I could and then swallowed it with reluctance. Reluctance because I thought of my suffering father who needed it even more than I, to keep up his strength for the operation and its aftermath. No one today can imagine what supreme effort of self-control it took not to finish any accessible food there and then.

To divert my attention from the alluring contents of the tin, which I kept, for most of the time, well hidden, especially from prying eyes, I reverted with extra diligence to a pastime forced upon us by our unwashed bodies during the last few weeks – delousing.

In vain! With the rage of a starved tiger, the emaciated body, combined with the irresistible urge and instinct for survival, made the interval between assiduous delousing and then feasting, even of tiny morsels, briefer and briefer until, by late evening, I came to my senses and realised, with shock and shame, that only about two little spoonfuls were left.

The guilt, which started then, is still with me: 'If not for your greed, your father might have survived,' goes the accusing voice.

'It wouldn't have helped him,' is the feeble defence. 'Anyhow, I couldn't get to him.'

'Did you try hard enough?' the accusation goes on, to which I have no satisfying answer.

* * *

The train was still stationary the next morning, 27 April 1945 – Liberation Day minus 8. The sliding door was opened, a prisoner entered. He came straight over to me and I knew what he was going to tell me. My father, my teacher, my closest friend – was dead. The last vestige of my world had collapsed and disappeared. I did not break down. I just sat there with a numbed stare; a solitary, small tear emerged and ran down my right cheek, drying out before it reached my chin – no more.

I remember numerous thoughts bursting simultaneously into my mind, none of them lingering long enough to reach any conclusions. 'I am all alone now – what matter – won't be long – why can't I cry, am I too weak? – What next? – Maybe mother and sister are still alive, what will they say? – Nonsense to believe that – Why don't I cry? – Maybe he is not dead – he smiled yesterday as he was sitting on that stool – he can't be dead, this man, who is much tougher than I ever was – unthinkable that his body should be without life – but, with that injury and no proper treatment ...'

*   *   *

That same day, I entered Mauthausen. I knew, of course, nothing about this camp, never even having heard of it. Were they gassing people here? Somebody said not. What luck!

Whether this reference about gassing was meant for us, I did not know. We were placed in a barracks, crammed with naked, emaciated bodies – all gas-chamber candidates. Instead of the usual delousing procedure when a new group entered the camp, they simply stripped us of all our clothes. Some, including myself, managed to get hold of a blanket.

The giant barracks was divided into two halves, both filled to capacity. I had hardly arrived when a tall, well-nourished man (my guess, the *Blockältester*), the only one among us who was dressed, approached me. Though I cannot remember what, I must have done something against the rules. He took me through the dividing door. There, he deprived me of my blanket, made me kneel on a stool, with my hands clasped behind my head. He then walked on. Before he had reached the far end of the long building, where he sat down at a table, I had got out of this most uncomfortable, even painful, position. Seeing him looking back, I pretended just to turn the stool 180 degrees, grinned at him and placed myself on it again. As there was no difference in discomfort, whichever way the stool was facing, I could swear that he had a smile on his face. How long did he intend to leave me like this?

None of the other inmates took any notice, nor would I have cared if they did. Two seconds after he turned away again, I was back through that door and, trusting that, if, indeed, he came looking for me, one naked shaven-headed *Muselmann* looked like the next, I mingled with the rest of them.

Now for the sleeping arrangements – oh God, those sleeping arrangements. Some memories fade, some disappear completely, others stay vivid to one's very end.

There were the usual three-tier bunk-beds lined up along both lengths of the opposite walls, thus creating a corridor from one end of the barracks to the other. Two sets of threes next to each other with small passages on either side. The space on my side was somewhat larger as there was a window in between. Below the window another table.

A table? I had not seen this sign of civilisation since 1942 – the 'good old days' in the ammunition camp of Klaj. I had worked on one of them – making graphs. A privileged prisoner with a room shared by only two others, one of them my father. After that, my living and resting space was my bed. Who could have dreamed that the time would come when I would call this kind of living luxury!

Here I shared the middle bunk, meant for a single person, with four others.

We had one blanket but not a stitch of clothing between us. We slept sardine-fashion – two on one side, three on the other. My feet were resting between two heads, on somebody's shoulders, at the far end of the bed. Forever alert, I managed to be one of a twosome. At first, I counted myself lucky to have only one neighbour until six legs, three pairs of feet, were pinning me down. On the other side, only the middle one suffered as badly as we did – unable to move all night. The outer ones were not to be envied either: part of their bodies were resting on the wooden frame. As if this were not enough, the one in the middle, opposite us, had diarrhoea. He was already too weak to get out of bed; he emptied his bowels where he lay, there was no avoiding it.

This was too much. I offered to leave the bed if they would give me the blanket – they accepted. The aforementioned table under the window was 50 cm wide and 80 cm long. On it, in a kneeling position, resting my head on my folded arms and, covered by my blanket, I spent the night.

28 April, Liberation Day minus 7. Whereas in Auschwitz a small loaf of bread was divided into four portions, here the same size of loaf was shared among six people. The tiny blob of margarine of previous camps had now disappeared altogether. At 6 p.m. a soup container was placed in the corridor. Since my 'bed' was in the middle of our half of the barracks it was only four yards away from me. At Auschwitz, the soup had contained the occasional bit of substance, but here it appeared to be coloured water with a few pieces of greens, or possibly grass, swimming forlornly in it. However faintly, I detected a taste which betrayed the fact that there must have been some meaty substance cooked in it. I could guess who had the good bits but, by now, I was conditioned not to expect better.

29 April, Liberation Day minus 6. How my bones hurt in the morning. A man, dressed in the usual concentration-camp uniform, came to our bed. He wrote in capital letters the word LEVI on the chest of our sick comrade. Peculiar. We were only numbers, how did that man (a doctor?) know the name. I had no answer to this procedure, I had never seen it before but I knew what it meant. Young Levi died later that day. His death left me completely without emotion. If anything, I felt an upsurge of joy that I could now share my bed with only three companions – plus the gain of a metal soup bowl and a spoon.

30 April, Liberation Day minus 5. After a more comfortable night my spirits had returned and, once again, I felt my old mischievous self. This morning's reduced bread ration (it was eight people to one loaf now) was taken with a shrug of my shoulders. 'I am going to survive anything they may dish out,' I said to myself, knowing full well that this display of bravado was to bolster my spirits and my never-diminishing will to live. It did nothing to stem the steady loss of my bodily strength and weight.

In the afternoon I was getting ready for the performance of my life.

The vessel containing the hot but watery soup had been put in its usual place and, through observation, I knew that it would be five to ten minutes before it was dished out. I intended to raid this locked container under the hungry stare of five or six hundred pairs of eyes.

My props for this feat were my newly acquired soup bowl and my blanket. I strode past the focal point of all the inmates, casually covering the top of it with my blanket which, for this purpose, I wore like a flowing robe on the right side of my body, leaving the left almost uncovered. At the fourth pass, I quickly bent down and, under cover, released the clasp which held the lid shut.

Another couple of dummy passes followed. Then, with the speed of a trained magician, again under cover of my blanket, I lifted the lid, dipped my dish into the hot liquid and, ignoring my scalded thumb, I moved triumphantly – but slowly – back to my bed. There, under my mattress, I groped for my hidden spoon. As I could not possibly eat openly, I lowered myself; then, kneeling down and putting my head under the bed, I tried to devour the spoils of my enterprise.

Before I managed to put the first spoonful into my mouth, I was surrounded by a pack of hungry wolves, showing with angry growling that they meant business. I had no alternative. Besides, I did not want anyone in authority to be alerted to what I had done. Holding the dish in front of me, I turned around and just managed to dip my spoon twice, before the bowl was empty. At least they left me alone when I was licking it clean.

My motive in procuring for myself the extra bit of watery substance was the illusion that: 'If they can last with this ration – I will last a little longer.' Whereas the acquisition of this extra ration had, I am sure, no bearing on my survival, the concentration of getting it, the scheming, the determination to survive, the fighting spirit, did.

The First of May 1945, Liberation Day minus 4. May Day, springtime – the very words lift people's hearts all over the northern hemisphere. They had no meaning for us. Another of my bedmates had died; so had many others. When I arrived, the population of this room was about 25 to 30 prisoners per four squares metres (two treble-tier bunks side by side). By now, it had gone down by nearly one-quarter. Although there was no bed with just a single person in it, there were many now with 'only' two or three occupants.

Yesterday's performance had been a flop. Too little reward for the danger and the effort. I occupied myself – what else was there to do – with scheming how else to obtain a little, life-giving, extra.

The soup arrived and was placed on its usual spot. I believe that there were more eyes looking at me than at the soup container. I

192

didn't move. As usual, two well-nourished inmates in prison garb were dishing out our 'dinner'. For this, we had to sit in our bed, awaiting our turn. The system was, first one side, than the other. We were first. My ever-watchful eye had spotted a bed, just across from us, with only two occupants. (They had lost one this very morning.) Our turn came. I took my time eating. The two distributors progressed at a slow pace and I bided my time for the right moment to move.

When they were at their furthest, I slipped across and joined the two in the 'underoccupied' bed. Two pairs of big eyes in skeletal faces stared at me in silence. Fearing they might give me away, I promised: 'I will share it with you.' Their angry expressions relaxed a little. Not a word was spoken as I dined with the two naked youngsters who looked as if they had died days ago. The taller of the two stooped forward a little as there was no room for him to sit upright. Like most of the others, they had no spoons and, using mine, I had to feed them and myself in turn, interrupted occasionally by a growl, indicating that the spoon was not full enough.

The second and third of May went by in similar fashion, except for two important events: the bread ration went down to one-tenth of a loaf per person and I came down with the dreaded diarrhoea. This malady probably claimed more victims among the pitiful remnants at the close of the war, and after, than any other disease connected with camp life.

At the end of the barracks was a larger partition within which there were three separate cubicles – ordinary water closets – all with separate doors. As we had by now sunk to the level of animals, no one bothered to close them. The poor wretches in the nearest dozen of bunks had to breathe the stomach-turning stench around the clock. Even thinned out to a certain extent, it reached the middle of our barracks where I was positioned. Since more and more prisoners began to suffer from this infirmity, combined with the general weakness of their bodies, many did not quite make it to their destination. Before one even reached the outer partition of the lavatories, the initial traces of excreta became more and more impossible to sidestep and in the end we, all barefoot, waded in the stuff. On such visits, I draped my dirty grey blanket around my neck to prevent it from being soiled. Leaving it behind would mean losing one of my three worldly possessions. When leaving this place, I would use the first clear spot on the floor like civilised people use a doormat – to clean and wipe my bare soles.

The more people became afflicted, the longer the queue. In these final days, nobody seemed to be in command, nobody was ordered to clean up the mess – and nobody did. It grew by the day. The lavatories themselves were functioning normally. With practically only liquid waste to go in and nothing to clean ourselves with, they were, at least, not blocked.

My weakened body could not take any additional strain. Death was approaching fast. I had no fear. Not even then could I believe or imagine that complete oblivion could or would happen to me.

4 May, Liberation Day minus 1. None of the almost hourly decreasing number of inmates talked. The eerie silence was interrupted only when the well-fed prisoners made their rounds taking away the dead. A Dantesque scene in the twentieth century. It was of no concern to me that, within two hours this afternoon, two of my bedmates stopped breathing and were duly collected. Initially I had exchanged a few words with them, I had slept and suffered with them, but I did not know them.

We knew nothing of the outside world, no news, no rumours. Unknown to us, almost all the camps were already liberated. Mauthausen's SS personnel had fled days ago and I still don't know who had replaced them or whether they were replaced at all. I am sure that all the German prisoners and, perhaps, many others had also fled the probably unguarded camp. The world was preparing for the big day – any time now. We, however, knew nothing of all this – we carried on dying.

A little life returned when the soup came in. I cannot remember if we had any bread at all that day. I was now too weak for a repeat performance of the last few days. The bed opposite, the venue of the most macabre dinner party of my life, was now empty. Stupor must have set in generally; there were beds with three occupants next to an empty one – it did not even occur to anyone to move into the vacated space.

That night I had a two-part dream. In the first I had a feast of chicken. How I hated to wake up to reality. The second was a repeat of previous dreams. Once again I had a machine gun, shooting into crowds of Germans – indiscriminately – non-stop. Again, as in previous dreams, I hesitated when I had small children in my sights except that, this time, when a voice warned me that they were innocent, I shouted angrily, 'So was my little sister' and I carried on mowing and mowing, as in a blind rage.

11

Liberation

It was late in the morning of 5 May 1945. Nobody in my part of the barracks had left their beds unless to follow a natural function or, having expired, to be carried away – on this of all days. My body had given up asking for food. Hunger was not painful any more and I do not recall whether we had any bread ration at all that day. An inmate, probably on his way back from the lavatory, climbed on to the little table on which I had slept for two nights during my stay here. He had observed something unusual and wanted to take a better look.

'Ein Amerikaner Soldat' he shouted in slightly imperfect German – and my insides erupted with uncontrollable convulsions. I did not know how this news affected my comrades around me. All was silent, I heard no screams of delight – no jubilation. Pulling my blanket over my head, I felt my tearducts' involuntary release, shedding streams which I would not have believed they had, especially as they had released only a single drop when my father died – just eight days ago.

One thought hit me to the exclusion of all others: I was now alone – all alone. If only I could have shared the triumph of survival against all odds with my dearly beloved father. But for a mischance, and fate's capriciousness following one wrong decision, he would have been with me now, the man whose will power and bodily constitution were far stronger than mine.

It was the fact of losing my closest companion – without whom I would have died long ago – so tantalisingly near to liberation and the chance to live again that would be the single greatest cause of many a sudden outbreak of tears during the rest of my life. It was also, to some extent, the reason why this book could not have been written earlier. Terrible self-reproaches and recriminations pursued me through the years to come. So many 'ifs' that might have meant the difference between life and death, not only for my father but for my whole family, were not relieved by any 'buts' and excuses, nor by the so-called healing effect of time. Mourning for the loss of my whole family in such unspeakably tragic circumstances will end only with my own death.

I wanted to share this incredible moment with someone. I looked at the last of my bedmates. He hadn't made it either.

*   *   *

That 5 May, the day of my rebirth, of which I ought to be able to remember, report and put on paper the minutest detail, a hazy gap, lasting several hours, occurred. Perhaps my weakened perceptive faculties could not take it all in, perhaps I was too dazed by the enormity of the event. Probably, against expectations, nothing worth remembering happened. The Americans, understandably, could not organise as fast as circumstances required. There was little change in the food for the first day and even part of the following one – that is, for those who were too weak to go out and help themselves.

I was among those who could not venture far. With the help of a long stick I could walk, not with normal strides but placing, or rather dragging, one foot alongside the other, very slowly, a few inches at a time.

It was late that afternoon when I noticed a little fire just outside the rear entrance of our barracks. My eyes, still being as sharp as ever, noticed that one of the inmates had 'organised' for himself three or four large potatoes. I got down on all fours and, like a prowling wildcat eyeing a potential victim, I began edging slowly towards him. Passing through the messy gangway outside the lavatories I silently pawed my way nearer and nearer. My blanket, which would have been a hindrance to my intended assault, I had left behind. He was just about to take his first bite when I pounced. Grabbing the boiled potato out of his hands, I put it into my mouth and, holding it with my teeth, triumphantly made my getaway – on all fours. That was the only way I could move fast enough to escape the wrath of the growling victim.

Perhaps he could not move very fast either, or was afraid to leave his other goodies behind. Instead of pursuing me, he threw the pot with boiling water after me. It landed with a splash just behind me, but near enough to scald my soles slightly. A direct hit would have killed me.

197

Was this the last in my long chain of near-misses, escaping death virtually by inches, or was it to be the first in a new life which, though with no comparable frequency and altogether in a different way, was marked with more than the average drama? Was it my unquenched lust for adventure or was it the fact that I was all alone now but for an inner voice telling me: 'The world is yours, nobody can tell you what to do and nothing can ever happen to you to equal your past,' that would guide and colour my life from now on?

These thoughts I had, of course, much later. At the time I was reminded of my prayer: '*Nor tzi iberleben – abee mit a trikkenem Kartoffel.*' (Oh to survive – be it with only a dry potato). I had survived and my first meal was – a dry potato. A memorable meal indeed.

* * *

On 6 May 1945 I awoke to a world in which, for the first time, I was no longer a prisoner destined to die. The same place, the same bed – all to myself. The same surroundings, the same people, still dying though on a lesser scale. Many likely victims, their spirits now lifted, found the reserves of strength necessary to hang on. I vaguely remember that the bread ration was slightly larger. I was weak, very weak, but I felt great. The new reality had now sunk in. Let's rise, shout, scream, kill the Nazis, embrace the world, the world – my world – it belongs to me. Nothing, nothing could ever happen to me to equal what I have been through, nothing the future might bring would make me sad or unhappy – all will be happiness and undiluted bliss. Up, let us rise and explore 'our' new world ...

Yet, to what the euphoric spirit aspired, the emaciated body could not match. Step by six-inch step, I shuffled to the front of the barracks. First through the dividing door in the middle where, on the first day of my arrival here, I was made to kneel on a stool. Then, through the main entrance into the sunshine. Just as I had felt in Auschwitz after leaving the gas-chambers, the sun epitomised glorious life, shining on the most beautiful and the most hideous scenes on earth. Hardly had I bathed in its warmth when, with serene equanimity, it illuminated the most gruesome sight I had ever seen or was ever likely to see again.

Two, very large, pyramids of corpses in varying states of decay. Grotesquely grinning, twisted faces looking at me and through me into nowhere. Faces distorted by pain and suffering, even in death.

198

This photograph of Belzec extermination camp in 1946 was taken by a special commission sent to gather the bones of the victims for reburial. The camp operated from May to December 1942 and was designed so that five trainloads of a thousand people each, could be murdered in a single day.

THE CONCENTRATION CAMPS

卐 Auschwitz concentration camp in which more than 4 million people were murdered between 1941 and 1944, including Jews, Gypsies and Soviet prisoners-of-war

■ Camps set up solely for the murder of Jews

卐 Other camps in which Jews and non-Jews were put to forced labour, starved, tortured and murdered in conditions of the worst imaginable cruelty. Most of these camps had 'satellite' labour camps nearby. *Courtesy of Martin Gilbert*

Layer upon layer, arms, legs, bodies entangled in all directions like discarded rubbish. Most of them were naked. Hardened as I was, my revulsion on seeing this obscenity showed that the spark of humanity in me was not yet completely extinguished.

Even when it occurred to me that, maybe, my father was among this multitude of human remains – yesterday's hopefuls – I could not bring myself to stay and look for more than a few seconds. As fast as I could I moved away from this never-to-be-forgotten sight.

There were very few people about. Those fit enough, and with an aim and a destination, had probably left. As yet, I had not seen my first American soldier. Nobody seemed to be in command. Maybe I should be on the lookout for some food. Except for the inside of my barracks I knew absolutely nothing of this camp which, so I learned much later, was among the most notorious. Slowly I shoved on towards the next barracks which (with a bit of wishful thinking) – I thought might be the kitchen or a foodstore. Lifting my eyes to look inside the darkened window, I saw yet another skeleton. Only its lively big eyes betrayed that their owner was still alive. As I moved away so, with identical movement, did the skeleton. It was the first time for years that I had seen a reflection of myself. Another image, seen only once and never to be forgotten.

Strangely, I was not upset at all by what I had seen; suddenly I was in high spirits: 'This *Muselmann* is going to live,' I assured myself. The image in the mirror waved back with a little smile.

I was getting tired and found an upturned bucket to sit on. Someone was walking towards me. Wearing a uniform and a helmet, a young American approached me with a camera in his hand. Though my English consisted of only a few dozen words, I understood that he wanted to take a photograph of me.

For reasons which will soon become apparent, I give a description of this photograph as best I can. I was sitting on the bucket with the barrack-wall right behind me. My only attire was my blanket, which I wore either around my shoulders or, more likely, around my waist. It is possible that I had my soup-bowl in my hands. In the faint hope that the taker of this photograph is still alive and may read this, I would beg him, or any of his descendants, to let me have a copy of this, for me, priceless memento. Needless to say, I would very much like to meet him again. It was my first encounter with a friendly uniform, my first confirmation that I really was a free man.

Nothing seemed to happen for a day or two, at least nothing that I could see and report. No news penetrated through to our group of the semi-dead and the dying. Within myself, I was sure that the Americans were doing what they could but it was not yet visible. On the morning of the third day I was taken to a large tent which served as a makeshift hospital. The floor was grass and the beds were stretchers. It was all very poorly organised – but I was not complaining.

One military man was in charge – but he was not a doctor. Some such person saw me briefly in the afternoon. No medical examination whatsoever; he was probably too busy or he could judge my state of health by the other hundreds (or thousands?) he had seen. I may do this man an injustice but it seemed to me that, seeing so many hopeless situations, he had adopted the attitude that either I would make it on my own – or I wouldn't. A case past medical help. However, a course of five large white tablets, given to me every four hours, even at night, was the result of this visit, presumably to stem my diarrhoea.

A container, of the same type that I had raided a few days ago, arrived. When its locked lid was opened I became very excited, my first proper meal. It contained: a watery soup. But there was a difference in taste and one could find a number of wide noodles swimming forlornly in that large drum. Inexplicably, I thought of my father as if he had told me before of such a situation and given me advice. I fished out the few solids I could find and poured most of the liquid away – then I asked for another portion which was not refused.

What I did not know then was the very sad fact that thousands of released prisoners were to die – from eating. Their digestive systems were no longer used to proper food and they did not know how to control their understandable greed for food. Many died while gorging themselves.

A boy was placed next to me. He was just 14 – the last surviving member of his family. 'What will happen to me, what will the Americans do with me?' he wondered. A large bottle was hung up above him. Without sufficient knowledge, I took it to be a sort of intravenous feeding. When I was woken up for my dosage of five tablets, I noticed him sleeping peacefully. In the morning, however, his place was empty – he had died.

The Americans were doing their best in the circumstances but they

200

could not arrest, not fast enough at any rate, the extent of mortality, which was by now of epidemic proportions. It was one thing to die during the *Churban* but quite another, having suffered it all, to survive it and then not be able to enjoy the deserved triumph. If there are any tears left, they should be shed for these, the most pitiable, luckless wretches whose umbilical cord with life had worn too thin to hang on.

The stretchers were meant to carry people, not serve as beds. The restricted mobility of the body caused severe soreness of the skin, especially on the unsightly, protruding and fleshless pelvis. I was given some ointment, which was no help. When I looked at myself, my thighs were non-existent – just thighbones covered in a parchment-like membrane.

After a few days, my diarrhoea had almost ceased, my food intake increased; an unknown feeling, an urge, made me get up and walk out. Out of the hospital, that is, and 'walk' is a pretentious description for the slow pace of my ambulation.

Following the photographer, the male nurse and the doctor, I now met my fourth American. He interviewed people and made notes. When I approached him, he asked if I had any relations in America. This was my first opportunity to make use of the few words I knew of the English language. I had prepared myself in my mind for this moment. True to character, in saying or doing the inappropriate or unexpected thing, I intended to ask him why Americans did not play football. My first attempt at being humorous failed miserably.

Was my brain (or rather speech) affected as well as my body? I was speaking haltingly and with a slur. After giving him the name and address (even there I made a mistake) of my aunt and uncle (Fanny and Sigi Muller) in New York, I gave up in embarrassment.

My name was then announced in the German language newspaper *Aufbau*, which was specially published for refugees. However, it was long after that before I actually communicated with them, and other relatives, by correspondence, and years before I actually met them.

There were other relatives who had emigrated in time. No doubt, especially after what had happened, they all would have been prepared to help me in starting a new life. That, however, if at all avoidable, was not in my nature to ask for – or to accept.

What next? If, by the remotest chance, my mother and sister (or one of them) had survived, it was my duty, and my yearning, to search for them. I had not yet learned that there were camps built for no other purpose than the destruction of human beings. Even during my stay in Auschwitz, where history's greatest single act of genocide took place within just a few square metres, and even at the time of liberation, I was unaware of the extent of the catastrophe which had befallen the Jewish race. At any given time during those murderous years, the eye perceived those around me – the living. Therefore, although quite aware of the enormous number of dead, the brain could not – or would not – accept the complete reality, not for a long time. The success of the Nazis can be measured by the time it took for the normal human mind to comprehend the incomprehensible, the sheer magnitude of it all.

This may explain why I hoped against hope that somewhere, somehow, the two loved ones had managed to survive and that I might meet them again. Today, I find it difficult to explain to myself how I could have clung to this absurd idea but I understand why my mind resisted, and still resists, the vision of how they met their end. Giving up on them meant writing them off, which I simply felt not entitled to do. So, in my mind, I worked out where they might go. First to mind came Frankfurt am Main, Germany. Why not? The tiger was toothless now, the hunters were the hunted.

Kraków was nearer to them but I reasoned that they would not expect us to chose this town as a meeting place. Besides, should we not have survived, neither Frankfurt nor Kraków would be of any interest to them. Thus, the destination to aim for would be Palestine, New York or London. In all these places we had relatives who had emigrated there before the war. Further reasoning and galling experience told me that, of the three areas, Palestine was probably the easiest to get to. Aunt Golda and Uncle Yehuda Brauner were there, the same kind relatives who, in 1935, were of great help to my parents when they were preparing to emigrate to Palestine. Unfortunately we missed the boat … Bitter thoughts lead me to reflect that the loss of my family, my years of misery, might have been prevented but for another 'if'. The Americans had operated a stingy, slow-moving quota for German Jews. If their system had been more liberal, my family and thousands of others might have been saved. If there is, or was, a plausible reason for this, then why was it possible for thousands of war criminals to make their home there? (A US

Justice official, Mr Allan Ryan, has said that, 'at a conservative estimate, as many as 10,000 Nazi war criminals might still be living in the US'.)

An office was established inside the camp for those who wanted to go to Palestine. After two weeks, I registered but only one minute before it closed down. Was it the fear of losing my independence which caused me to hesitate? Also, I could not see myself fitting in now with anybody who, not having experienced the *Churban* themselves, would certainly not have given up any of their religious practices, or call it habits of a lifetime. Not being a hypocrite, I would probably offend these good people with my anti-religious thinking and behaviour. The thought of standing in prayer just made me angry.

Although I had started the journey to Palestine, I did not reach it until many, many years later. After I had added my name to those who wished to emigrate to the Holy Land, we were told that it would take two more weeks to organise.

Meanwhile, I was getting stronger. Now my body demanded food which even the increased ration could not satisfy. A sort of trading had developed among those still in the camp – the major currencies being cigarettes and eggs. A schooling, a foretaste in miniature form of my activities of the near future – the black market.

Four weeks had passed since my 'rebirth' and since I had seen my reflection in a window. I could walk again. Another look in the window (we had no mirrors) showed a pleasing change. A face, still thin but starting to fill out, a short crop of hair covering the formerly shaven skull. I cannot remember how I acquired the greyish-brown shirt with short sleeves, which I had to wear open-necked as it had no buttons, nor the pair of grey shorts and ankle-high boots. In addition, I 'bought', for a few cigarettes, a green straw hat to complete this ridiculous outfit.

Four of us decided to go for an extensive walk – any direction would do. About two kilometres from the camp we spotted a small farmhouse. We braced ourselves, we would show these bastards who was master now. Needless to say, I did not have the machine gun which I had dreamed about – nor any other weapon. Nevertheless, I was quite keen to confront anything and anybody, not quite knowing what I would do. A woman in her forties opened the door, a peasant's wife in simple working dress and apron, visibly frightened by our appearance. She stared at us, voiceless but with questioning eyes. 'We want food,' I said, with much less harshness than I had intended. She led us into the kitchen and busied herself at the stove. A boy of four and his slightly older sister rose from a wooden bench at a table where the four of us sat down. The tender age of these infants made me think that the woman must be much younger than she looked. Not since the summer of 1942 had I seen children of that age. I stared at them. Were these the children on which, in my dreams, I would wreak revenge?

Two fried eggs, bread and butter and, best of all, a large glass of fresh milk were put in front of each of us. Slightly confused, I broke away from my thoughts and addressed myself to the comestibles in front of me. Her demeanour was as if there had never been a war, nor that one of the most notorious concentration camps was practically on her doorstep – less than two miles away.

We might have just dropped in for a casual breakfast. At the time I gave it no thought that a single slice of the bread in front of me almost equalled a day's ration in Auschwitz – let alone Mauthausen – nor that it was about five years since I had had a complete breakfast like that. I ate with relish, with satisfaction but also with a growing anger.

Here we were sitting at the table of a deadly enemy and enjoying food, of which they had deprived us until we had nearly died. They were Austrians and, as far as I was concerned, as guilty as the Germans.

Today I know better. If I had shot a thousand Austrians with my imaginary machine gun and then a thousand Germans, statistically, I would have eradicated a much higher percentage of people infected with the antisemitic virus in the first batch. It took years of indoctrination in Germany to bring people to the same level of Jew-hatred as they (the Germans) found when they entered Austria. Those who fled from the Nazis, via Berlin, were reported to have found that, after five years of intensive Nazi propaganda, there was less harassment there than in Vienna after only five days.

Hitler's oratorical skill, his promises of work for all, at a time of immense unemployment, fell on many eager ears. A Volkswagen, a car for the people, was a thing many people could only dream of. His ranting against the Jews was welcomed by those already infected with antisemitism but taken with indifference by most others – it did not concern them. 'I'm all right, Jack' is the English term for it.

LIBERATION

I doubt if anybody, before the war, thought of the wholesale murder of the Jews as it was finally contrived at the Wannsee Conference, early in 1942, and carried out under the cover of war. That must include most Jews as, otherwise, they would all have stampeded out of Germany. There were plenty of signs for those in exalted positions that the Nazis would, ultimately, not allow them to continue. The average, the masses of Jews often heard what was also said to my father: 'We (the Nazis) are not after you, it's "the others" we're after.' We expected deprivations, destitution – but murder?

To illustrate the lethargic attitude of the average German towards the Jews, I quote the famous German, Pastor Niemöller:

> First they came for the Jews and I did not speak out
> because I was not Jewish
> Then they came for the Communists and I did not speak out
> because I was not a Communist
> Then they came for the Catholics and I did not speak out
> because I was not a Catholic
> Then they came for the Trade Unionists and I did not speak out
> because I was not a Trade Unionist
> Then they came for me and there was no-one left
> to speak out for me.

We had nearly finished our meal when a gaunt-looking man entered the kitchen. With his wrinkled and weatherbeaten face, his well-worn but clean working clothes and equally well-worn cap, he gave the impression of a hard-working but not very well-to-do peasant. He looked about 50 but, like his wife, was probably younger. His casual 'good morning' made me explode. Maybe I had expected everyone to run away from us, knowing what they were guilty of, or show some signs, any sign, of guilt or remorse – but a casual greeting as if there wasn't a major camp of human destruction in the vicinity?

I laid it on, verbally. I told him all about what I was sure he already knew, watching his reaction closely. His not too bright face looked at me with genuine, unfaked astonishment. When I finished he spoke, with an unforgettable simplicity in his Upper Austrian dialect, the unforgettable sentence: '*Ay, dess hum mer yor gornet gevoost,*' which I can only translate as 'Ay, we didn't even know that.' I was shattered but I believed him. With satanic cunning, the Nazis had hoodwinked the Jews, the world and a very large number of their own people by plying them with lies, and blinding them with slogans, to cover up their foul deeds within barbed-wire surroundings.

Of course people knew of concentration camps and their 'harsh' regime. They also feared it, because many a German dissenter was taken there, some who spoke incautious words against the regime, others among them who listened to foreign broadcasts. They were betrayed by neighbours, often for jealous or vindictive reasons – not always for Nazi ideology. But those camps, where, ultimately, no one was to survive, were built far away from Germany, in places where they were also assured of the willing co-operation of the local populace. Those who committed the atrocities were not likely to talk – and rarely did.

While suffering what I suffered, while seeing what I saw, I wasted no time speculating whether or not there were people in Germany (I did not think of Austria as a separate country) whose hands were not bloodied, if not directly then indirectly. This encounter with this peasant family was only the first of many such shocks to come.

*　　*　　*

Six weeks after liberation, several canvas-covered military lorries left the camp, destination Italy – and thence on to Palestine. On the way we were joined by others until our convoy consisted of 35 vehicles. The Jewish Brigade (an attachment of volunteers to the British forces, from what was then called Palestine) had been organising, if maybe not initiating, this exodus. In the evening we were told to keep quiet and not to lift the canvas while we were crossing the borders.

Although complying with this order, I felt real anger welling up inside me. It did not at all conform to my idea of 'liberation' and 'the world belongs to me now' concept. Were not the Italians allies of the vanquished Nazi Germany? Who did they think they were to object to our passing through on our way to 'our' country! It did not cross my mind that it might have been the British government which should be kept from knowing about our intentions. It would not have occurred to me, even in my wildest dreams that, after what we had been through, any government in the world could want to block our way to our homeland.

Nobody told us how long to maintain this silence, so we kept quiet for hours. The monotonous humming of the engines was the only sound to break the stillness of the night. The excitement of tomorrow soon made me forget my irritation. Strangely, the fact of being smuggled, the very act of this 'illegal' crossing of borders, awakened in me a long-dormant feeling. Adventure, danger! Not of the one-sided kind of my recent past but the sort where the cards are evenly stacked, where the challenge and the consequence were my own doing and my own responsibility. My spirits were overflowing. Yes, tomorrow I would challenge the world; normal law did not apply to me, it applied only to ordinary, 'normal' people of whom I did not regard myself as one.

Had I not, immediately after liberation, been too weak, had I gone wild, had I killed masses of Germans, had I robbed banks, I would, possibly, not even have received a reprimand. I did nothing of the sort and I felt that there were massive credits in my book. I wondered what kind of character had emerged out of these camps, where no one who did not develop a certain measure of cunning and, quite often, of unscrupulousness, could have endured. This does not mean that all who survived had become antisocial individuals. Not at all. Most of them acclimatised themselves (became normal human beings) in a very short time. As for me, with an added inborn lust for adventure, it was to be years before I would accept the laws of normal society.

Epilogue

We are, inevitably, the sum total of our past, and our behaviour – and our belief – evolve accordingly.

My new life had begun. No parental supervision, no religious fetters, no respect for authority – nor, for that matter, for anybody else. Visions and memories of occurrences, alien to most human beings, were partial to the evocation of a philosophy where yourself and chance were the masters of your destiny.

This guideline prevailed for a significant period after liberation. A time when I indulged in freedom and adventure, endeavouring to make up in all spheres of life for lost years. A time when I delighted in challenging officialdom, the elements and fate. Then, with the euphoria of my rebirth gradually subsiding, when introspection began in earnest, sadness and bitterness set in. Although my balanced nature managed to prevent them from taking permanent hold, they recurred spasmodically, invading my dreams, affecting my moods and my life. When, after more than a quarter of a century my mind turned again to religion, they guided my thinking process and shaped and swayed my reasoning even to this day.

When overcome by these visions of the past, I sometimes believe that I only turned to God to vent my embittered feelings, and my prayers were often interrupted by a monosyllabic question – why?

*   *   *

What will future historians make of these incomparable events which still cause their victims nightmares and whose perpetrators largely managed to escape to foreign lands and punishment: events that are harrowing the innermost being of grieving and frustrated survivors, haunted by unparalleled memories to their dying moment – yet are beyond the most eminent writer to convey and impossible for non-participants to apprehend?

208

EPILOGUE

Analysing present trends, these events may well be presented to future generations like this:

'Once upon a time, before Germany became a European province, it was ruled by an evil tyrant. He had three major objectives: to conquer the world, to annihilate all the Jews and to establish the German Reich which was to last a thousand years. He unleashed the Second World War and gained many victories. He promised his people that, soon, his scientists would create a miracle weapon, the atomic bomb, which would overcome the enemy and guarantee the conquest and mastery of the world by the German "master race" and the glorious German Army.

'But, like all the tyrants in history, he did not ultimately succeed. His policies of hatred deprived him of the one man who could have helped him to build this miracle weapon, a Jewish scientist called Albert Einstein. So, once again, good prevailed over evil. Instead of conquering the world, his country lost the war and for many years was split in two halves. Instead of annihilating all Jews, he managed to kill only a third, and the Third Reich, which was to last a thousand years, ended after only twelve.'

Although nothing could compensate me for the loss of my family, seeing Nazi Germany defeated, the elite of the 'master race' running for cover, hiding their once arrogant identities to save their impoverished little souls and then, after 2000 fateful years, experiencing the rebirth of the State of Israel was the one consolation, the only satisfaction to help me in my grief. If I were asked to name a single event which was worth surviving for, there is no doubt in my mind – it was winning back the Land of my Fathers.

The Jews who, for about two millennia, were about the only people who adhered to the Christian doctrine of offering the other cheek, suddenly said: 'Enough is enough!' They learned how to fight, gained their self-respect, the respect of the world and, finally, regained their homeland. Whenever I recall this momentous day in April 1948, I walk erect, I grow tall. It gave me back my pride in belonging to a people which, I shamefully confess, I once wanted to desert. It was, as it were, my step back to the fold but not – not yet – to God.

*   *   *

For more than a quarter of a century I suspended all thinking about religion. Having, since then, acquired a new outlook and a new religious philosophy, I cannot, in all honesty, say whether I am happier now or in those long-gone golden years after liberation. Golden, because they were carefree – I consciously made them so.

I can say, however, that I am reasonably happy. I have the proverbial 'wife in a million' and two lovely daughters. As I approach old age and look back to the years preceding my present 'respectability', I have no regrets other than having, artificially, drawn out my youth. In other words, I should have married the girl of my life years before I did.

Did I adhere to the pledge: 'Oh to survive, be it with only a dry potato', to which I bound myself when misery and fear were my permanent companions? Did I adbide by my promise to ask no more from life than the bare minimum to sustain it?

I have now begun writing the second part of my life story (or is it the story of my second life?) and I have named it 'The Dry Potato'.

It is my sincere wish that relatives and friends will content themselves with what they have read in this book and, for the rest, take me as they have found me – as they know me now.

6   The author in Rome, December 1945, seven months after liberation